'We shape
our tools
and
thereafter
our tools
shape
us.'

MARSHALL MCLUHAN

BISPUBLISHERS

DELFT
DESIGN
GUIDE

DELFT UNIVERSITY OF TECHNOLOGY FACULTY OF INDUSTRIAL DESIGN ENGINEERING

PERSPECTIVES
MODELS
APPROACHES
METHODS

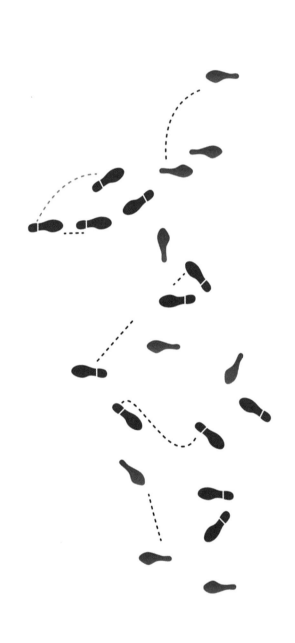

INTRODUCTION

Ever since its founding in the 1960s, the Delft Faculty of Industrial Design Engineering has taken a methodical approach to design education. But the methods were never uncontroversial. The Dutch writer Godfried Bomans asserted: "In the realm of the mind a method is comparable to a crutch; the true thinker walks freely."

Many designers share his thoughts. Good designers seem to need no methods. They tend to attribute their successes to intuition, creativity and expertise, and not to the use of particular methods.

Now, nobody believes anymore that designers can do without intuition, creativity and expertise, as research into the problem-solving behaviour and thought processes of designers has convincingly shown how essential these capacities are. But that does not mean that methods have no role to play in design.

Despite criticism and doubt – some godfathers of the 'design methods movement' of the 1960s became critics of their own work – methods have not disappeared from the scene. Methods are often used as means of teaching design. The development of better methods is probably the most important driver of design research. And it is not uncommon for design consultancies to advertise themselves on the basis of their specific methodological approaches.

Since 1991, industrial design students at the Delft University of Technology have been raised with the book Product Design: Fundamentals and Methods that I wrote together with Johannes Eekels. The genesis of this book goes back to our lectures in the 1970s, but much of its content is still relevant. However, the field of design has changed greatly. Nowadays, industrial designers also design services and social and economic artefacts. In product development, the social and behavioural sciences have come to play a major role alongside engineering. Our awareness of the limits of production and consumption has increased enormously and unprecedented technological possibilities have emerged for the development of design tools.

Such developments have led to numerous new methods. I am extremely excited that finally a new Delft textbook that also addresses these new methods has been published. But there is more to it. Methodological textbooks usually focus on detailed descriptions of methods and barely address their application. The authors of this book have explicitly opted for the latter perspective. As good descriptions of methods are sufficiently available, they confine themselves to short characterisations of methods and refer to relevant sources for more information. How should a project plan be designed given specific objectives and available resources, when and in what situation and how should a particular method be used, and what can and cannot be expected from the use of a method? This book gives answers to these and other such questions.

Thanks to this specific focus, this book provides an important contribution to the literature on design methods. Given the success of the first edition, this book has a promising future ahead.

Norbert Roozenburg

Associate Editor of the International Journal Design Studies.
First graduate at the Delft Faculty of Industrial Design Engineering in 1971.

FOREWORD

In the beginning of my career, I had the chance to work alongside the Australian designer Marc Newson on the simple, yet ingenious Ford concept car 021C. This was Marc's first experience in automotive design. During some of the more intense moments, he described it to me as *'trying to design 500 products at the same time'.*

Cars are incredibly exciting, but also amazingly complex objects. In a way, they are the pinnacle of design in terms of their complexity, impact on society and the way we live our lives. What Marc experienced is daily life for my international design team. About 550 members in 6 studios - from Sao Paulo to Shanghai - are working on 50 to 60 projects at any given time. Which is why I admiringly refer to our team as a creative design machine.

In these projects we work upstream and downstream in close collaboration with market researchers, product planners, engineers, program teams, manufacturing, suppliers, marketing & sales, communication and many other partners. To many people the creative process is very elusive. Design models, approaches and methods help to increase the transparency and timing of the creative process, therefore it facilitates collaboration with the many other disciplines involved.

To do this harmoniously and with a joined understanding of our mission, we use powerful design methods and processes. They are needed to guarantee that our projects address the right future challenges, target the right customers, advance the brand values and progress on time and on budget with the necessary quality while respecting the various rules and regulations.

The car industry is in the midst of a profound transformation towards mobility that is more electric, connected, autonomous, and shared. There is a gradual shift from ownership to mobility as a service, driven by macro-trends such as the growth of metropolitan cities. We search for environmentally responsible solutions while providing freedom of movement and fulfilling people's wishes to connect. And there is a societal desire to reduce accidents to zero, to improve well-being and give people back their precious time. These once-in-a-lifetime transformations are asking for new solutions. And new solutions need new methods.

Of course, strong design methods don't guarantee creative and effective solutions. This still depends on the talent, intuition and skill of each individual designer. But the methods provide structure that creates serenity, a space to think, and time to reflect. From my personal experience I know that it takes time to get 'into the zone' and to be truly creative.

It is therefore my great pleasure to introduce you to the completely renewed 2nd edition of the Delft Design Guide. I was not only happy (and a bit relieved) to recognize many of the methods being featured; I also know their value, because we use them on a daily basis. But more importantly, the Delft Design Guide asks stimulating and challenging questions and offers new models and approaches for the reader to try out.

The proposed perspectives, models, approaches, and methods in this Delft Design Guide are what instruments are to a composer; it is perfectly possible to come up with a beautiful melody using only a flute, but why not use the full spectrum of an orchestra and compose a sweeping symphony?

Laurens van den Acker
Executive Vice President Corporate Design Groupe Renault
Graduated at Delft University of Technology, faculty of Industrial Design Engineering in 1990

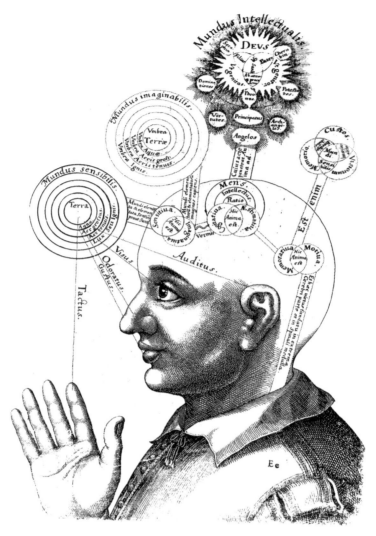

Microcosm diagram of the mind designed by physician Robert Fludd, beginning 17th century; below an exploded view of a modular smartphone, beginning 21st century.

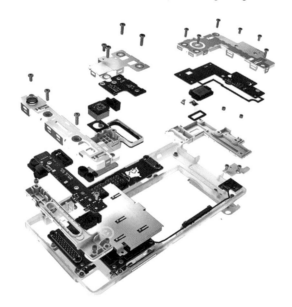

PREFACE

The Delft Design Guide originated from the need for a more comprehensive overview, deeper insight, and stronger assistance in choosing and understanding the right perspective while establishing the design goal, understanding theoretical models, and selecting appropriate approaches and methods that help with the actual development of products, services, and other manifestations of a creative process. We are truly pleased to know that the book is now used in many different places around the world, both in the educational institutions and in practice. The book has also helped in shaping a common image and language that contributes to the Delft design culture that has found its way around the world through this book. Additionally, the graphic design and layout of the book helped to make it an inspiring and accessible reference work, and for this we thank Yvo Zijlstra of Antenna-Men. As a result, the Delft Design Guide is currently used in various design disciplines and at different schools around the world. Thanks to one of our Chinese alumni, the Delft Design Guide has even been published in Chinese since 2014. Since 2015, there is also a Japanese version.

This is a completely revised Delft Design Guide. Like the first edition, published in 2013, this book once again offers a collection of perspectives, models, approaches, and methods that are used in the design education at TU Delft. The book offers a toolbox, an important asset for designers and it offers insight into the distinct Delft Design Thinking. We are proud that the Delft Design Guide is a project of co-creation and the result of a bottom-up approach, in which we created the content together with our many colleagues.

Our field is rapidly changing; after six years, we deemed that the time was ripe for a comprehensive review and renewal. The integration model of People, Technology, and Organisation is still central. The discipline is shifting from a focus on mostly physical products and individual users to a zoomed-out level in which products and individuals are part of a larger system. Non-physical designs, such as in services, and indirect users also play a role in that larger system. There is also more attention to the effect of design on people, the environment, and society: the raison d'être of design. Design therefore becomes increasingly complex and requires new or adapted working methods.

The new Delft Design Guide distinguishes itself from the previous edition on several points. First, more than one-third of this book consists of new content and pages. Second, this book is organised into a clearer structure with distinctive categories (perspectives, models, approaches, and methods). Third, some topics have been removed, whereas others have been merged. Finally, all subjects are improved and enriched with the 'mindset' component that explains the underlying values and principles.

We wish everyone good luck and an enjoyable learning experience with this new Delft Design Guide!

Editors
Annemiek van Boeijen
Jaap Daalhuizen
Jelle Zijlstra

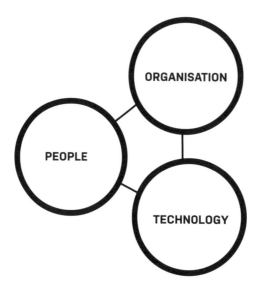

DELFT UNIVERSITY OF TECHNOLOGY
FACULTY OF INDUSTRIAL DESIGN ENGINEERING

ACKNOWLEDGMENTS This book could not have been written without the contributions and expertise, inspiration, and skills of design researchers and design educators and the support of the faculty management team. Our special thanks go to the contributors of this book who all worked as staff members, former staff members or students in the faculty of Industrial Design Engineering in Delft. The editors hope that the book will justify their dedicated work. Cheers!

Aadjan van der Helm, Anton Jellema, Arjen Jansen, Armağan Albayrak, Arnold Vermeeren, Bas Flipsen, Bert Deen, Carlos Cardoso, Chen Hao, Chèr van Slobbe, Conny Bakker, Corné Quartel, Corrie van der Lelie, Dirk Snelders, Elif Ozcan Vieira, Ellis van den Hende, Elisa Giaccardi, Elmer van Grondelle, Elvin Karana, Ena Voûte, Erik Jan Hultink, Erik Roscam Abbing, Esther Zijtregtop, Frido Smulders, Froukje Sleeswijk Visser, Gerd Kortuem, Gert Pasman, Gert Hans Berghuis, Giulia Calabretta, Ingrid de Pauw, Jan Buijs (in memoriam), Jan Schoormans, Jan Willem Hoftijzer, Jasper van Kuijk, Jeroen van Erp, Johan Molenbroek, Joost Vogtländer, Jos Kraal, Lilian Henze, Lianne Simonse, Katrina Heijne, Koos Eissen, Maaike Kleinsmann, Marc Tassoul, Marcel Crul, Marieke Sonneveld, Marielle Creusen, Marina Bos-De Vos, Mathieu Gielen, Matthijs van Dijk, Mieke van der Bijl-Brouwer, Nazli Cila, Nancy Bocken, Norbert Roozenburg, Nynke Tromp, Paul Hekkert, Peter Vink, Petra Badke-Schaub, Pieter Desmet, Pieter Jan Stappers, Pinar Cankurtaran, Remco Timmer, Remke Klapwijk, Renee Wever, Richard Goosens, Roos van der Schoor, Roy Bendor, Ruud Balkenende, Sicco Santema, Stefan van de Geer, Stella Boess, Sylvia Mooij, Thomasz Jaskiewicz, Valentijn Visch, Wilfred van der Vegte, Wouter Kersten, Wouter van der Hoog, Students of the master course Design Theory Methodology 2018-2019

DELFT DESIGN GUIDE

PERSPECTIVES - MODELS - APPROACHES - METHODS

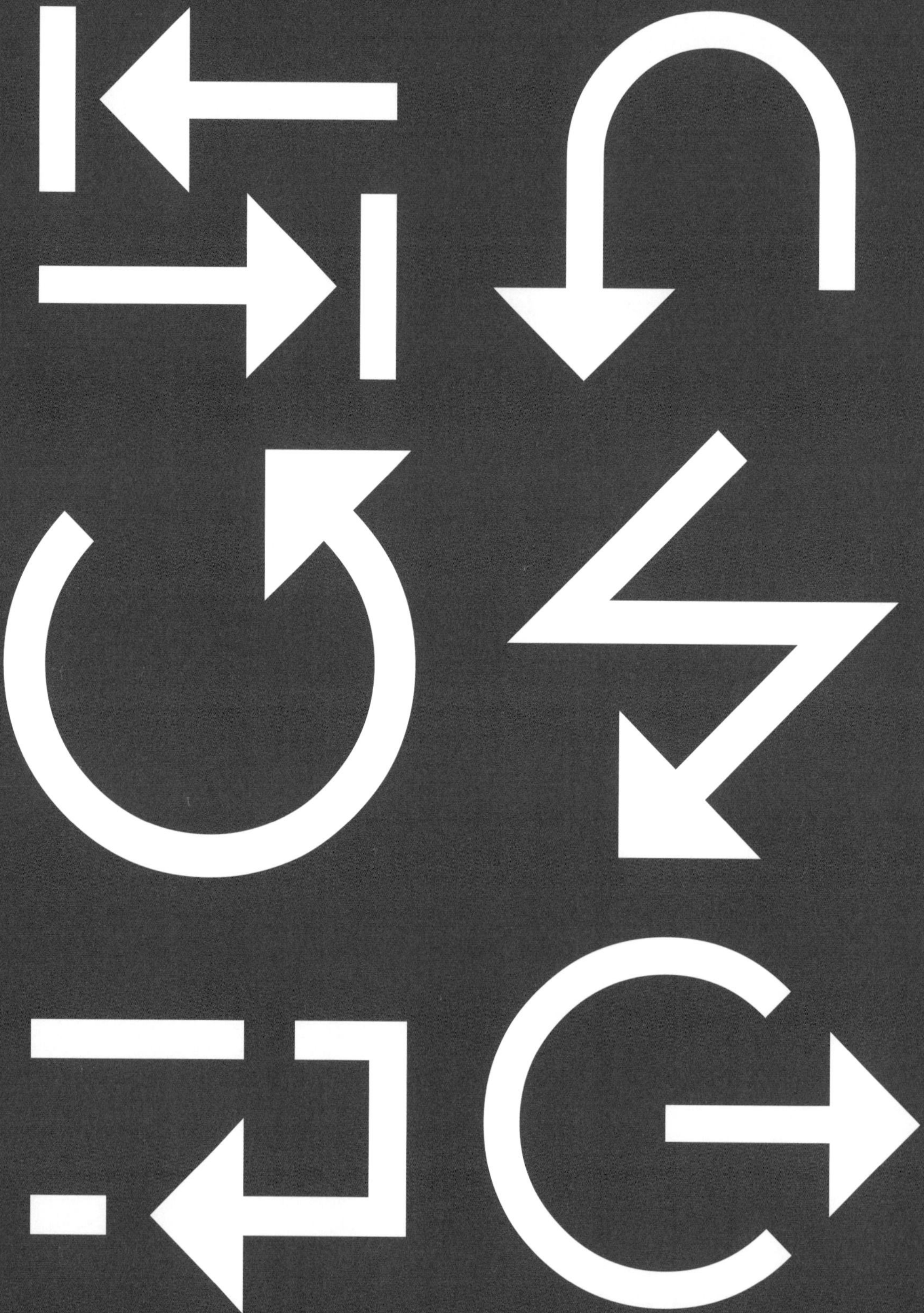

A guide to the Delft Design Guide

You have the completely revised and extended Delft Design Guide in your hands. This guide is meant for everyone that is - or aspires to be - a designer. It should help you to understand how a designer thinks, what a designer does and how this is done, the Delft way. The diversity of perspectives and methodologies presented in this guide shows that design is a rich field with many applications and a network of ways of working and tools to use. The Delft Design Guide offers you a set of perspectives, models, approaches, and methods that serve four distinct purposes.

First, to help you to diverge or converge in your design project in a structured way, identifying and selecting options to solve your design challenges. Second, to help you determine what information and knowledge to find and use to allow you to make decisions and progress the design process. Third, to document and communicate a way of working that helps others to participate and collaborate with you. Finally, to develop yourself as a designer with a strong identity and rich toolbox to tackle the challenges ahead!

BUILD A MINDSET

The domains and application areas that design contributes to are becoming increasingly complex and turbulent. For example, designing interventions that help bring about positive change in the healthcare system, or that change our relationship with the climate are immensely complex and require skills, creativity and thoughtful actions, and productive collaboration. The content of this book can help you in achieving impact, yet it is not enough on its own. Much of what is needed is embedded in the culture and values of our faculty, the missions of the design challenges we collectively work on, and can be identified in the principles of our way of working. In these we can see a strong common denominator that is what makes up the Delft designer. For example, we believe in being human-centric and evidence-based. We also believe in iteration and co-creation. Methodology provides the building blocks, yet you and the people working with design need to build a design mindset to bring these together into effective and meaningful ways of working. This

is why we have added a section on mindset to each method in this new edition. These mindsets help you understand how and why a method can contribute to achieving a certain goal. Your first priority however, should always be to succeed in solving your design challenge and to have maximum impact for your cause.

BE REFLECTIVE

We see design as a goal-directed discipline aimed at creating change. This is not a new idea: Nobel Laureate Herbert Simon already wrote in 1996 in his book *The Sciences of the Artificial*: 'To design is to devise courses of action aimed at changing existing situations into preferred ones'. Design is inherently uncertain and this can be traced back to the core elements in Simon's definition. Designers explore new and sometimes untrodden territories when they ask: *what would be a preferred situation?* They discover and define opportunities for innovation and improvement. They ask what would be meaningful and valuable for people in their context and dare to take a stance to steer innovation. Designers challenge the way tasks or problems are framed and formulated when they ask *what is problematic about the existing situation?* They will keep asking questions until they find root causes and core values that form the starting point for good design. Designers facilitate and drive the development of design solutions that can realise the *preferred situation when they ask: what courses of action will best realise the preferred situation and who should I involve to make it happen?* They make ideas and visions tangible and iteratively explore their potential in realising the desired change. They will keep asking how to realise maximum effect with minimum means for people and within the complex systems that we find ourselves in today.

The Delft Design Guide embodies a diverse and rich set of perspectives, models, approaches and methods that can help you in navigating uncertainty and realising your design goals. There is one major prerequisite: you need to take the steering wheel and always reflect on what ways of working are most likely to help you achieve your goals. In doing so, you need to reflect on both your own values and beliefs as well as the ones of the organisation and community you are working with or for. This means that there are three core questions to ask yourself continuously: 1. what do I want to achieve or contribute? 2. What is the best way to reach these goals? 3. Am I still on the best path to get where I need and want to be? In short: be reflective!

BE A CO-CREATOR AND FACILITATOR

Design is an integrative discipline. Designers work with clients, stakeholders in the organisation, external stakeholders, experts from other disciplines, users, et cetera. An important role of the perspectives, models, approaches and methods is to provide a common structure and language for innovation projects and practices that facilitate productive collaboration, trust and coordination amongst the diverse sets of people that are typically involved in design.

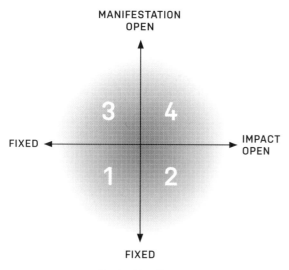

Navigation Canvas.
(Source: Jeroen van Erp)

BE A NAVIGATOR

A design assignment is typically framed along two dimensions: *impact* and *manifestation*. *Impact* refers to a desired effect of the design. M*anifestation* refers to the way the design manifests itself in the world, for instance, a physical product, a service, an app or a game. For both impact and manifestation, an assignment can either define what is expected, or leave it open for the designer. The position of an assignment in one of the quadrants gives direction to the kind of approach and/or methodology that is appropriate and likely to help you achieve your aims. Of course, the world is not as black and white as the matrix suggests, it should be used as a canvas. The more experienced you are as a designer, the more you know how to play with the model.

1. **Impact fixed, manifestation fixed.**
   The classic design assignment: how the design should be manifested and what impact it should have is fixed. A good example is the assignment for a ticket vending machine for public transport. Both impact and manifestation are given from the start.

   For this kind of assignment, you can work with a user-centred design approach to structure the overall process. Various methods like interviews or focus groups can be used to elicit and validate specific user needs. The WWWWWH method can be used to generate relevant questions for the problem analysis and a list of requirements to capture and manage all requirements to inform solution development.

2. **Impact open, manifestation fixed.**
   Assignments of this nature often focus on generating new business models or expanding current businesses. The manifestation in this case is often tied to the assets of the organisation, for instance, its current production facilities, technology expertise or distribution channels. A good example is TomTom, who became famous with its GPS navigation products. When smartphones were introduced, the company realised that selling hardware products to consumers would not be a sustainable business model anymore. Tom Tom successfully changed its strategy and moved from a business-to-consumer to a business-to-business approach, building on the available assets.

For this kind of assignment, you can work with the product innovation process to structure the overall process. Methods like SWOT and brand DNA can help to analyse and understand the current situation of the company. Methods like business modelling, and list of requirements to define the design brief and creative problem solving approach to develop and test solutions.

3. Impact fixed, manifestation open.

Assignments like these often have a strong drive to realise change in a specific domain or situation. Hester Le Riche got her PhD in 2017 and developed the so-called Tovertafel (Magic Table). This is a device that creates 'moments of happiness for people living with dementia and the people around them'. The assignment started with a clear aim to positively impact the lives of people suffering from dementia, yet the manifestation was not determined at that point.

For this kind of assignment, you can work with a user-centred design approach, and use methods like contextmapping and observations as well as research to gain insight into the domain of interest. These insights can be synthesised using, for example, the Persona and Journey Mapping methods. Creativity methods like brainstorming or How-Tos can then be used to develop ideas, and storytelling and experience prototyping for testing and improving concepts.

4. Impact open, manifestation open.

An assignment in this quadrant often aims for exploring future possibilities in a domain, for instance, healthcare or mobility. There is a need to look beyond the current and to create a future vision. A good example is the Redesigning Psychiatry project. This is a consortium of companies and institutions that wanted to improve mental healthcare, with a horizon of 2030. Redesigning Psychiatry envision a future in which mental healthcare is no longer a rigid system but a dynamic network.

For this kind of assignment, you can work with the Vision in Product Design approach to structure the work and explore and define a future direction in terms of impact and solution direction. Then, creativity methods like brainstorming or How-Tos can be used to develop ideas, alongside with storytelling and experience prototyping for testing and improving concepts.

THE ASSIGNMENT JOURNEY

A design assignment will not stay stuck in a quadrant. As your project progresses, you move through the quadrants until you end up in quadrant one. For example, Boyan Slat started his quest with an open attitude, starting in quadrant three. As he progressed, he found out that 1000 rivers bring 80% of the plastic to the ocean. 'Closing the tap' - as he calls it - would heavily contribute to a more plastic free ocean. That led to the idea of the Interceptor moving his project into quadrant one. Sometimes an assignment has unclear or even conflicting aims, making it hard for you to determine where it is positioned. It is a good idea to ask questions and figure out with the relevant stakeholders what is really the aim!

Start-ups often 'float around' on this canvas. They often start with an insight, an idea or a hunch of how a certain technology can be brought to the market; manifestation rather clear, impact open. Yet, they might progress and find out that their initial idea for a manifestation was not the right one, flipping between quadrants two and three. They move back and forth between exploring user value and business opportunity. Once matured, they scale-up and stay in a single quadrant for a longer period.

'Let us get used
to looking at the
world through the
eyes of others.'
BRUNO MUNARI

PERSPECTIVES

Perspectives are descriptive in nature. That is, a perspective focuses on specific intended effects and qualities to strive for when doing design. For example, Design for Sustainability describes the intended effect of the design and explains its importance. Many perspectives are linked to an approach and/or one or more methods that help to achieve the desired effect when doing design.

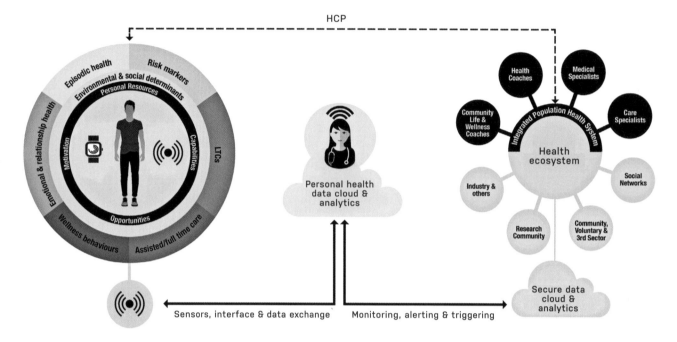

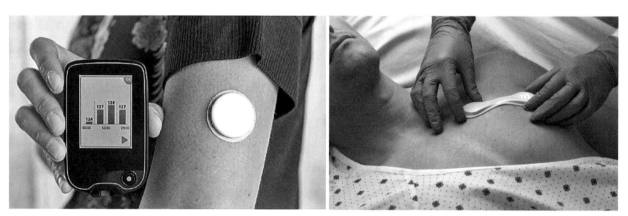

Biosensors are wearable medical devices that are radically different from wrist trackers and smartwatches. A biosensor is a self-adhesive patch that allows patients to move around while collecting data on their movement, heart rate, respiratory rate, and temperature. These devices can lead to significant reduction in patient deterioration into preventable cardiac or respiratory arrest. This demonstrates the ability wearables have to improve patient outcomes and possibly reduce staff workload.

Design for Health and Well-Being

Design for Health and Well-Being offers a perspective for designers to understand the complexity of healthcare systems, to identify the needs and expectations of the different stakeholders, and to design innovative and sustainable solutions with an added value for human health.

WHAT & WHY? The healthcare context is the physical, informational, and organisational environment in which healthcare processes take place. This can be a confusing experience for people who need care. Health services and care pathways are often part of these very intricate processes, including different kinds of interactions between patients, healthcare professionals, products, and services. Such processes are often highly regulated with evidence-based protocols and ethical considerations. Multiple stakeholders are involved, ranging from patients, caregivers, and a multidisciplinary group of healthcare professionals. All these individuals have different backgrounds and different interests, making interaction and communication between them 'multilingual' in a way.

The way in which care is provided has been continually changing. Due to increasing healthcare costs and the shortage of personnel, there is a need to try different approaches for maintaining sustainable and high-quality healthcare. These new challenges make care processes even more complex. Prevention will play an increasingly more important role in our future health. While at present the care system is primarily focused on treating the sick, in the future the focus will be more on preventing people from falling ill. Personal data such as health data will play a crucial role, which can potentially overwhelm a number of healthcare stakeholders as they need to manage a seemingly endless flow of data.

Dealing with this growing complexity and challenges asks for a holistic approaches. An integration of the knowledge and insights into meaningful and sustainable solutions will be the key approach here. In this way, designers today can offer added value to human health in the future.

MINDSET: Design for Health and Well-Being asks designers to look for solutions that are part of sociotechnical systems. Such systems should be designed to be meaningful and sustainable and should anticipate changes in the healthcare system. This means that you need a holistic view and to work in multidisciplinary collaboration.

HOW? Challenges in complex healthcare systems are addressed with design approaches such as Human-Centred Design, Contextual Design as well as participatory approaches such as Co-design and Co-creation. Within these approaches, the ones that are typically used are Patient Journey Mapping, Patient Profiling, Contextmapping, and Personas.

TIPS & CONCERNS
Go through a research cycle to understand the challenges, design and propose sustainable solutions, as well as evaluate the impact on the health system.

It is essential for you to have a solid understanding of the healthcare systems and processes in order to create meaningful and sustainable solutions.

LIMITATIONS
Design for Health and Well-Being needs to rely on a multidisciplinary collaboration of the different stakeholders during the whole design process.

It is very important to create solutions with an added value for all the stakeholders.

REFERENCES & FURTHER READING: Carayon, P. & Wooldridge, A.R., 2019. Improving Patient Safety in the Patient Journey: Contributions from Human Factors Engineering. In A.E. Smith (Ed.), *Woman in Industrial and Systems Engineering: Key Advantages and Perspectives on Emerging Topics*. Springer International Publishing. / Simonse, L., Albayrak, A., & Starre, S., 2019. Patient journey method for integrated service design. *Design for Health*, 3(1), 82-97. / Groeneveld, B.S., Melles, M., Vehmeijer, S.B.W., Mathijssen, N.M.C., Dekkers, T., & Goossens, R.H.M., 2019. Developing digital applications for tailored communication in orthopaedics using a research through design approach. *Digital Health*, 5, 1-14. / Ridder, E. de, Dekkers, T., Porsius, J.T., Kraan, G., & Melles, M., 2018. The perioperative patient experience of hand and wrist surgical patients: An exploratory study using patient journey mapping. *Patient Experience Journal*, 5(3), 97-107.

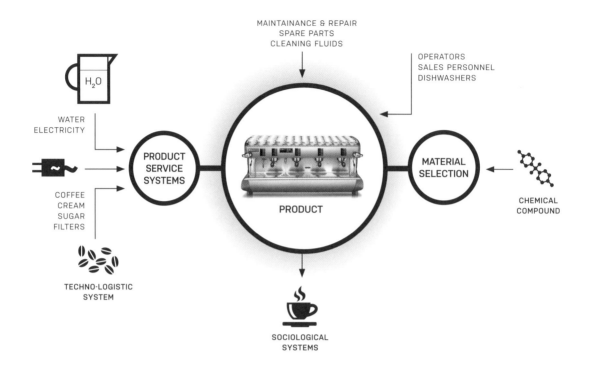

No product exists in isolation. Focussing on just a tiny segment of the Grand Universal Hierarchy, the one that ranges from our social-technical systems down to chemical compound level, the domain of actual products is wedged between the domains of product service systems and available material choices. Design for sustainability is an approach that puts the well-being of people and the environment first. In addition it implies thinking in systems (deciding how things relate to their larger system); dematerialisation (get more 'service' from less product renewable, natural materials); think of materials and components as being in a 'nutrient' cycle.

Design for Sustainability

Any product or product-service system that you design will have an impact on society and the natural environment. Design for Sustainability (DfS) aims for net-positive impacts, namely beneficial outcomes for society and the natural environment. Understanding how to design for sustainability is a fundamental design skill.

WHAT & WHY? DfS means designing products and product-service systems that benefit the natural environment, enhance the well-being of communities around us (especially underprivileged and disadvantaged populations), and are conducive to economic prosperity.

Sustainability is essential to our well-being as well as to human survival in the long run. Designers have a responsibility to pay attention to the sustainability impacts that their work can have. This is not easy, and there is a tendency to treat sustainability as a desirable quality of the product-service system that should only be considered once other priorities have been established. We need to recognize that sustainability is not in competition with other requirements – it is a fundamental precondition for the continued existence of the product-service system, and it influences each design decision that is made.

Sustainability is not a problem that can be solved; it is more of a challenge that we should respond to intelligently and learn from while doing so. Sustainability is also systemic by nature. When you deal with one aspect of sustainability such as choosing a renewable material, you will automatically influence other aspects such as biodiversity loss. As a designer, you have to become a system thinker – any design intervention aiming to address a particular challenge will have co-benefits, spillover effects, and negative side effects, and these need to be understood in order for you to design an intervention with sustainable impact.

MINDSET: The most important values a designer can bring to DfS are a sense of responsibility and a willingness to think in systems. Doing sustainable design means creating synergy between human well-being, planetary health, and economic prosperity. A design is not considered sustainable if it has many benefits for the well-being of people but results in ecological losses.

HOW? There are a number of approaches, each with advantages and drawbacks. If you are new to DfS, you could start with the Ecodesign Checklist and the Ecodesign Strategy Wheel, which together provide a good overview of the field. The drawback of Ecodesign is that it focuses on incremental improvements of existing products. If you want more fundamental approaches to DfS, you can try Biomimicry, Cradle to Cradle, or Design for a Circular Economy. The Product Journey Map and the Sustainable Business Model Canvas are useful when designing for a circular economy.

Use the 10 Golden Rules of Design for Sustainability as a memory map. You should always take these 10 rules into account, no matter which DfS approach you choose!

TIPS & CONCERNS

Do not to let other priorities overtake the urgent need to address sustainability.

Address sustainability right from the start of any product and service development project.

LIMITATIONS

The success depends on many factors, not all of which can be controlled by designers.

You need to be patient and even stubborn enough to keep bringing up the topic including its opportunities with clients and colleagues.

You will have to deal with a lack of reliable data and other uncertainties in the projects you do.

You need a long-term view and an open mind to keep monitoring societal and scientific developments, and you will need to adjust your design approach accordingly.

1 **Toxicity:** Limit the use of toxic substances and, where such substances are essential, try to arrange closed material loops.
----
2 **Housekeeping:** Review your routines to minimize energy and resource consumption in production and transport.
----
3 **Weight:** Choose materials and designs that minimize the weight of the product.
----
4 **Energy:** Think about how the end product will be used and try to minimize the user's energy and resource consumption.
----
5 **Upgrading:** Design the product to allow upgrading and repair, especially for long lifespan and system-dependent products.
----
6 **Lifetime:** Optimize the product for its intended working life.
----
7 **Protection:** Invest in durable materials and surface treatments to protect the product.

8 **Information:** Prepare for upgrading, repair and recycling through accessibility, labeling, modular construction and manuals.
9 **Mixing materials:** This affects recyclability in a negative way. Try to use as few materials as possible in simple forms.
----
10 **Construction:** Use as few joining elements as possible, avoid the unnecessary use of screws and bonding, and look for intelligent geometric solutions.

REFERENCES & FURTHER READING: Shedroff, N., 2009. *Design is the problem. The future of design must be sustainable.* Rosenfeld, USA. / Crul, M., Diehl, J.C., Ryan, C. (Eds.). 2009. *Design for Sustainability, a step-by-step approach.* United Nations Environment Program. / Papanek, V.J., 1985. *Design for the real world. Human Ecology and Social Change.* Academy Chicago Publishers. / Bakker, C.A., 2019. *Ten Golden Rules of Design for Sustainability.* Proc. PLATE 2019, Product Lifetimes and the Environment, Berlin.

This zebra crossing - a concept first introduced in New Delhi, Inda - applies a cleverly-detailed optical illusion causing fast drivers to slow down. On the right: Operating on the theory that exposure to blue light has a calming effect on one's mood, rail stations in Japan began installing blue LED panels as a suicide-prevention measure. According to a study by researchers at the University of Tokyo data analyzed over a 10-year period shows an 84 percent decline in the number of suicide attempts.

The Camden bench is a prime example of hostile architecture, a controversial type of urban design aimed at preventing people from using public spaces in undesirable ways. It can come in the form of spiked or sloped benches, bolts installed on shop doorsteps and windowsills, and even water features that operate at surprising intervals on flat surfaces. The Camden bench required that people couldn't sleep on it, stash drugs in it, or skate on it.

Design for Behavioural Change

Design for Behavioural Change (DfBC) concerns designing products and services with the aim to change people's behaviour. A behavioural change project is multi-disciplinary in nature. Design interventions often support people to create awareness and help them either realise an intended behaviour or maintain a preferred behaviour.

WHAT & WHY? Designers are increasingly asked to create interventions via products, services, or combinations that support the realisation of a behavioural change.

In Design for Behavioural Change, models are used from psychology and social science that aim to describe the psychological process of behaviour. From psychology it is known that when people change their behaviour, they often go through three stages: '1. Awareness of the new behaviour including contemplation and the intention to try the new behaviour, 2. Action preparing and starting the new behaviour, and 3. Maintenance maintaining and habituating the new behaviour. You should be aware of these stages of change with respect to your intended users and then tailor your design accordingly. A change in behaviour is often the main indicator of success, and it can be measured either during the interaction with experience-oriented measurements; directly after the interaction with intention-oriented measurements; or after a longer period following the interaction with behaviour- and attitude-oriented measurements. Design for Behavioural Change is not limited to a behavioural aim in a strict sense, which is understood as an execution of bodily action. It can also target raising awareness, influencing a social change, or facilitate a cognitive change.

For example, when you design a smart pill box that selects the right daily amount of medication and sends persuasive reminders to patients when they did not take it, the behavioural goal of the designed device is clearly communicated to the patient. In this case, ethical concerns might involve questions regarding patient dependency and trustworthiness of the system. In nudging practices, the behavioural design goal is often not clearly communicated to the user. For instance, a candy shop may try to persuade people to buy their candies by placing them at a grabbing level near the counter. In these cases, people are influenced by product placement without knowing it, and this might even conflict with the person's personal behavioural intentions, such as to eat healthy.

MINDSET: DfBC raises ethical questions. The importance of an ethical discussion depends on the product or service and the situation.

HOW? Various approaches and methods are developed to support Design for Behavioural Change. Persuasive Game Design in this guide offers a design recipe for a behavioural change involving motivating game elements. The card set *Cards-for-Change* can be used for discovering and selecting existing behavioural change techniques that can be used in your design.

TIPS & CONCERNS
Take ethical issues into consideration. See the section 'Mindset'.

For a good understanding of individual behaviour, you need to understand the sociocultural context people live in.

Work together with multiple stakeholders and disciplines, such as those in psychology and anthropology, implementation partners, and intended users.

Focus not only on quick and short-term motivations for behavioural change but also include long-term motivational strategies.

Anticipate the possible unexpected outcomes as well as the difficult and sensitive situations.

Design processes for behavioural Change are typically iterative and involve co-creation sessions and observations.

LIMITATIONS
Influence of designers through design is limited. In practice there are many, sometimes unforeseen factors on a personal and societal level that will influence a person's behaviour and the effect of your intervention.

REFERENCES & FURTHER READING: Prochaska, J.O., & DiClemente, C.C., 1983. Stages and processes of self-change of smoking: toward an integrative model of change. *Journal of consulting and clinical psychology*, 51(3), 390. / van der Kooij, K., Hoogendoorn, E., Spijkerman, R. & Visch, V., 2015. Validation of games for behavioral change: connecting the playful and serious. *International Journal of Serious Games*, 2(3), 63-75. / Cash, P.J., Hartlev, C.G., & Durazo, C.B., 2017. Behavioural design: A process for integrating behaviour change and design. *Design Studies*, 48, 96-128. / Darnton, A., 2008. *An overview of behaviour change models and their uses*. GSR Behaviour Change Knowledge Review (p. 81). Retrieved from https://research.fit.edu/media/site-specific/researchfitedu/coast-climate-adaptation-library/climate-communications/messaging-climate-change/Darnton.-2008.-Behaviour-Change-Models--Uses.pdf

Designs which tap into the user's emotions are considered to do more than just respond to their stated needs and provide a greater level of user experience. Musicians can form highly beneficial relationships with their instruments. Research results showed that many musicians express feeling 'at one' with their instrument. Those considering it as 'part of themselves' experiencing more confidence and less anxiety when performing. Image: violinist and conductor David Oistrakh (1908-1974)

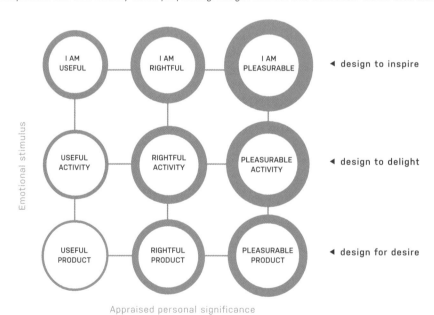

Humans form emotional connections with objects on three levels: the visceral, behavioural, and reflective levels. Plutchik's Psycho-evolutionary Theory of Emotion helps categorize emotions into primary emotions and the responses to them.

Design for Emotion

Design for Emotion is a perspective on design that takes the intended emotional impact as the leading principle in the design process.

WHAT & WHY? Design for Emotion offers a systematic approach to designing products with predefined emotional intentions. The approach can be used to (a) define an appropriate emotional effect, (b) gather relevant user information so that this emotional effect can be achieved, (c) envision concepts that evoke the intended effect, and (d) measure to what extent the design concept evokes the intended emotion. The approach is based on a basic model of emotion in design where designers distinguish between the different layers of emotion that should be taken into consideration in design processes.

The key variables in the model are stimulus and concern. With regard to stimulus, design can provide emotional stimuli on three levels: object, usage, and context. With concern, there are three types of user concerns that are relevant here, namely the goals, standards, and attitudes of users. These two variables combine to form a matrix of nine sources of product emotion.

MINDSET: The perspective is based on a cognitive approach to analysing emotions that builds on an evolutionary perspective of human experience. Emotions play a central role in the human ability to understand and learn about the world. Positive experiences kindle our curiosity, and negative ones protect us from repeating mistakes. It requires an analytical view on emotions and a research-informed design approach.

HOW? You can use various methods to measure emotions, such as PrEmo (see 'Product Emotion Measurement Instrument'). You can also use interview techniques to explore the relationship between emotions and the underlying goals and needs:

Concerns: Determine the underlying concerns of the user by asking three questions. First, what are their goals? These can refer to objectives such as things they want to accomplish or see happen. Second, what are their standards? This can involve the expectations and beliefs about how they themselves, other people, and objects should behave or act. Lastly, what are their attitudes? This refers to dispositional likings or dislikings for qualities of objects, people, or activities. All these concerns should be formulated

not only in relation to objects – as in, the product to be designed – but also in relation to the activity that is enabled or supported by the use of the product and in relation to the people (including the user) who are involved in the context of use.

Response: Observe current emotional responses in the context of use. This can help you determine user concerns. These existing emotions are used as entry points in interviews to understand underlying concerns.

Conflicts: Formulate possible conflicts between user concerns. These conflicts are then used to formulate new design solution spaces. The emotional impact of concepts can be tested with the use of PrEmo.

TIPS & CONCERNS
At least 25 different emotions can be experienced in human-product interaction. In the design process, the intended emotions should be defined because different emotions require different designs.

Design for Emotion involves designing for concerns; therefore, this approach always requires a research stage in which user concerns are determined.

Concerns should be formulated as 'I want...', 'I should / someone should / a product should...' or 'I like....'

The formulation should be concrete, and concern sets should include not only goals but also standards and attitudes.

LIMITATIONS
Design for Emotion focuses on emotional effects of design, but it does not necessarily take other relevant aspects or requirements into consideration. The approach should therefore be incorporated into regular design approaches rather than used in isolation.

Although the basic concepts in the approach are easy to understand, using them in design processes does require some experience.

REFERENCES & FURTHER READING: Desmet, P.M.A., 2012. Faces of Product Pleasure; 25 Positive Emotions in Human-Product Interactions. *International Journal of Design*, 6(2), pp. 1-29. / Desmet, P.M.A., Fokkinga, S.F., Ozkaramanli, D., & Yoon, J., 2016. *Emotion-driven product design.* In: H.L. Meiselman (Ed.), Emotion Measurement (pp. 405-426). Amsterdam: Elsevier. / Desmet, P.M.A. & Schifferstein, N.J.H., 2012. *Emotion research as input for product design.* In J. Beckley, D. Paredes, & K. Lopetcharat (Eds.), Product Innovation Toolbox: A Field Guide to Consumer Understanding and Research (pp. 149-175). Hoboken, NJ: John Wiley & Sons. / Ozkaramanli, D. & Desmet, P.M.A., 2012. I know I shouldn't, yet I did it again! Emotion-driven design as a means to subjective wellbeing. *International Journal of Design*, 6(1), pp. 27-39.

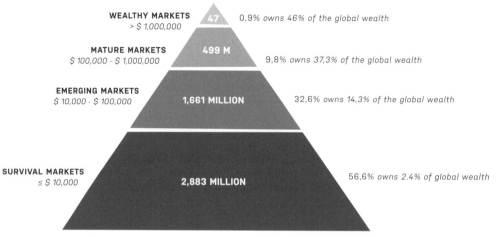

WEALTHY MARKETS > $ 1,000,000	47	0,9% owns 46% of the global wealth
MATURE MARKETS $ 100,000 - $ 1,000,000	499 M	9,8% owns 37,3% of the global wealth
EMERGING MARKETS $ 10,000 - $ 100,000	1,661 MILLION	32,6% owns 14,3% of the global wealth
SURVIVAL MARKETS ≤ $ 10,000	2,883 MILLION	56,6% owns 2.4% of global wealth

Most companies focus on the top markets, while three quarters of global adult population that fit into the bottom echelon of the wealth pyramid largely go unlapped. In developed countries, about 20 percent of adults fall within this category. 2.7 billion people live on less than $2.50 a day. (source: Credit Suisse global wealth report 2019)

Liter of Light is an open source design by Alfredo Moser (Brasil) for a low-cost light tube to provide daytime interior lighting for dwellings with tin roofs. The device is simple: a transparent two-liter bottle is filled with water plus a little bleach to inhibit algal growth and fitted into a hole in the roof. During daytime the water inside the bottle refracts sunlight, delivering about as much light as a 40–60 watt incandescent bulb to the interior. A solar bottle can last up to 5 years. Liter of Light has installed more than 350,000 bottle lights in more than 15 countries and taught green skills to empower grassroots entrepreneur .

Design for The Majority

Design for The Majority means designing products and product-service systems for the world's less fortunate people. Often these people live in nations with emerging markets that are characterised by rapidly growing production and consumption.

WHAT & WHY? Most products are designed for the top of the world's economic pyramid (ToP). These products are unsuitable for the majority of the world's population, who from an economical perspective belong to the Base of the Pyramid (BoP). ToP products are typically too expensive, unavailable for people living in poor areas, and are often not appropriated enough to local situations and possibilities. Designers are often not familiar with the socio-economic context of the BoP population. They need thorough contextual research to gain an empathic understanding of the intended users and context of use. Another major challenge in designing for the BoP context is the variety and complexity of the stakeholder landscape. Such projects often involve not only a company but also governmental and non-governmental organisations, aid foundations, and knowledge institutes, all with different backgrounds and interests.

MINDSET: Designers working for BoP projects believe that welfare and well-being should be distributed more equally worldwide. When designing for unfamiliar contexts, you need an open attitude – at least open enough to question your own presumptions about what the norm is, what design should do, and what good design is. Furthermore, you need to prepare yourself for uncertain and unexpected situations and be flexible enough to deal with them.

HOW? You can use existing models, approaches, and methods, but often they need to be attuned to the local context. For example, you need to adjust participative methods to the targeted culture (see Culture-Sensitive Design). When designing for a BoP context and emerging markets, pay extra attention to the following principles:

Affordability: The challenge for you as a designer is to propose affordable solutions. There are several strategies to make products cheap, but overall a holistic approach is needed. You need to take into account not only the production costs of a single product but also the entire system so that each actor or component can benefit from the new product, including entrepreneurs.

Accessibility: The solution should be accessible to the intended users, especially those living in areas with poor infrastructure.

Availability: If the products are manufactured locally, the availability of materials and skills should be taken into account.

Reliability: Solutions should be reliable and easy to maintain and to repair locally; this is to prevent people from becoming too dependent on outsiders.

Sustainability: Solutions need to be sustainable and should not harm the often vulnerable living environments.

Acceptability: You must have a thorough understanding of the opportunities and preferences of the targeted people, the intended users and other people that are influenced by your design. Realising they are both members of a cultural group and members of the global community.

These principles are part of an integrated, holistic, and multi-disciplinary design approach that stimulates local and international entrepreneurship.

TIPS & CONCERNS

As an 'outsider', you need to do your homework first! The way people live and behave is usually based on a long history. Before you intervene, it is important to understand the intrinsic reasons of why people do what they do.

Additional aspects that should be taken into account include building trust, understanding otherness, checking biases, and dealing with poor infrastructure. So you will need more time than what you may be used to.

Contextual design research methods should be attuned to the local context.

For organisations in BoP contexts, producing for Western markets often involve another interpretation of requirements such as product quality, consumer preferences, and safety.

For a good understanding of the local situation, you need to experience the local context yourself.

The world is rapidly changing. Concepts such as 'developing countries' and 'East versus West' are becoming outdated, and they do not reflect nor justify reality.

LIMITATIONS

The success of a product or service depends on many factors, and many new designs simply do not enter the market. It is especially difficult in the BoP context, and therefore the collaboration with local and experienced people is important.

REFERENCES & FURTHER READING: Jansen, G.J. & Crul, M.R.M., 2012. *Sustainable Product Innovation: A Do-it-yourself Toolkit for SMEs in Emerging Economies*. Delft: Delft University of Technology. / Kandachar, P.H., de Jongh, I. & Diehl, J.C., 2009. *Designing for Emerging Markets-Design of Products and Services*. Delft: Delft University of Technology. / van Boeijen, A.G.C., 2015. *Crossing Cultural Chasms: Towards a culture-conscious approach to design*. Doctoral Thesis, Delft University of Technology, Delft. / Mink, A. 2017. *Design for Well-Being: An Approach for Understanding Users' Lives in Design for Development*. Doctoral thesis, Delft University of Technology.

The $ 890,- Balaclava Jumper of luxury brand Gucci is made of black wool with a turtleneck that extends over the mouth. The jumper was part of a collection 'inspired by vintage ski masks'. On its release in 2018 it created uproar on social media with some calling it 'haute couture blackface for millenials'. Blackface is a form of theatrical make-up used by non-black performers to represent a caricature of a black person. These sort of practices continue to contribute to the spread of racial stereotypes. Gucci deeply apologized for the offense it unintentionally caused and withdrew the sweater from its collection. (Gicchi, Wikimedia Commons)

PERSPECTIVES
Culture-Sensitive Design

Culture-Sensitive Design (CSD) is a perspective that highlights the influence of culture regarding a designer's background, the process of designing, and the generated designs. A sensitive 'eye' for the cultural context helps with finding opportunities and overcoming barriers due to cultural influences.

WHAT & WHY? In design projects, usually both individual and universal values and needs are examined. The cultural perspective is often forgotten or implicitly included. However, the cultural context influences the perception of design in a two-way fashion.

In a globalized world with interconnected societies and with the complexity of multicultural subgroups, designers are confronted with the challenge of people sharing different beliefs, values, and practices. This may be seen as a problem needing to be tackled in order to avoid cultural mistakes. It can also be seen as a positive attitude change towards people living in different cultural contexts (such as different regions, professions, or families) or people dealing with different situations, climates, economic situations, demography, and politics.

Culture-sensitive designers are aware not only of the cultural context that they design for but also the influence of their own cultural backgrounds on their design.

MINDSET: Developing cultural awareness and sensitivity can only result from a curious attitude, an open mind, and a broad social and historical interest. CSD requires you to reflect on your own cultural background to understand how it influences your values and beliefs, as well as what it means for your own work.

HOW? CSD offers models that help designers sharpen their lens in looking at culture, appropriating existing methods, or exploring cultural contexts. Theories are adopted from other disciplines such as anthropology, design history, and sociology, and these are attuned to the designer's needs. An example is the circuit of culture, a comprehensive model that entails five processes that influence the cultural meaning of things: these processes are production of meaning, consumption (daily practices), social regulation, representation by media, and identity.

In line with Persona, a new method called Cultura has been developed that helps designers gain insights into people's cultural contexts and build intercultural empathic understanding in the early stages of a new product or service development. A set of sociocultural dimensions and the Crossing Culture Chasms card set can help designers raise culture-specific questions and generate ideas based on specific value orientations.

TIPS & CONCERNS

Culture is a comprehensive term that is not easy to delineate and cannot be cast into concrete. Therefore, you need an open and flexible mind and a broad interest.

Individuals often do not consider themselves as representatives of a cultural group. A helpful analogy is the forest: we can classify a group of trees into different types of forests, such as a tropical rain forest or a Mediterranean forest. While each type is different, together they have something in common.

Culture-sensitivity helps you attune your design research methods to intended users and to develop your own stance regarding what your design should do in the cultural context.

It also helps you specify who is or isn't included in the context.

LIMITATIONS

CSD is based on viewing people as members of groups; therefore, less attention is given to individual differences.

It does not highlight what most individuals have in common, such as the universal principles of human behaviour.

To avoid blunders, culture-sensitivity should be incorporated into regular design processes.

REFERENCES & FURTHER READING: du Gay, P., Hall, S., Janes, L., Mackey, H., & Negus, K., 1997. *Doing Cultural studies: The Story of the Sony Walkman*. London: Sage Publications (in association with the Open University). / Hao, C., van Boeijen, A.G.C., & Stappers, P.J., 2017. Generative research techniques crossing cultures: a field study in China. *International Journal of Cultural and Creative Industries*. / van Boeijen, A.G.C., 2015. *Crossing Cultural Chasms: Towards a culture-conscious approach to design*. Doctoral Thesis, Delft University of Technology, Delft. / van Boeijen, A.G.C., 2020. *Culture Sensitive Design: A guide to culture in practice*. Amsterdam: BIS Publishers.

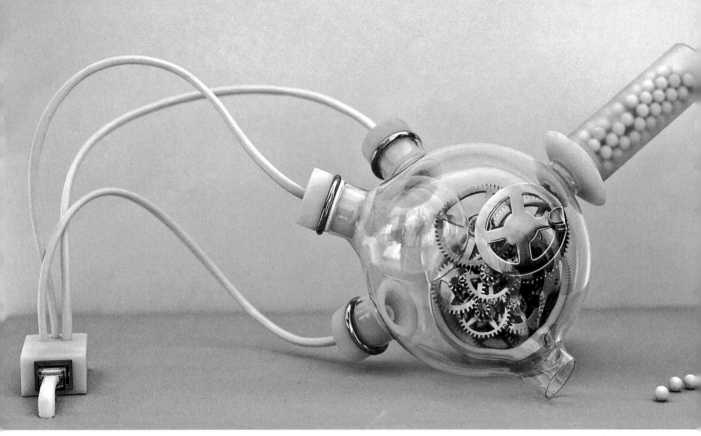

This Artificial Biological Clock highlights the complex social pressures and expectations that dictate a woman's reproductive potential in contrast to the body's natural rhythms. A woman seeking a clearer understanding of her circumstances could look to the clock, which is fed information by her doctor, therapist, and bank manager via an online service. When these complex factors align, the clock lets her know that she is ready to have a child. (Revital Cohen, 2008)

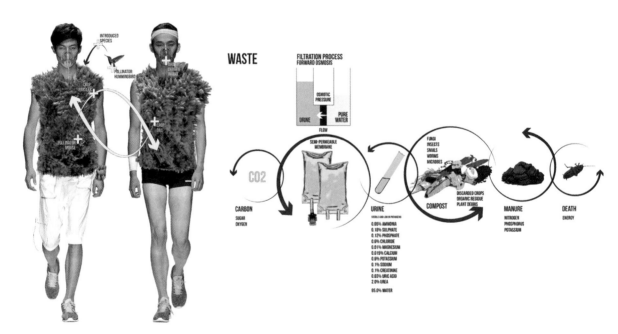

Posthuman Habitats is a wearable landscape system, The garments promote healthful diet and lifestyle, as the gardens are fed and nourished by bodily wastes, and inspire outdoor exposure to optimize photosynthesis. Distinctive subjects, isolatable artifacts and environment are blurred and hybridized. Here, bodily systems and plant ecologies are symbiotic and the 'human' becomes part of a larger habitational field. (www.foreground-da.com)

Speculative Design

Speculative Design seeks to create and promote critical discourse around important social issues. By giving future possibilities a provocative and tangible form, designers attempt to disclose and challenge our social imaginaries. Speculating about the future using this mode can serve as a means to problematize our current conditions and contemplate future alternatives.

WHAT & WHY? Speculative Design uses the future as a backdrop for engaging with social dilemmas, and it allows designers to break free from some of the cognitive, normative, and behavioural constraints of the present. This method creates an imaginative space for designers to consider and convey the consequences of contemporary and future ways of being. Speculative Design can be seen as a form of communication – it invites users to reflect and debate matters of concern, perform the future situation or 'try it on for size', and discover alternatives to current conditions.

The imaginative nature and future orientation of Speculative Design make it especially suitable for engaging with complex and even 'wicked' problems. Such problems often display a puzzling array of emergent, interrelated causes and dynamics, and therefore they do not lend themselves to traditional forms of problem solving by design. Speculative Design allows designers to inquire about the various dimensions of the problem without attempting to solve it outright, thus opening up the problem space to new perspectives.

MINDSET: Speculative Design operates on multiple temporalities, thereby suggesting alternative pasts, presents, or futures. To do this effectively, both designers and users are asked to suspend disbelief in the designed outcome. This involves replacing plausibility: *'Will this come true in the future?'*, **with credibility:** *'Does it feel like this future could come true?'* **as a criterion for evaluating outcomes. Reference to a real world 'out there' is substituted for a sense of internal – or diegetic – consistency.**

HOW? Speculative Design processes often start by projecting the current social, cultural, and technological trends into the future. Future possibilities are then crafted into provocative, imaginative scenarios, and these scenarios can be materialised through a variety of design tools, techniques, and media.

While there is no single 'standard' or conventional way to conduct Speculative Design, most speculative designers make use of techniques drawn from futures studies (or futurology). These techniques include Trend Foresight and Horizon Scanning, but also more commonly Written Scenarios, which consists of positing 'what if' questions and following them to their logical conclusions (see Trend Foresight and Written Scenarios). Pluralizing the future in this way may lead to unanticipated, evocative results.

Since Speculative Design often proceeds as a form of storytelling, it makes use of fictionalizing techniques. These are meant to create compelling narratives and situations that are credible yet provocative.

TIPS & CONCERNS

The significance lies in provoking the imagination and the sense of possibility in both the designer and the user.

Speculative Design should not be confused with other future-oriented design techniques such as Design Fiction in particular, which can be seen as ways to prepare for the future instead of illustrating the future's malleability.

The construction of thought-provoking situations often works well with more nuanced rhetorical strategies such as humour, irony, and grotesque exaggeration.

Create a sense of personal relevance and affect while maintaining a critical distance from the design itself.

LIMITATIONS

The success of Speculative Design processes relies on the fit between the chosen scenario, including its time-frame, cultural context, and protagonists. And the user's interpretive strategies, such as their existing social imaginaries, cultural tropes, and background.

It is important to remember that the outcome may feel more like fanciful fantasy than critical speculation if the designed outcome is situated too far into the future, if the situation lacks credibility, or if the interaction lacks consistency.

REFERENCES & FURTHER READING: Dunne, A., & Raby, F., 2013. *Speculative everything: design, fiction, and social dreaming.* Cambridge, Mass.: MIT Press. / Wakkary, R., Odom, W., Hauser, S., Hertz, G., & Lin, H., 2015. Material Speculation: Actual Artifacts for Critical Inquiry. *Aarhus Series on Human Centered Computing*, 1(1), 97-108. / Wilkie, A., Savransky, M., & Rosengarten, M. (Eds.)., 2017. *Speculative Research: The Lure of Possible Futures.* Abingdon, UK; New York: Routledge. / Bendor, R., van der Helm, A., & Jaskiewicz, T. (Eds.)., 2018. *A Spectrum of Possibilities: A Catalog of Tools for Urban Citizenship in the Not-So-Far Future.* Delft: Faculty of Industrial Design Engineering, Delft University of Technology.

The Māori tribes in New Zealand do not consider themselves masters of the universe but part of it. They fought a 140 year-long legal battle to grant the Whanganui River the same legal rights as a human being. They finally won the case in 2017 meaning that it would be treated as a living entity, as an indivisible whole, instead of treating it from the perspective of ownership and management. That perspective is not an anti-development, or anti-economic use of the river but one that begins with the view that a river is a living being, and then consider its future from that central belief. (wickimedia commons)

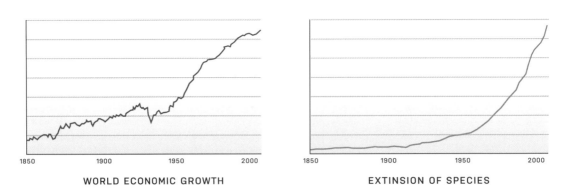

WORLD ECONOMIC GROWTH

EXTINSION OF SPECIES

Graphs of economic growth are deeply political. They simplify and exclude a more troubling and complex reality. Apart from a few hiccups we've been moving upwards over the past hundred years. Moving up to no idea where. When seen against another graph, but this time that of species which have gone extinct in the same period, one realizes that this kind of progress can only be celebrated as a victory in isolation. (source: University of Idaho)

More-Than-Human Design

More-Than-Human Design considers the knowledge and behaviour of non-human entities – from plants to animals to intelligent things – and it aims to craft new capacities for meaning and action at the intersection of humans and non-humans.

WHAT & WHY? Through design, we are transforming the planet to meet user needs and desires. While it is reasonable to assume a beneficial intent to design, the consequences of design are not always positive and such consequences can range from climate change to resource depletion to surveillance capitalism. A more-than-human perspective acknowledges that humans are more than users: they are part of an ecosystem. Within this ecosystem, it is not exclusively humans who act and produce effects; in fact, plants, animals, and intelligent things can create new possibilities too.

MINDSET: More-Than-Human Design promotes the idea that to explore the futures we might face, we need to inquire what happens when we step out of an anthropocentric view of the world. Such an inquiry is necessary not because humans matter less but that society has largely become a sphere that threatens inclusion, diversity, and well-being due to the design ideal that humans are users of products to be consumed.

HOW? With a More-Than-Human Design approach, you can experiment with ways to access and include the knowledge and behaviour of non-human entities in design work. In doing so, the method contributes to the development of a next generation of co-design methods. Non-human perspectives are the 'views' of plants, animals, or intelligent things, namely what they can 'see' and contribute to the understanding of a context. Such perspectives are usually included in the design process by means of multispecies ethnography and science and technology studies, and this can be realised with the aid of intelligent cameras, computational or bio-based sensors, and algorithms. It should be noted that this is not about how to see like a pigeon and how to empathise with the pigeon. It is about critically enhancing, complicating, and possibly challenging human blind spots and biases, specifically at the intersection of the data and trajectories that non-humans give access to and the theoretically informed analysis that humans bring to it.

An example in this guide is the Thing Ethnography approach, which can be applied when designing connected products that can sense data, exchange them, and autonomously act upon the data across decentralised computational networks. The aim of the method is to map the interdependencies of a product ecosystem and its potential societal impact. However, the methods in this guide that are originally developed for human-centred design could be extended to explore and articulate the knowledge and behaviour of animals, plants, and intelligent things as well.

TIPS & CONCERNS
The development of a design sensitivity to non-human scales and types of knowledge is a major challenge for designers using a More-Than-Human perspective.

For example, what does it mean to access the knowledge of a river that has existed and has played a role in a specific context for hundreds of years? What are the boundaries of the investigation? How can we map insights in a way that they can be discussed in multidisciplinary teams?

Develop skills for recognising, understanding, and making palpable the potential discomfort, tension, and compromise that is required to forge new alliances with non-human entities in design. How can animals be enlisted as participants without being harmed? What data can be collected and used with respect to people's privacy?

LIMITATIONS
Our understanding is inherently limited by what we humans know regarding the actions and behaviour of living and computational organisms. We can gather a lot from a More-Than-Human perspective, but this kind of consideration concerning the impact of design on the interplay between human and non-human systems is far from trivial.

REFERENCES & FURTHER READING: Clarke, R., Heitlinger, S., Light, A., Forlano, L., Foth, M., & DiSalvo, C., 2019. More-Than-Human Participation: *Design for Sustainable Smart City Futures*. Interactions26 (3), 60-63. / DiSalvo C., & Lukens, J., 2011. *Nonanthropocentrism and the Nonhuman in Design: Possibilities for Designing New Forms of Engagement with and through Technology*. In M. Foth, L. Forlano, C. Satchell, & M. Gibbs (Eds.). *From Social Butterfly to Engaged Citizen*. Cambridge, MA: MIT Press. / Giaccardi, E. & Redström, J., Technology and More-than-Human Design. *Design Issues*.

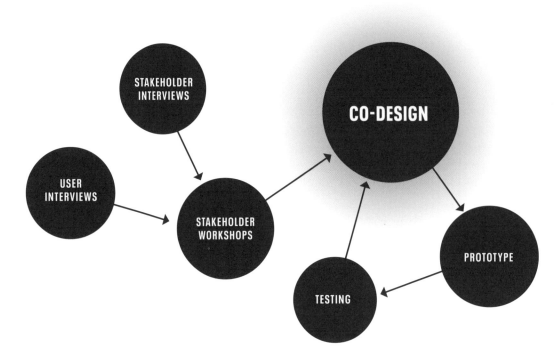

Balinese pedagogy named 'maguru panggul' or 'teaching through the mallet' implies a strong kinaesthetic feeling of being led by one's hands. As the name implies, maguru panggul refers to almost entirely practice-based learning. The teacher plays, often at or near performance tempo, the students try. The teaching and learning process feed into creativity for which both teacher and pupil are essential as the pupil also gives knowledge to the teacher. The clever pupil asks the teacher 'what is a good way of playing?' So the teacher finds out what's even better so that he is not outdone by them. (Fotocollection Dienst voor Legercontacten Indonesia)

Skilful Co-design

Skilful Co-design is a perspective that values reciprocity – meaning a balance in the concerns of both the designers and the participants. This concept applies educational principles within the regular co-design process to improve the design skills of participants and consequently the quality of their contributions.

WHAT & WHY? When users are involved in the design process they can enrich these processes with their context-specific and personal experiences. However, they may not have developed creative thinking and other design skills; this in turn impedes their contribution.

Key principles in Skilful Co-design include sharing learning goals, scaffolding, and providing intermediate feedback on the developed design skills. These allow for reflection on the design processes. The permanent growth in design skills brings value to the participants in exchange for their contribution, meaning that participants may be able to deploy these skills elsewhere. Due to the rapid changes in contemporary society, there is a need for people and organisations to tackle problems using approaches and methods from the design realm.

When designers embed learning activities in the Co-design process they receive higher quality contributions from more skilled participants. In addition, users are more willing to participate in Co-design sessions. In this way, users and their environment may become more sensitive and open, both to the final designs and to design thinking in general.

MINDSET: In the perspective of Skilful Co-design, designers strive for a reciprocity in the investments and benefits between designers and participants.

TIPS & CONCERNS

Because learning principles are included in the process, participants can work more independently, and therefore it becomes possible for them to work with larger groups.

Designers embedding educational principles may experience cognitive overload at first when they have the responsibility to achieve both learning and design output.

When collaborating with teachers these trained educators can guide part of the Skilful Co-design process, and doing so can assist them in integrating the learning principles.

LIMITATIONS

Although design skills are improved, it may take some time before the learning has an effect on the quality of participants' contributions..

HOW? Design skills do not need to be present yet; they can be developed consciously by embedding the following three educational principles:

Goal 1 – Sharing learning goals: When you as a designer can clarify the learning goals and can share concrete success criteria with participating users, the users are able to monitor and evaluate the quality of their own design processes and products. Learning goals are shared in parallel to the design goals, and this usually takes place before the actual design activity starts.

Goal 2 – Scaffolding: Scaffolding gives people support to perform tasks that they are not able to do without help. Providing examples and demonstrations are a way to apply scaffolds. For

instance, a facilitator may demonstrate creative Brainstorming out loud. It was found that managers who received such a demonstration can generate roughly twice as many ideas and that their ideas were much more varied compared to managers receiving a normal instruction.

Templates can be used as a scaffolding strategy as well. In primary schools, using a template that helps to formulate design critique in constructive and inspiring phrases can avoid defensive reactions and improve the reception of such critique.

Goal 3 – Feedback to skill development Learning by doing requires moments of reflection on what has happened. It is crucial that the participants involved in a Co-design process receive timely feedback, as feedback is necessary for them

in the process. Mid-term pauses during design activities enable participants to evaluate their own learning. Try focusing on a specific design skill and on related success criteria. For example, after sharing on how to think divergently, allow the participants to check after taking their break whether they think divergently and can understand how they can improve their thinking in the next brainstorm round.

The principles described here can be applied throughout the Skilful Co-design process and can be used with different user groups, such as primary and secondary schools that have prioritised creativity and design thinking on the educational agenda. They can also be used in organisations that promote design skills among their non-design staff.

REFERENCES & FURTHER READING: Your Turn, toolkit for skilful co-design for use with 8 – 14 year old children: English version: www.tudelft.nl/codesignkids. Dutch version: www.tudelft.nl/yourturn / Klapwijk, R. & van den Burg, N., 2019. *Formative assessment in primary education- Involving pupils in clarifying the learning goal of divergent thinking*, PATT37, 3-6 June, Malta, 277-287. / Schut, A., Klapwijk, R., Gielen, M., van Doorn, F., & de Vries, M., 2019. Uncovering early indicators of fixation during the concept development stage of children's design processes. *International Journal of Technology and Design Education*, 1-22. / Gist, M. E., 1989. The influence of training method on self⊠efficacy and idea generation among managers. *Personnel psychology*, 42(4), 787-805.

Graphic novelist Chris Ware has become synonymous with his ability to visualise the most banal into the extraordinary. Ware called comics 'not a genre, but a developing language' dealing with the weird process of reading pictures, not just looking at them. His works visualize our every day struggles with modern life. As in all things catastrophically 'innovative' we'll have to adapt and, most importantly, mature from within to master it, or it will master us. (Disconnect, Chris Ware 2012)

Visualising Interactions

This pertains to a set of methods that help to express and understand existing interactions, and to conceive and develop future ones. When designing for interactive products, user experiences, or services, designers need to envision how user experiences unfold over time, and comprehend the relations between people, products, and their environment.

WHAT & WHY? These visualisation techniques help to express how activities take place over time and between people, how cause and effect transpire, and what the people involved do and feel. The strength of visualisation techniques lies in their capacity to make abstract considerations visible for the designer and in a team discussion.

Interaction Visualisations can help to document an existing situation and discuss this with stakeholders. They are also a means of envisioning a new situation or 'sketching your way' into a future interaction.

MINDSET: Visualising Interactions supports analytical and intuitive thinking for individuals and groups. As a reader, you can step into the user experience just like a cinema audience does and step back to understand the technology and services that are at work. The visualisation helps viewers to literally 'lay a finger' on the many abstract considerations.

HOW? Step 1: Think of story ingredients and determine what aspects should be told: Where is the story happening? Who is involved? What are the important points to show? How does the story start and end? Does the story describe a minute, a day, or a week?

Step 2: Put the elements in sequence and start with a clear indication of the situation with a clear development and conclusion. Keep the story manageable. Storyboards often consist of five to seven pictures.

Step 3: Give each visualisation a clear title to prime the viewer for the core message. It can be powerful to make several storyboards displaying the variations of design or situation and put them side-to-side in a discussion.

Step 4: Link these visualisations to Role Playing, Wizard of Oz, and Cinematic Prototyping. Role Playing can be used for creating imagery for a storyboard (Photoboarding) or exploring variations of a scenario or a storyboard.

Timeline: Give a visual indication of how long the parts of an interaction take, where it is intense, or emotional, or boring. Visual markers indicate specific moments.

Written Scenario: Use a few lines of text to tell a story, making clear the where and why a user does something.

Storyboarding: This is a sequence of pictures to tell the story, each picture complemented with an annotation to explain the whys and whens of the actors in the story.

Journey Mapping: Extend the annotations of storyboards to a series of parallel 'swimlanes', each describing how one factor develops through the interaction, for example, the user emotion, actions by technology or service provider, external conditions, and design criteria. This supports the design team to make visible relations between the factors at points in time or over time, and how one factor may depend on another.

Flowchart: Flowcharts from software design show the moments where choices are made, and the timeline can follow different paths.

TIPS & CONCERNS

Make the storyboard captions convey the points that are not obvious from the visual. For example where the story takes place, what the protagonist is trying to achieve, or why a certain reaction occurs.

Captions are typically read on first encounter, and they are referred to only occasionally afterwards.

When making a journey map, avoid the mistake of only including the touch points when user and service meet.

Do not overlook the time which can be important for the user experience: Anticipation, waiting, or the technology: Preparation, delivery.

In consultations, allow participants to put their finger on, and write on, your visualisation.

Make the visualisation a 'shared space', not a fleeting illustration flashed in a slide presentation.

LIMITATIONS

All of the techniques listed above show a single timeline, but real interactions can unfold in different ways as people make choices.

One means of addressing this issue is to tell several stories. Another way is to express these aspects with a flowchart.

REFERENCES & FURTHER READING: Van der Lelie, C., 2006. The value of storyboards in the product design process. *Personal and ubiquitous computing*, 10(2-3), 159-162. / Van der Lugt, R., Postma, C. E., & Stappers, P. J., 2012. Photoboarding: Exploring service interactions with acting-out and storyboarding. *Touchpoint: the Journal of Service Design*, 4 (2) 2012.

The Tadrart Acacus prehistoric cave paintings are scattered over a large mountain range in the Sahara Desert. These paintings can be dated back to 12,000 BC and are one of the most significant prehistoric cave paintings, depicting hunting scenes of animals and humans with hunting tools. Below: Boeing art director William Fetter was the first person to draw a human figure using a computer. This figure is known as the 'Boeing Man'. In 1960, Fetter coined the term 'computer graphics' in a description of his work on cockpit design for the Boeing Company.

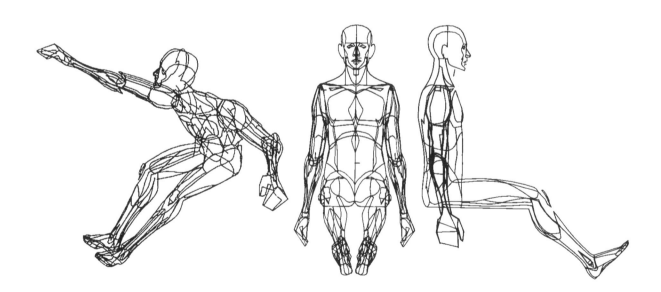

PERSPECTIVES
Design Drawing as a Language

Throughout the entire design process, design drawing can serve as a visual language for exploring options and communicating final or intermediate outcomes. Drawing can facilitate thinking, boost creativity, kick-start conversations, and explain concepts. Drawing can be done on paper or a tablet; it offers flexibility and adds the designer's signature to a proposal, and it is universally understood.

WHAT & WHY? Drawing represents an early sign of culture, an expression of mankind's unique creative capabilities and an example of our near-exclusive usage of tools. The activity of drawing or scetching has characterised human beings since prehistoric times: it was utilized for communicating long before writing was present and served as a basis for written language.

Drawing supports a range of methods and creativity in general in all stages of the design process. Visualisation helps externalise our thoughts. It serves aesthetic, behavioural, cognitive, and communicative purposes. In a design context, sketching serves these four purposes with a focus on collaboration, cognitive development, and communication. Drawing is a method for developing knowledge, thoughts, concepts, ideas and for communicating these with others such as peers and clients. Use it to discuss or present concepts, or to provoke a reaction. Sketches convey information and provide signature.

The word 'sketching' literally meanis 'improvise', which characterises the dynamic and developmental function that it has in a design context. The creation, preservation, and transfer of knowledge have always been important functions of drawing and sketching. Especially for designers sketching constitutes an essential asset for their visual language, which is akin to writers using text for communication.

MINDSET: Feel free to use any technique, drawing tool or other means at your disposal to to visualise your observations and thoughts.

TIPS & CONCERNS
Utilize a drawing language that emphasises a well-considered structure, viewpoints and composition using clear lines and tonal values, both for concrete and for abstract representations.

Sketching requires practice in order for us to use the full potential the method offers.

Start by drawing basic shapes, and then slowly increase the complexity and creative exploration while practising motor skills and raising your awareness of perspective and composition.

Maintain and improve your skills; sketch every day!

See also: Design Drawing in the four stages of this book.

LIMITATIONS
In later stages, alternative formats come into play, such as graphic design, movies, animations, and CAD renders, which usually need to be preceded by sketches as well.

HOW? Artist and painter David Hockney stated that with drawing you can express all kinds of ideas that might otherwise be lost. Art critic John Ruskin said that the discipline of drawing tunes the sensitivity of the drawer to a higher pitch; it refines the drawer's vision.

Sketches can be representations of either existing things and situations or of conceptual thoughts and imaginary concepts. This limitless medium allows for exploring and creating visions and scenarios that can involve anything.

Designers draw throughout the entire design process. The appearance of the sketch or visual representation differs according to its purpose. Various factors are involved, such as the designer's intention, the subject or field, the audience, the type of decision to be made, the direction of the information flow, and the stage of the design process.

The four design stages of Discover, Define, Develop, and Deliver (the Double Diamond Model) are taken as a starting point for distinguishing the various process parts for sketching. These stages and the ways in which sketching and visualising can contribute to the stages are discussed in the subsequent sections of this book.

REFERENCES & FURTHER READING: Eissen, J. J., & Steur, R., 2009. *Sketching.* Amsterdam: BIS Publishers. / Robertson, S., & Bertling, T., 2013. *How to Draw.* Design Studio Press. / Tversky, B. (2011). Visualizing Thought. *Topics in Cognitive Science*, 3(3), 499-535./ *www.delftdesigndrawing.com/basics.html*

'Have no fear of
perfection -- you'll
never reach it.'

SALVADOR DALI

MODELS

Models are descriptive in nature. That is, they describe how design happens. For example, the Basic Design Cycle describes how designers fundamentally think while designing. A model offers a generic description of design activity, often in a non-normative manner.

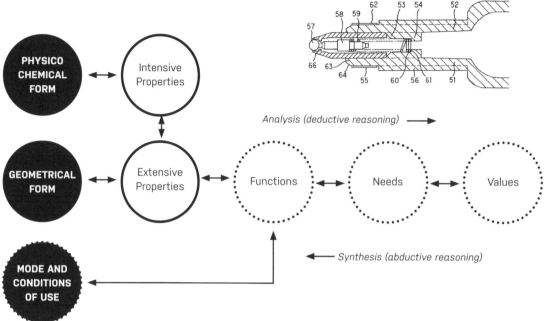

PHYSICO CHEMICAL FORM ↔ Intensive Properties

GEOMETRICAL FORM ↔ Extensive Properties

MODE AND CONDITIONS OF USE

Extensive Properties ↔ Functions ↔ Needs ↔ Values

Analysis (deductive reasoning) →

← Synthesis (abductive reasoning)

62 53 54 52
58 59
57
66 63 64 55 60 56 61 51

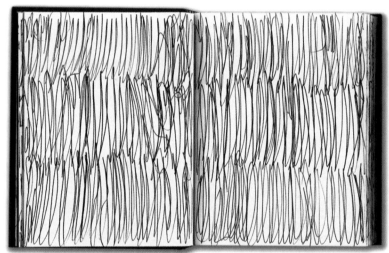

FORM	PROPERTIES	FUNCTIONS	NEEDS	VALUES
• forms • materials • colours • sizes • textures.	• weight • stiffness • colour • comfort	• transfer ink to paper • display brand name (intended functions) • fixate hairdo (alternative function).	• expression • communication	• profits • education • status

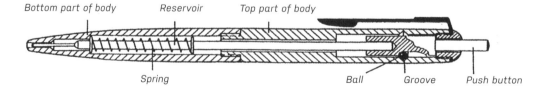

Bottom part of body   Reservoir   Top part of body

Spring   Ball   Groove   Push button

Reasoning in Design

The Reasoning in Design model is a generic representation of how designers process their ideas in a logical manner when designing. The model is primarily based on the design of tangible products, but it can be applied to services as well. The model helps to reflect on the different levels of reasoning while designing.

WHAT & WHY? Products and services are designed to serve specific usage functions; they are made in a way where they can fulfil specific needs and support certain values. To design a product is to conceive its use and to find a suitable geometrical and physio-chemical (or material) form that fulfils the intended function and the desired needs and underlying values. The kernel of designing lies in the reasoning process that occurs when we examine these values via needs, functions, and properties, and then bring them to a final form.

The functioning of a product depends on its form, use, and context of use. This means that if you know the geometrical and physio-chemical form of a product, you can in principle predict its properties. Along this line, if you also know the environment where the product will be used in and how it will be used, you can predict whether the product will work as intended. This kind of reasoning is called an *analysis*. However, for designers the essential mode of reasoning is to reason from function to form – this is referred to as *synthesis*, which is a process that starts with the values and needs of the potential user, and ends with the form of a product that can satisfy those values and needs.

MINDSET: This model suggests an analytical and structured way of thinking. A mindset that some designers may not be aware of in practice. Therefore, articulating the different levels in an explicit way leads to more informative discussions during the design process.

TIPS & CONCERNS
Both the form and also the mode and conditions of use determine how a product will function in action. The context of use counts as much as the product itself, and therefore you will need to pay equal attention to both these areas. In a sense, designing a product should include designing its use.

LIMITATIONS
Intuition and creativity have an indispensable role to play in design. Notwithstanding the importance of scientific knowledge, systematic approaches, and modern possibilities for simulation, we can say that design processes would come to a standstill without intuition and creativity.

HOW? You can use the model in several ways, such as structuring your thoughts, communicating with others during the design process, generating questions, and structuring insights from research. The model is described as follows:

Form: The geometrical and material form of a product is specified in its design. The parts that make up a design are realised in the production process.

Properties: Due to its form, a product has certain properties, such as weight and stiffness. Properties describe the expected behaviour of a product under certain circumstances, and they can be intensive or extensive. Intensive properties are completely determined by the material of a part, such as its weight. This kind of properties and the geometrical form determine the extensive properties. For example, both the material used and the geometrical form determine the strength of a component. As a designer, you would typically focus on the extensive properties, as they are the most direct component in determining the functioning of a product. We need to remember that these properties have both desirable and less desirable consequences. For example, steel is stiff and durable, but it is heavy and also rusts, while aluminium is light and does not corrode, but it is less stiff. The art of designing is to give the product a geometrical form such that the product still has the desired extensive properties along with its intensive ones.

Function: Properties and functions both describe the behaviour of things. Statements on properties are objectively true or false. For functions, this is not necessarily so: Functions express what a design is made for, and

while these depend on the intentions of the designer, they also depend on the preferences, objectives, and goals of users. The designer of a ballpoint pen may have kept specific functions in mind, such as the need to transfer the ink to the paper or that the pen should display the brand name. Users may have considered the alternative functions of a pen, such as its ability to keep a hairdo in place. As we can see, functions can have a variety of traits – they can be technical, ergonomic, aesthetic, semantic, economic, societal, and more.

Needs and Values: Through their functions, products can satisfy the needs of users and realise values. For example, a ballpoint pen can help individuals satisfy their need of expressing themselves in writing and thereby support aesthetic, cultural, or economic values.

REFERENCES & FURTHER READING: Roozenburg, N.F.M. & Eekels, J., 1995. Product Design: *Fundamentals and Methods.* Chichester: John Wiley & Sons. / Roozenburg, N.F.M. & Eekels, J., 1998. *Productontwerpen: Structuur en Methoden.* 2nd ed. Utrecht: Lemma.

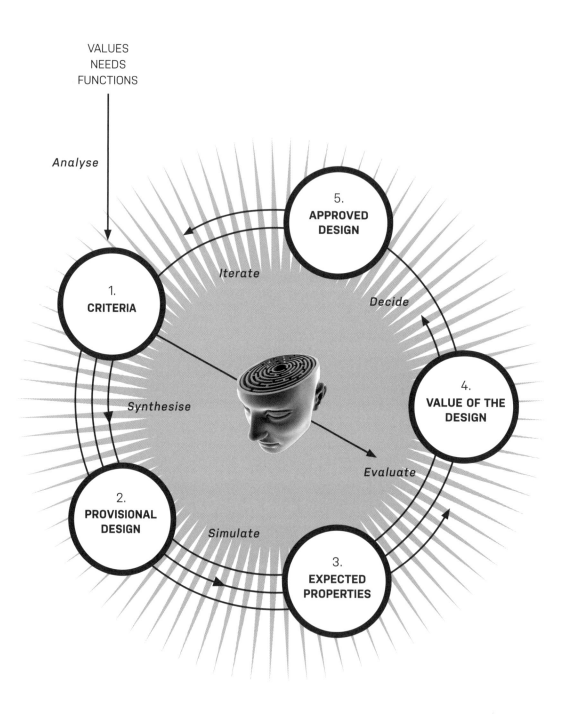

VALUES
NEEDS
FUNCTIONS

Analyse

1.
CRITERIA

Iterate

5.
**APPROVED
DESIGN**

Decide

4.
**VALUE OF THE
DESIGN**

Synthesise

Evaluate

2.
**PROVISIONAL
DESIGN**

Simulate

3.
**EXPECTED
PROPERTIES**

The basic building block of the design process is this circle of thought, action and decision. Designing is like a fractal: zooming in or out results in a similar image. Designing is an iterative process where you sometimes have to take a few steps back – 'back to the drawing board!' – in order to go a step forward later on. Being aware of the basic cycle that you are going through, up to a few times per minute, helps you as a designer to organise your thoughts and design activities. (After Roozenburg and Eekels, 1995)

MODELS

Basic Design Cycle

The Basic Design Cycle is a model that represents the fundamental reasoning steps in the process of designing. It consists of a sequence of conscious reasoning steps that are repeated in empirical cycles. The knowledge of both the problem and the solution increases with each cycle.

WHAT & WHY? The model describes the different basic reasoning steps a designer goes through when solving a design problem purposefully and consciously. Theoretically, you can go through only a single cycle, but you usually perform many cycles across the various phases of any design process. The basic design cycle consists of five reasoning steps that are logically connected. Novice or naïve designers often tend to 'jump' over some of the steps, which might harm the quality of the design outcome. For example, one might immediately 'jump to solutions' when presented with a design brief, without thoroughly analysing the problem. This reasoning might result in a design that does not address the actual problem. Ideally, you spiral from problem to solution, from abstract to concrete, and from function to product geometry. This process is usually iterative, in which you sometimes have to take a few steps back – 'back to the drawing board!' – to go a step forward later on. You might also enter into the cycle at different steps, as long as you complete the cycle each time. Being aware of the basic cycle that you are going through on different resolution levels – from a cycle within the time span of a minute to cycles that span several weeks – helps you to organise your thoughts and design activities.

MINDSET: The Basic Design Cycle represents a fundamental cycle of reasoning that is inherent in conscious, purposeful design problem solving. This means that a designer who desires to do so needs to critically reflect on how his or her own thinking corresponds to basic reasoning logic.

HOW? The model describes five reasoning steps, each with its own purpose. As mentioned, these steps can happen, for example, in a span of a few seconds or over a period of weeks depending on the resolution level you take.

Analyse: In this step, you examine the aspects related to your design goal or a design problem. Overall, analytical reasoning yields information that informs your design criteria and eventually the requirements.

Synthesise: In this step, you generate possible solutions. Synthesis yields (elements of) design proposals that potentially offer valuable (parts of) solutions to the problem.

Simulate: In this step, you create imagined, digital, or physical representations of (elements of) design proposals. Simulation yields representations either in your mind or externalised with which you can evaluate their potential value.

Evaluate: In this step, you reason about the potential value of design proposals through their simulated representation. This happens in relation to design criteria. Evaluation produces an understanding of the current value of (an element of) your design proposal and informs design making.

Decide: In this step, you reason about the relative value of (an element of) your design proposal and you decide on how to proceed. Decision making informs the next cycles of design: whether to repeat a cycle, proceed to (an element of) your design proposal, or focus on other elements instead.

TIPS & CONCERNS
Do not confuse the five reasoning steps with the phases of a design process. The Basic Design Cycle is a model describing the fundamental reasoning steps and their relative logical order, which happen throughout any conscious, goal-directed design process.

This means that there is not one phase in which you synthesise, but that you must engage in synthesis throughout the design process.

When you 'get lost' in your ideas and thoughts, you might find it helpful to consider which step of the basic cycle you are in and identify which reasoning steps you might have missed that might get you back on track.

Discussion with others often helps in effectively doing these reflections.

LIMITATIONS
'Analyse' is the first step in this model, and this might suggest that it should also be your point of departure. However, that step is not necessarily your preferred point for starting your design cycle.

Depending on your preference, you can enter into the cycle at different points.

45

REFERENCES & FURTHER READING: Roozenburg, N.F.M. & Eekels, J., 1995. *Product Design: Fundamentals and Methods.* Chichester: John Wiley & Sons. / Roozenburg, N.F.M. & Eekels, J., 1998. *Product Ontwerpen: Structuur en Methoden.* 2nd ed. Utrecht: Lemma.

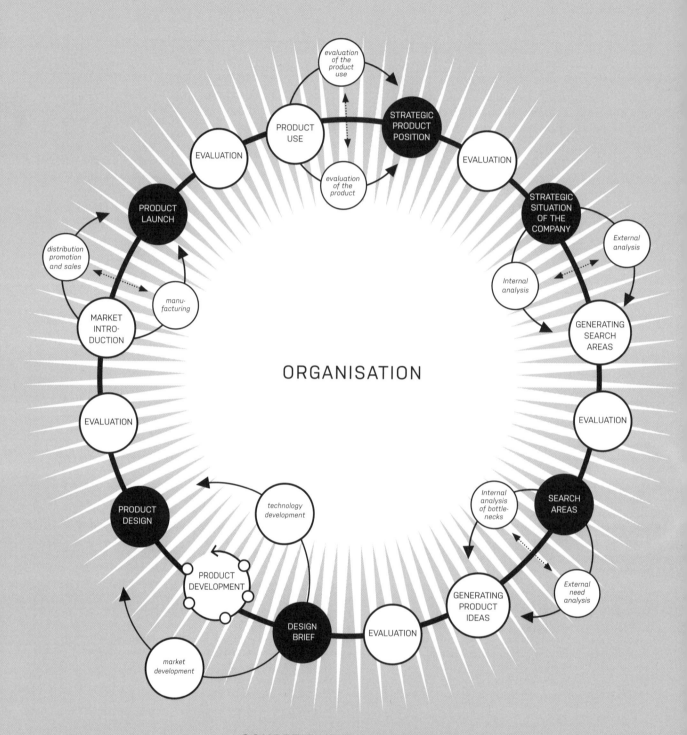

ORGANISATION

COMPETITIVE ENVIRONMENT

It never ends: the Product Innovation Process is a continuous circular process. An organisation moves through the cycle all the time, developing new products and redeveloping existing products, sometimes simultaneously. (After Buijs, 2012)

Product Innovation Process

The Product Innovation Process model describes the overall process of product innovation, along with an emphasis on the fuzzy front end. The model can help designers plan for and manage innovation as well as to keep an overview of the process while innovating.

WHAT & WHY? A company often responds to changes inside and outside its organisation by developing new products. This kind of development can be seen with the Product Innovation Process, which is a model that describes innovation as a process of experiential learning in a continuous loop. Several stages are seen in this loop: the development can begin from people using an existing product, to the company forming its strategic product position, to the project undergoing stages of product development, and finally to the product launch where people are using the new product. The model can help you to organise and align all activities in this loop.

The Product Innovation Process model advances a stepwise approach to product design and development, and it is intended for active use by designers to set agendas and collaborate with others in innovation.

MINDSET: Broaden in your mind the position of design in innovation and make a departure from the tradition that describes design as a function to bridge a world of production with a world of consumption.

HOW? The process consists of five stages that are visually similar in terms of building blocks, shape, and size. Each stage ensures creativity in innovation by requiring divergent thinking and by forcing innovators to consider the company's internal and external environment. For each step in the model, various methods are developed to support research and development, as well as other activities in the design process. For example, for the strategy formulation stage (Step 5), you can use methods such as Strategy Wheel and SWOT & Search Areas. In the development stage (Step 4), you can try several different approaches for creativity.

Step 1 - Product use: The use of the company's existing products is seen as the starting point for the next innovation round. This stage involves connecting product use with the next step – which is referred to as a strategy formulation for the company – thereby initiating the next innovation cycle.

Step 2 - Strategy formulation: This stage starts with determining the current strategic situation of the company using an internal and external analysis of the company. By combining these two analyses, you can formulate search areas, which are strategic ideas for innovation and are potential new business opportunities. When evaluating these search areas you can check their validity in a number of ways such as expert interviews, looking at patents, or observing potential customers and users.

Step 3 - Design brief formulation: In this stage, the selected search areas are transformed into product ideas, which

TIPS & CONCERNS
The visualised innovation process, a circular model, suggests that there is neither a beginning nor an end. This is true because a new product on the market will lead to reactions from competitors. These reactions will eventually eat away the competitive advantage of the new product, and this would necessitate the start of a new Product Innovation Process.

LIMITATIONS
In theory, the model could also be applied to the innovation of digital services in highly networked eco-systems. However, in those cases, you need to be aware that it is hard to make a distinction between the analyses (internal and external) and between the human factors (users and providers).

The model was not conceived for more agile forms of innovation, where ideas are quickly prototyped and marketed for faster learning cycles. In agile innovation, certain stages in the model can be skipped in order to speed up the innovation process.

------

are then formulated in a design brief. This brief describes the ideas in a way that an internal or external design team can start developing the product or service. The brief can include a vision statement, a program of requirements, and other guidelines to steer the design direction.

Step 4 - Development: This stage involves traditional design activities that are related to product design, and such activities include creating a marketing plan and assessing the required technology for the product and its production. A number of essential components will result from this stage, such as working prototypes, technical documents and assembly schemes.

Step 5 - Market introduction: This stage entails the further development of a full-scale manufacturing process as well as marketing, encompassing sales, promotion, and distribution. The final result is the product launch.

REFERENCES & FURTHER READING Buijs, J. A., 2012. *The Delft Innovation Method; a design thinker's guide to innovation*. The Hague: Eleven International Publishing. / Buijs, J. & Valkenburg, R., 2005. *Integrale Productontwikkeling*. 3rd ed. Utrecht: Lemma. / Buijs, J., 2003. Modelling Product Innovation Processes: from Linear Logic to Circular Chaos. *Creativity and Innovation Management*, June, 12(2), pp. 76-93.

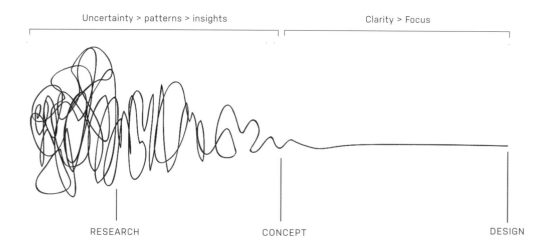

Uncertainty > patterns > insights   Clarity > Focus

RESEARCH   CONCEPT   DESIGN

Decades before agile's inception, Dwight D. Eisenhower famously declared plans useless. But many forget the second half of his declaration: 'In preparing for battle, I have always found that plans are useless and planning is indispensable.'

Agile Design & Development

Agile is an approach to design and development. Its purpose is to accelerate the process and add flexibility. Agile values and principles originated in software development, and they are being applied to more and more disciplines, including design.

WHAT & WHY? Innovation is often being slowed down due to delays and rework, particularly in the phase of delivery. Writing elaborate plans or project initiation documents often takes a lot of time, and once delivered, these plans and documents take away most flexibility to adapt to new insights, changes in context, and so on. People are often seen as interchangeable resources to be moved around, rather than part of teams that drive innovation. Clients are also viewed as legal entities rather than collaborators. Speed is essential in innovation, especially towards delivery. Agile comes into play at this stage; it helps to put well-performing teams in the driver's seat of innovation and fast-track development while keeping maximum flexibility in what to deliver.

MINDSET: Agile is a mindset that is based on four values that are formulated in the Agile Manifesto. Value individuals and interactions over processes and tools; working results over comprehensive documentation; customer collaboration over contract negotiation, and responding to change over following a plan.

TIPS & CONCERNS
A common means of making the progress visual is working with a Scrum board and Post It notes. All these could easily camouflage that the actual Agile mindset itself is absent, and these boards and notes only serve as innovation theatre.

LIMITATIONS
The Agile mindset is a rather abstract set of values and principles. It takes effort and practice as well as an open mind to grasp and internalise it.

HOW? Agile in itself doesn't tell you what to do next: it is a set of values and principles, which is mostly about mindset, not about the process to follow. To be agile, designers should cherish the diversity in the team, be comfortable in not knowing what the exact outcome will be, be proactive to inspect and adapt their work and way of working, and naturally share energy, information, and results.

The *Manifesto for Agile Software Development* is based on 12 principles which can be applied to innovation processes in general:

----

1. Provide customer satisfaction via early and continuous delivery.
----
2. Welcome changing requirements, even late in development.
----
3. Deliver working results frequently, for example, in weeks rather than months.
----
4. Create close, daily cooperation between business people and developers.

5. Build projects around motivated individuals, who should be trusted.
----
6. Practice face-to-face conversation, which is the best form of communication.
----
7. Utilise working results, which is the primary measure of progress.
----
8. Attain sustainable development to be able to maintain a constant pace.
----
9. Continuously focus on technical excellence and good design.
----
10. Recognise the necessity of simplicity, or the art of maximising the amount of work not done.
----
11. Realise that the best constructions, requirements, and designs emerge from self-organising teams.
----
12. Allow the team to regularly reflect on how to become more effective and to adjust accordingly.

REFERENCES & FURTHER READING Jongerius, P., Offermans, A., Vanhoucke, A., Sanwikarja, P., & van Geel, J., 2013. *Get Agile!: Scrum for UX, Design & Development*. BIS Publishers.

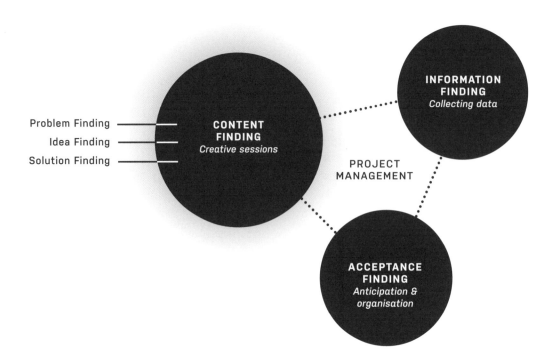

Problem Finding ——————

Idea Finding ——————

Solution Finding ——————

CONTENT FINDING
Creative sessions

INFORMATION FINDING
Collecting data

PROJECT MANAGEMENT

ACCEPTANCE FINDING
Anticipation & organisation

Modern composers like Thelonious Monk no longer write detailed scores to be meticulously reproduced, but instead compose within a personal idiom based on parameters that support systems of change and interaction. Ideas are generated and implemented on the spot, tested and improved until the music 'works'. Solutions need to be found for musical problems like expressing a certain mood or feeling or for going from one tempo to another. During solos, individual musicians are given the floor to show their skills and creativity. Creative processes are all about postponing judgement, fresh ideas need a safe environment and time to grow into better ideas. (Photo: Eugene Smith 1959)

Integrated Creative Problem Solving

Integrated Creative Problem Solving (iCPS) is a structured, iterative model that helps with developing novel and useful solutions to open problems in groups. It comprises four interdependent sub-processes that work together: Content finding, information finding, acceptance finding, and project management.

WHAT & WHY? Whenever a creative session is needed for generating novel and useful solutions within a group, iCPS is a powerful approach you can use. The model is integrated into the entire innovation trajectory – including the periods before, in-between, and after creative sessions. In iCPS, the roles of facilitator, problem owner, and resource group are clearly delegated and supported. The main principle of iCPS is the clear separation between the diverging, reverging, and converging stages.

MINDSET: The needed mindset is very different for each stage because iCPS is based on the principle of a strict separation between the five steps in the iCPS basic module. (see below). This separation is essential.

HOW? ICPS includes the following three sub-processes which need to be managed simultaneously. The project management process leads the creative sessions and embeds the project into the larger organisation.

----

1. Content Finding: is the process of finding the actual goal – such as a need, a wish, or an opportunity – and is often conducted within one or more creative sessions. Content finding includes three stages:

- **Problem finding:** Explore and identify the goal, wish, challenge, or opportunity, with an aim to clarify and formulate the problem.
- **Idea finding:** Generate novel and useful ideas to solve the identified problem.
- **Solution finding:** Move from the idea to an implementable solution, develop the criteria for success, and anticipate the follow-up.

Each stage entails five steps: Task Appraising, Diverging, Reverging, Converging, and Reflecting. Navigating through these steps is guided by the facilitator. There are numerous methods and techniques that can be used for content finding, such as Brainstorming, Brainwriting, WWWWWH, SCAMPER, and Synectics.

----

2. Information finding: is the process of collecting data and information that could be used to influence and stimulate the creative sessions on the content level.

----

3. Acceptance finding: is the process of anticipating and organising the future implementation of the generation solutions, which goes beyond agreement on implementation plans.

TIPS & CONCERNS

Create a safe environment where the resource group feels free to share any thoughts and ideas.

Use a structured process and clear rules to manage the creativity in the resource group.

A clear problem statement is a critical success factor.

LIMITATIONS

An independent facilitator should guide the creative session.

One pitfall is that the problem owner takes the role of the facilitator and has a tendency to steer the resource group into a predetermined direction, thereby limiting the creative output.

A facilitator should focus only on guiding the creative process, not the content.

51

REFERENCES & FURTHER READING Buijs, J., & van der Meer, H., 2013. *Integrated Creative Problem Solving.* The Hague: Eleven International Publishing. / Heijne, K. & van der Meer, H., 2019. *Road Map for Creative Problem Solving Techniques - Organizing and facilitating group sessions.* Amsterdam: Boom Uitgevers. / Parnes, S.J., 1967. *Creative Behavior Guidebook.* New York: Charles Scribner's Sons. / Tassoul, M., 2006. *Creative Facilitation – a Delft Approach.* Delft: VSSD.

Hermes was was the 'messenger of the gods'. Also considered to be the inventor of language and speech, an interpreter, a liar, a thief and a trickster. As Socrates noted, words have the power to reveal or conceal and can deliver messages in an ambiguous way. These multiple roles made Hermes an ideal representative for hermeneutics. Phenomenology is the study of experience and the ways in which things present themselves in and through experience. What are people doing? What are they trying to accomplish? How exactly do they do this? What specific means or strategies are used? How do people talk about and understand what is going on? What assumptions are they making? (image: Adolf Hirémy-Hirschl 'The Souls of Acheron', 1898)

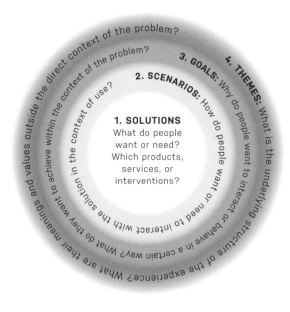

1. SOLUTIONS
What do people want or need? Which products, services, or interventions?

2. SCENARIOS: How do people want or need to interact or behave in a certain way? What do they want to interact with the solution in the context of use?

3. GOALS: Why do people want or need to interact or behave in a certain way? What do they want to achieve within the context of the problem?

4. THEMES: What is the underlying structure of the experience? What are their meanings and values outside the direct context of the problem?

Needs & Aspirations for Design & Innovation

Needs & Aspirations for Design & Innovation (NADI) is a model that aims to make designers become aware of the different levels of depth in qualitative human insights. NADI also helps designers to identify which insights they need, as well as evaluate and present design proposals in relation to these levels.

WHAT & WHY? As human-centred designers, we may find it difficult to explain how having an insight into needs and aspirations can contribute to designing innovative solutions. In design innovation, there is a growing tendency to focus on 'deep customer insights', but it is unclear what these 'deep' insights are. The NADI model helps to distinguish these levels of depth and explaining how each level influences a design process.

A theme is defined as the 'structure of experiences'. Phenomenological themes are closely related to human values, and they describe patterns in our experiences. One theme that underlies the experience of teaching is the 'drive to make a difference'. When we consider what it means to have such a drive, one element of this pattern is that teachers need feedback on their efforts to sustain their drive. If teachers know their students are learning, they remain motivated to teach. Working with the theme level is particularly useful in multi-stakeholder contexts as these experience patterns are often shared.

MINDSET: The theme level requires a deep understanding of human experiences. The interpretation of others' experience is always subjective as it is not possible for us to look directly into their minds and their hearts, which means that our interpretations are based on our own experiences. Therefore, designers are invited to reflect on their personal experiences and interpretations when investigating themes.

WHEN? The NADI model can be especially useful in the discovery phase of design. It can help you when you work on certain tasks such as formulating questions for design research, making sense of qualitative research data, as well as evaluating and exploring how the envisioned solution can meet needs and aspirations on different levels.

HOW? The NADI model has four levels:

Level 1: The top level describes what types of solutions people want or need; aptly referred to as the solution level.

Level 2: Describes how people want to interact with solutions in certain scenarios; this is often presented in a narrative journey or storyboard.

Level 3: Is the goal level which explains what someone wants to achieve in a certain context.

Level 4: The deepest level is the theme level, which describes aspired experience patterns that can be explored outside the problem context.

A market researcher might identify a colour range for products. The scenario level explores how products and services provide positive and seamless user experience journeys. The goal level is the higher-level of constraints and requirements to be used to evaluate proposed designs. The theme level gives input to the reframing of problems the generation of innovative solutions.

TIPS & CONCERNS

In early phases, you may often need to fill the model with assumptions and draw on personal experiences to generate questions and initial problem frames.

In an iterative process, this rough sketch can then be validated and adjusted based on qualitative research about needs and aspirations of different stakeholders.

The NADI model does not prescribe a strict process. Feel free to jump from one level to another and go back and forth between the levels.

When looking at the theme level, try to focus on aspirational experiences instead of merely negative ones
----
There is no 'right' theme to focus on. You are encouraged to work with multiple themes.

Try to be aware of how values and cultural differences might influence the themes.

LIMITATIONS

The model focuses on the needs and aspirations with regard to experiences. It does not take any other concerns or requirements into account.

Be aware of using the term 'solution' in complex social *innovation* contexts because such complex challenges often involve multiple uncontrollable factors and thus cannot be 'solved' easily.

REFERENCES & FURTHER READING van der Bijl - Brouwer, M. & Dorst, K., 2017. Advancing the Strategic Impact of Human-Centred Design. *Design Studies* 53, pp. 1-23. / van Manen, M., 1990. Researching Lived Experience: *Human Science for an Action Sensitive Pedagogy*. Albany, New York: State University of New York Press.

'Your work
isn't a high stakes,
nail-biting professional
challenge. It's a form
of play. Lighten up and
have fun with it.'
SOL LEWITT

APPROACHES

Approaches are prescriptive in nature. That is, they describe ways for how to go about a design activity. An approach offers a comprehensive process for design that spans across phases. Many approaches are linked in turn to a set of methods and tools that are appropriate to use in combination, for example, because they adhere to the same mindset as the overall approach.

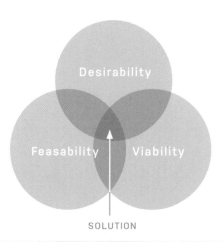

Desirability

Feasability · Viability

SOLUTION

A 'basted fitting' is when you try on a custom suit jacket that has been temporarily stitched together with white basting thread. Initial measurements that were carefully taken during your first fitting were used to create this 'working' jacket. This jacket is used to finetune the fitting. The basted fitting is also the customers first opportunity to try on the custom made suit. It may not look like much, but it will still feel like it was made for you.

User-Centred Design

User-Centred Design (UCD) is a design approach that focuses on the user perspective to create valuable and usable products, interfaces, services, or systems.

WHAT & WHY? UCD is a problem-solving approach that focuses on the needs, desires, properties, and capabilities of projected users of a product, service, or system. This is contrary to taking technological possibilities or business considerations as a starting point. A UCD process is believed to positively influence the level of usability and the quality of the user experience.

UCD helps designers to predict what aspects of the design might be problematic for future users. At the start of a project designers know little about their users' needs, workflows, and limitations. On the other hand, designers typically know too much, because they are overly familiar with their own life and work. This makes it hard for designers to predict what aspects of the design might be problematic for future users.

Base your design on evidence from sources such as user observations, interviews, and data. Avoid assumptions and personal views and accept the fact that you might be wrong.

MINDSET: Listening to users and observing what they do is not the same as blindly doing what they say. You need a determined attitude with perseverance. Be prepared to see that your initial ideas, assumptions and preliminary designs might be off the mark, and always strive to evaluate them with projected users. Front-end user research and user evaluations require investments, and so does making design choices that result in better products.

WHEN? UCD is relevant in any domain where there is a gap between designer and user. The approach can be used throughout the design process, both for setting the design goalas well as for the creation of the design.

HOW? UCD is about learning from the active involvement of participants that represent the projected user group. User involvement is performed from the start to prevent taking important design decisions without knowing the user perspective. When it is not possible to include users, the user perspective can be sought through user representation methods (also called analytical or inspection methods). There are multiple models of UCD, which share the following types of activities that can be linked to the Basic Design Cycle.

Step 1 - Front-end user research: Know the user group, their needs, capabilities, and the context of use. (Interviews, Focus Groups, User Observations, Contextmapping, Cultural Probes, Questionnaires, Usage Analytics, Anthropometric Design)

Step 2 - Define: Set goals, requirements, and limitations; describe user group and context of use. (Problem Definition, Persona, Cultura, List of Requirements)

Step 3 - Create: Synthesize a solution that incorporates knowledge from users and capture a new, desired state. (Storyboarding, Design Drawing to Develop, Journey Mapping)

Step 4 - Prototype: Create simulations that allow participants to experience the future product, service, or system. (Written Scenario, Storyboarding, Three Dimensional Physical Model, Experience Prototyping, Cinematic Prototyping, Wizard of Oz)

Step 5 - Evaluate use: Assess the use and user experience of the design through user involvement and/or representation. (Product Concept Evaluation, Product Usability Evaluation (lab or field), Focus groups).

TIPS & CONCERNS

Use appropriate ways to involve participants In every phase of the design process.

Realise that people are not only users but often also owners, observers, buyers, and so on.

Compared to UCD, Human-centred design has a more holistic perspective.

The overlap between the two approaches, in terms of methods applied and the required attitude, is considerable.

In many situations the experience of products and systems is a critical issue, which requires attention in its own right.

LIMITATIONS

There is no guarantee that by going through the specified steps, a design will be usable or will have an excellent user experience, since in addition to the process, UCD is also very much about having a user-centred mindset throughout decision-making.

REFERENCES & FURTHER READING: ISO. 2010. ISO 9241 Ergonomics of human-system interaction. In: Part 210: Human-centred design for interactive systems (formerly known as 13407). Switzerland: International Organization for Standardization. / Nielsen, J., 1992. The usability engineering life cycle. *IEEE Computer*, 25(3), 12-22. / Norman, D., 2013. *The design of everyday things:* Revised and expanded edition. Basic books. / Van Kuijk, 2010. *Recommendations for usability in practice* (card set). Delft: Delft University of Technology.

	WORLD LEVEL	MEDIATION LEVEL	ARTEFACT LEVEL

DEBRIEFING ▶ **ANTICIPATING THE FUTURE** ▶ **GOAL SETTING** ▶ **DEVELOPING THE INTERVENTION** ▶

1. Domain
2. Context factors
3. Context structure

4. Statements

5. Interaction
6. Idea
7. Validation

Russia-Georgia (Abkhazia/ South Ossetia). Double barbed-wire fence fixed on metal bars and studs. Illegal occupation barrier in violation of human rights.

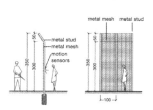

Morocco-Algeria. Metal mesh fence fixed on metal studs. Features motion sensors. Conflict and anti-terrorism barrier.

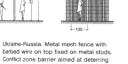

Ukraine-Russia. Metal mesh fence with barbed wire on top fixed on metal studs. Conflict zone barrier aimed at deterring terrorism and weapons smuggling.

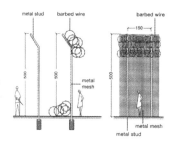

Israel-Egypt. Double fence with barbed wire fixed on metal studs. Anti-illegal immigration barrier.

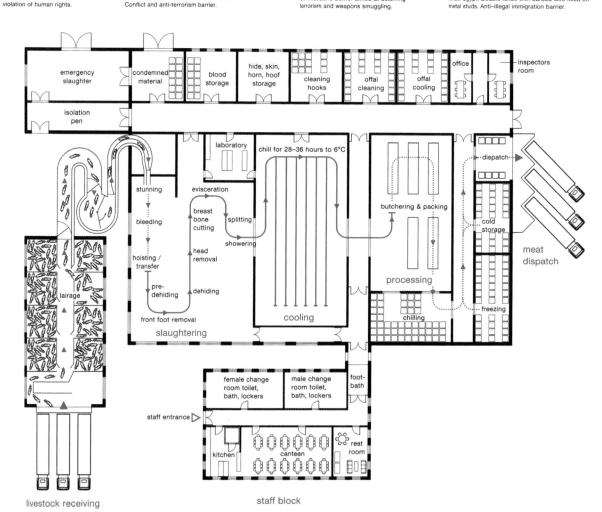

Samples from 'The Handbook of Tyranny' by Theo Deutinger, which raises questions on the problematic relations between political power, territoriality, systematic cruelties and design. The 21st century shows a general striving for an ever more regulated and protective society. Yet the scale of authoritarian intervention and their stealth design adds to the growing difficulty of linking cause and effect. (Lars Müller Publishers)

Social Implication Design

The Social Implication Design (SID) approach supports designers in developing interventions for societal challenges. Designers are encouraged to align societal goals with user needs or desires, thereby creating products or services that make prosocial behaviours meaningful to the individual.

WHAT & WHY? Many designers are interested in designing for the common good, and increasingly the organisations in public sectors recognise the value of design. It is important to understand how typical designer's skills are valuable in light of complex societal issues on the one hand, and of the fact that society-centred design is not the same as User-Centred Design on the other. This approach aims to do just that – expand the repertoire of designers by building on their key qualities so that they can create things that are meaningful to people.

The approach builds on the effect-driven design approach Vision in Product Design, by integrating mediation theory and social dilemma theory.

MINDSET: You need to be able to translate abstract social implications into concrete means. You also need to be motivated to explore concepts and principles from the social sciences, apply system-as-cause thinking, and be bold in taking a stand and in defending your ideas.

WHEN? The method offers an appropriate approach when designers either wish to design for society – meaning they wish to primarily contribute to the common good – or they wish to take responsibility for the potential social implications of their products and services. The method supports the general stages of Discover, Define, and Develop of design. It helps designers with understanding where to intervene and how to intervene, as well as for them to evaluate and ideate iteratively. Nevertheless, it can easily be combined with other more detailed tools and techniques, and it does not facilitate the actual detailing of the design intervention.

Although organisations from the public sector are logical clients for this type of design, it does not exclude the commercial sector. Some commercial organisations wish to take their social responsibilities seriously, and many start-ups do operate commercially while primarily striving for societal goals.

HOW? The method involves four stages with seven design steps.

Stage 0 - Debriefing: Explain the activities before the real project kicks-off to explore client's expectations and their earlier attempts to solve the problem. This stage also involves understanding the conditions for success.

Stage 1 - Anticipating the future: Set the domain of the project (Step 1). This domain explains the boundaries of the phenomenon under study, and it typically explains an area of collective life or an aspect of society. It is typically a larger scope than the problem and is neutrally defined.

The domain defines what factors are relevant in data collection (Step 2). Factors describe trends, developments, states, and principles that help with understanding how the phenomenon is about to change in the future. Finally, this stage ends with a coherent vision of the future context in which your design intervention should become meaningful. This vision is created by building a context structure (Step 3).

Stage 2 - Goal setting: Define the effect you wish to achieve for both users and society. This effect is specified in a statement (Step 4) that describes:
• The behaviour you wish to support through design.

• The social implications of this behaviour and the way in which this can address or contend with collective concerns based on societal values.
• What meaning this behaviour has or will have for people due to individual concerns based on user values.

Stage 3 - Developing the intervention: This intervention is an iteration between defining the interaction between the intervention and users (Step 5), developing ideas (Step 6), and validating either crucial assumptions underlying the idea or the idea as such (Step 7). For the Steps 2, 4, and 7, the book *Designing for Society* offers several tools and techniques.

TIPS & CONCERNS
Remind yourself that taking a step back takes time and avoid 'jumping to solutions' or go for the quick-wins. Doing this will increase the chance your intervention will fundamentally change the world for the better.

Remember that your design intervention will NOT solve the social issue you are designing for. It is impossible to solve complex social problems with a single intervention.

Learn to gain satisfaction from taking small steps into the right direction and from having little pushes to system transformation.

LIMITATIONS
The approach is meant to be used with additional tools and techniques. The book under further reading offers some suggestions but is by far not conclusive here.

REFERENCES & FURTHER READING: Tromp, N. & Hekkert, P. (2019) *Designing for Society-Products and services for a better world.* London: Bloomsbury. / Tromp, N., & Hekkert, P. (2016). Assessing methods for effect-driven design: Evaluation of a social design method. *Design Studies*, *43*, 24-47. / Theo Deutinger, Brendan McGetrick, *Handbook of Tyranny*, Lars Müler Publishers, 2018, 9SBN 78-3-03778-534-8, English

When people think of a refugee camp they imagine a collection of tents, hastily erected and soon to be removed. Few refugeecamps conform to this image and develop into permanent settlements. The Concrete Tent designed by The Decolonizing Architecture Art Residency (DAAR) is a gathering space for communal learning. The urgency and idea of a space for cultural activities and social meetings emerged as a possibility to materialize and give architectural form to narrations and representations of camps and refugees beyond the idea of poverty, marginalization and victimisation. (www.decolonizing.ps)

Co-Design & Co-Creation

The terms Co-design and Co-creation refer to a collaborative design effort where designers work with users, experts, or other non-designers in doing design activities together. The degree and amount of this can vary; it could be done in certain parts or all parts of the design process, depending on the availability and need.

WHAT & WHY? In design, you may find yourself working on problems that test your limits: You may not have enough knowledge about the problem or enough ability to create solutions, or you may find it difficult to influence the organisations involved. Collaborate with others, including stakeholders, to tackle this. When this collaboration goes beyond asking for input and becomes a process of working together creatively, we speak of Co-design or Co-creation. By involving others into the design activities, they become actors in the creative process. In this way, they can bring unexpected insights and ideas for solutions.

There are three reasons to involve users or other stakeholders. The first is an ethical reason since users and stakeholders will be affected by the solution. They should have a say about the design and what it becomes. Secondly, when users express their needs and abilities, they can provide designers the knowledge to make a better solution. Finally, the stakeholders need to gain support from relevant parties.

MINDSET: Co-design and Co-creation require your respect for each participant as a source of meaningful active contribution. As facilitator, you are responsible for supporting and managing the process. To do this, you will need to set up activities so that participants can bring their contributions despite the fact that they are not trained designers.

WHEN? Co-design and Co-creation can by used in different phases of the design process. You can use this when you do not know the user's life situation (referred to as co-design with intended users), when you want to include a combination of new technologies (co-design with experts), or when you want other people in the company to own the resulting insights so that they can work further on it (co-design with colleagues).

HOW? There are many ways to carry out Co-design and Co-creation. You can involve your collaborators throughout the design process, or you can use only one Co-creation session. You can engage with them in a one-on-one setting, in a group session, or through social media. The key challenge is to equip participants with the language, tools, and the design topic – all of which should be adapted to support them in bringing in *their* expertise (see 'Context-mapping').

TIPS & CONCERNS:

Have a clear idea about what you want to achieve in your project and what the contribution of the participants can be.

Be open to unexpected contributions, but set the activity in a clear direction.

Manage the expectations of participants who may think they only have to provide their opinion about something you have made. Or you giving them your opinion or permission.

Ask participants to bring a creative contribution and connect their thinking to that of others.

Think of what could be an appropriate reward for them. This may be payment or the fact that the event is pleasant for them – it can even be fun!

A checklist for preparation includes: support from higher management; materials; an introduction; instructions; a script for the interaction; an agreement form if you want to record a session.

Use Co-Design for collaboration with users throughout the design process and Co-Creation for single session collaboration with experts within an organisation, as in focus groups.

LIMITATIONS:

Organising participation can be a lot of work, and this requires time and budget, especially if it involves a large group of people.

It is often difficult to get hold of experts in busy professions and people with busy lives, but they can bring important input.

REFERENCES & FURTHER READING: van Doorn, F. A. P., Gielen, M. A. & Stappers, P. J., 2014. Involving children and elderly in the development of new design concepts to become active together. *Interaction Design and Architecture (s)*, 2014(21). / van Rijn, H., & Stappers, P. J., 2008. *Expressions of ownership: motivating users in a co-design process*. In Proceedings of the Tenth Anniversary Conference on Participatory Design 2008 (pp. 178-181). Indiana University. / Sanders, E. B. N. & Stappers, P. J., 2008. Co-creation and the new landscapes of design. *Co-design*, 4(1), 5-18. / Sanders, E.B.-N. & Stappers P.J. (2012) *Convivial Toolbox: Generative research for the front end of design*. Amsterdam: BIS Publishers.

The myth of designing for the 'average' person - since there are no people whose body dimensions are all at the 50th percentile. Body dimensions aren't linearly correlated so people with short arms don't necessarily have short legs. While the use of the 5th and 95th percentiles on one body dimension may exclude 10% of the population, the use of these on 13 dimensions actually can exclude 52% of the population.

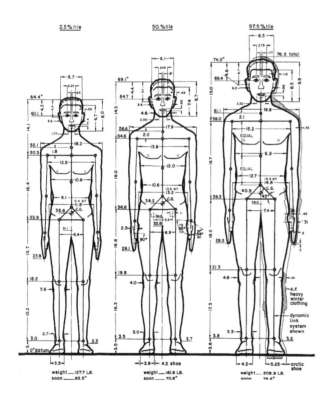

Anthropometric Design

Anthropometric Design is an approach to be used through the design process to ensure the optimal fit of products to the people using them. Doing so will help you to design and make decisions on adjustability, size, and shape throughout the design process.

WHAT & WHY? The interior of a car, a train seat, an office chair, safety equipment, or a hand tool, should accommodate the variation in shape and size of the targeted users. As the average user in terms of size, weight and shape doesn't exist, designers need to gain insight into the variation within their target group with the help of statistical measures such as percentiles and correlations between different body measurements.

Using scientific databases that include anthropometric information requires demographics about the users, such as birthday, age, and gender, because human size, weight, and shape widely vary across populations. You also need to determine which anthropometric parameters are relevant for the design at hand. Therefore, you need to study the interaction between the human body and the product and describe how users will handle the product, in what postures, and which movements they possibly will make.

MINDSET: Be aware of your user group and be aware of who will be excluded by certain design decisions. Children are very different from adults and so are people who are disabled in any type or form. An important principle is to always aim to design for all within your user group; to practice inclusive design. On the other hand, a personalised design or a design made for a very limited user group might prove to be useful for a larger group of users. For example, an easy-to-open jar lid that is specifically designed for the elderley is easy to open for all. Such a well thought-out design strategy facilitates the comfortable, safe, and efficient use of products.

WHEN? Anthropometric data can be used in different stages of the design process, preferably right from the discovery phase because this ensures an optimal outcome, instead of trying to adjust the design at the end of the design process.

TIPS & CONCERNS

It is important to mention that the size, weight, and shape of the population in the world is continuously changing (secular trends) due to ageing, lack of nutrition, overeating, or sedentary lifestyle.

Why not design for P0.1–P99.9? The standard use of P5–P95 to define your target group will lead to the exclusion of 10% of the population per anthropometric variable.

The closer the product needs to fit on the body, the more important the knowledge about shape becomes. 3D scan data can be of great help.

Some industries have developed advanced software representations of humans (Digital Human Models).

LIMITATIONS

Many modern products and systems integrate both physical and non-physical elements such as services and digital interfaces, for which additional data are needed.

HOW? First the future user group is defined. Then decide whether a product should be one-size-fits-all, have a size system, be made adjustable, or be fully personalised. Depending if the additional costs and complexity are worth the gain in ergonomics. The method involves 5 steps:

Step 1: Define the target population, taking into account demographic variables as well as relevant abilities and disabilities. Describe the context of use: posture, movements, and sequence of movements; socio-cultural influences; artefacts (clothing, tools, equipment) and physical environment. Observing how similar products are used can be very helpful in this stage.

Step 2: Search for anthropometric data, for example, in the DINED database (dined.nl) or scientific papers. Consider representativeness (demographic variables), precision, and presentation type (1D, 2D, 3D). If no data are available, determine whether there is time and budget to perform measurements for the missing data; otherwise, make estimations (based on the correlation between known variables).

Step 3: When all the data have been collected, add allowances for worn garments and use of tools and equipment For example, stature +20mm for shoe sole thickness.

Step 4: Establish the anthropometric design guidelines. Prototypes are needed to evaluate the fit, comfort, force exertion, interaction during short use or prolonged use, and interaction with the environment while using the tool.

Step 5: The use of statistics and databases is a simplification of the reality; the proper evaluation of the final concept based on a mock-up is necessary. This process is often iterative, and a fifth step to search for additional anthropometric data could be necessary.

REFERENCES & FURTHER READING: Jellema, A., Galloin, E., Massé, B., Ruiter, I., Molenbroek, J., & Huysmans, T., 2019, *3D Anthropometry In Ergonomic Product Design Education.* In I. Whitfield (Ed.), In proceedings of the 21th International Conference on Engineering and Product Design Education, Glasgow. / Lee, W., Molenbroek, J., Goto, L., Jellema, A., Song, Y., & Goossens, R., 2019. *Application of 3D scanning in design education.* In S. Scataglini, & G. Paul (Eds.), DHM and Posturography, (1st ed., pp. 721-731). Academic Press. / Robinette, K. & Hudson, J., 2006. *Anthropometry.* In G. Salvendi (Ed) Handbook of Human Factors and Ergonomics (3rd ed, pp. 322-339). John Wiley & Sons, Inc. / Verwulgen, S., Lacko, D., Vleugels, J., Vaes, K., Danckaers, F., De Bruyne, G., & Huysmans, T., 2018. A new data structure and workflow for using 3D anthropometry in the design of wearable products. *International Journal of Industrial Ergonomics,* 64, pp. 108-117.

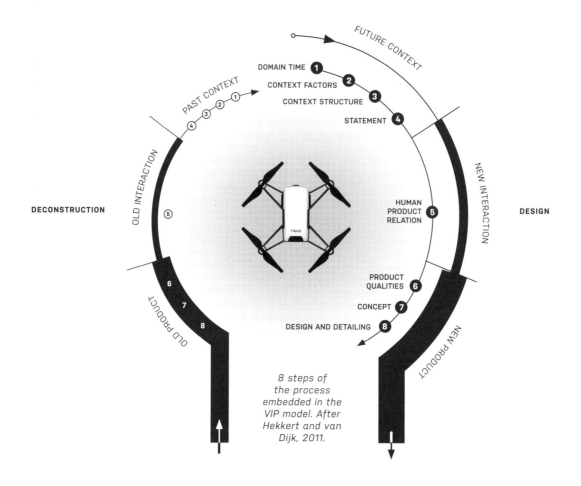

DECONSTRUCTION

FUTURE CONTEXT

PAST CONTEXT

OLD INTERACTION

NEW INTERACTION

DESIGN

1 DOMAIN TIME
2 CONTEXT FACTORS
3 CONTEXT STRUCTURE
4 STATEMENT
5 HUMAN PRODUCT RELATION
6 PRODUCT QUALITIES
7 CONCEPT
8 DESIGN AND DETAILING

OLD PRODUCT

NEW PRODUCT

8 steps of the process embedded in the VIP model. After Hekkert and van Dijk, 2011.

How personal is your relationship with your PC? The ViP approach focuses on the relationship between user and product and how it changes when moving into the future. For example, IBM was the main manufacturer of large mainframe computers during the 1970s. Extrapolating from their business at that time, they predicted that a handful of their machines per country would be enough to do all necessary calculations. They did not realise that the relationship between people and computers would become much more personal, as Microsoft and Apple proved.

Vision in Product Design

Vision in Product Design (ViP) is an approach that supports innovators of any kind to 'design' the vision, the reason 'why', or the 'raison d'être' underlying their design or intervention. This method considers products, services, or systems as carriers for change in a future society.

WHAT & WHY? The key to ViP is to design for future goals instead of solving today's problems. Today's problems reflect design decisions from the past that have inadvertently led to the problematic situations we face today. Trying to solving them would most likely maintain the old undesired situation. ViP aims to understand how we take a position in a future world – as in what is meaningful to people in a future society based on a shared worldview and value-framework. ViP can inform you on your role as a co-shaper of society, and it offers a step-by-step approach in developing a responsible and authentic design vision that steers ideation and conceptualisation. This vision includes the explication of what you wish to offer people in a future context before defining the means by which the design achieves this. This aspect of the method makes it suitable for innovation processes of any kind. It leads to designs with meaning and a soul – that is, appropriate and authentic products that reflect the vision and personality of their creators.

MINDSET: In the ViP philosophy, designing entails responding to a future worldview, not reacting to the present. This means that a designer needs to take responsibility to shape such a worldview and take a stance on how to achieve change within this scope. This inadvertently requires some subjective judgment by the designer, and thus the authenticity of those choices is paramount.

WHEN? Use ViP alongside the Discover, Define, and Develop stages. It usually ends with a detailed design proposal (a carrier for change), after which detailed design and implementation follow in the deliver stage.

HOW? ViP involves a deconstruction phase and a designing phase.

Deconstruction phase: In this phase, examine the current product (the what), the product-user interactions (the how) and context (the why) of those interactions. This deconstruction will help you make sense of the urgency to start acting explicitly, and it also makes you be respectful to the complexity of design.

Designing phase: In this phase, you develop the future context, interactions, and design. Describe the future context or worldview using a set of conditions that will steer how future attitudes, opinions, and behaviours of people are manifested in this future context. By carefully selecting and discussing the factors shaping these conditions, you build the worldview underlying the design. To

act upon this world, you need to take a position, also called 'the statement'. In this statement, define the raison d'être of the final solution by asking yourself, *what do I want to offer people? What do I want them to understand, experience, or do?* This is a step that you can perform together with the organisation and stakeholders you work with, thereby creating a shared purpose.

The statement is not directly translated into an intervention; the intervention is just a means for triggering appropriate actions, interactions, and relationships. Hence, you are encouraged to consider the interaction first, such as by looking for appropriate analogies. The statement, interaction, and product vision – as in the qualitative characteristics that the product has to embody – form the basis for further ideation, conceptualisation, and materialisation.

TIPS & CONCERNS
ViP is value-free. You can use it for 'good' or 'bad'; the method makes you fully responsible for the values you take into account when taking a position in the future world and the effects that you foresee with end-users.

ViP links visionary, strategic, and operational design stages to ensure business and societal appropriateness of the designed intervention.

ViP applies to Social Design, Sustainable Design, Experience Design, or any other Design movement.

ViP allows you to design in any domain, such as democracy, finance, mobility, healthcare, culture, or consumer goods.

Although the structure of the method reflects a clear rationale, it helps for you to move back and forth through the steps of worldview, statement, interaction, and product vision.

LIMITATIONS
ViP postpones the development of product ideas as it supports designers to consider its meaning to people first. Be willing to set aside enough time to do so.

ViP does not provide answers to questions; rather, it asks you to pose the right questions. It is up to you to take a position and argue for this position consistently and convincingly.

REFERENCES & FURTHER READING: Hekkert, P. & Van Dijk, M.B., 2011. *Vision in Design: A guidebook for innovators.* Amsterdam: BIS publishers. / Tromp, N. & Hekkert, P. 2019. *Designing for Society: Products and services for a better world.* London: Bloomsbury.

Risk is a fact of life. Today, technology unicorns, governments, startups, financial institutions, and open source projects are embracing collaboration with hackers to identify their unknown vulnerabilities in an ever changing digital context. The technology world's mass migration to the cloud has resulted in increased risks from vulnerabilities like Server Side Request Forgery. The image shows a Privacy Phone that has been designed in response yet, critics claim the problem is not the hardware but the ever changing software and digital environment. (image: McAfee)

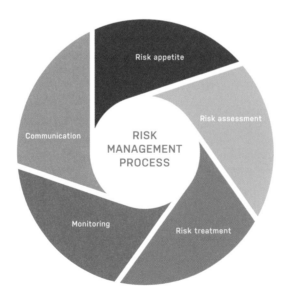

The ever changing context makes organised risk management a neccesity for digital security.

Context Variation by Design

Context Variation by Design (CVD) is an approach that encourages designers to take contextual variations of a problem into account before the design task is set. Consequently, the design outcome is adaptive towards multiple contextual scenarios rather than an optimised product or service for a specific context. The result is a design that is prepared for upscaling.

WHAT & WHY? In current practice, the design brief often zooms in on one specific context because a limited scope can provide clarity and focus. The design outcome is then optimised for that context. However, most societal problems occur in multiple contexts – which are often interdependent – and each context has different requirements. Working with the initial design outcome as a base is often seen in practice; such an approach can result in a mismatch with these requirements and may require an expensive redesign. This could in turn postpone or even block substantial large-scale positive societal impact.

The CVD approach approaches the task differently by applying systematic variation before the design task is set, not just during the design process. The problem definition covers the problem from different contextual angles. By including information from these different angles, you can enhance the richness of the conceptual design space where the information is widely sourced in non-arbitrary directions. The rich, multi-layered, multi-perspective, and interconnected design space enhances the quality of information to base decisions on in a stage where this information is still low-cost. Investments for production and distribution have not yet been made by this point. The design outcome is an architecture that is adaptive to be able to cover requirements from a relevant variety of contextual scenarios with intent – hence the term 'by design'.

MINDSET: The main mindset when using CVD is to acknowledge that a diversity of requirements reflects reality. This improves the initial design outcome, and having such a mindset can both represent and enable a longer term perspective regarding costs and time-to-markets instead of only designing for the first market.

WHEN? CVD is particularly relevant as an approach to address large-scale societal problems. In these cases, it is possible to foresee how a design process that focuses on one particular context will not cover the diversity of requirements that are associated with larger scale issues. Using CVD is therefore essential before the design task is set.

TIPS & CONCERNS
To be used together with other methods and tools in this guide.

To prevent getting lost, the multiform design task covers the relevance of multiple non-arbitrary contexts. The search space within the design task is therefore at the same time wide *and* well-directed.

The decision of when to move from opening up the search space (divergence) to focus (convergence) is driven by intuition, just like with any other method.

The unpredictability of the short-term outcome of a CVD-driven process may be higher than for a contextually focused (market) design process. However, once the architecture is known, there is much more clarity about *the potential for scalability* across multiple contexts ('markets').

LIMITATIONS
Using CVD may require an allocation of more resources at the early stage. If the assignment represents a well-defined (re) design with specified short-term results, managers may not consider this to be worth it.

HOW? Step 1: Systematically identify and analyse several contexts that are relevant to the general problem. Choose relevant contexts that are likely to result in different requirements by varying key dimensions of the problem.

Step 2: Define the multiform design task (formalised in a brief) based on a range of non-arbitrary contextual variations of the problem that are different enough and can still have touchpoints.

Step 3: Specify the main intelligence in the form of insights per context. Then feed these into a rich conceptual design space that results in shared insights. These are the main input for creating design concepts.

Step 4: From this set of design concepts, develop a draft version of the adaptive architecture with well-informed choices regarding generic, modular/optional, and context-specific elements.

Step 5: Check that version against the list of requirements derived from the multiform design brief. If this is not satisfactory, return to the rich design space.

Step 6: Finalise the architecture, which is adaptive towards a range of contextual scenarios. While the design outcome is suitable for implementation in multiple contexts, management priorities determine the actual sequence.

REFERENCES & FURTHER READING: Kersten, W.C., 2020. *What Leonardo could mean to us now. Systematic variation 21st century style, applied to large-scale societal issues.* Doctoral Thesis, Faculty of Industrial Design Engineering, Delft University of Technology. / Diehl, J.C, van Sprang, S. Alexander, J.W. & Kersten, 2018. *A scalable clean cooking stove matching the cooking habits of Ghana and Uganda.* Global Humanitarian Technology Conference, San Jose, CA, USA. / Kersten, W., Diehl, J.C., & van Engelen, J.M.L., 2019. Intentional Design for Diversity as Pathway to Scalable Sustainability Impact. In *Innovation for Sustainability*, 291-309. Springer.

Swapfiets is the first company in the world that provides a bicycle with full service for a fixed monthly fee. The concept started in 2014 in Delft and is extending it's program with e-bikes. Swapfiets is a bike service spreading accross Europe where you pay a monthly fee in exchange for a robust bike and a support team at the end of a phone call. Swapfiets guarantees that customers will never go more than 2 days without a bike, including if it's been stolen. Swapfiets aims to provide and promote the most efficient mobilty in big cities.

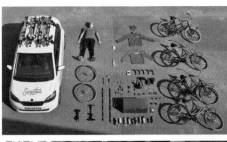

Service Design

Service Design involves designing longer-lasting interactions between the provider and users, which are possibly supported with IT, intangible components, and services provided by people. Where product design can be said to end with a mass-designed product, services typically come into being at the time of use, and their form and content develop after launch.

WHAT & WHY? Service design is an interdisciplinary approach that focuses on the service that an organisation provides to the user. For example, a message app on a smartphone is meaningless without an Internet connection to a central server or to other users; it may start out with minimal functionality but gets updated and extended every few weeks. Another example is the carsharing company Greenwheels, which requires an end-to-end system for car maintenance, administration, billing, and providing access to vehicles. Applying for personal care is also an example of service design where care providers, informal caregivers, the municipality, and the financial system need to operate together to fit the needs of a patient over time.

The active participation of users and other stakeholders is regarded as essential for understanding the complexities involved. The final deliverables of Service Design can be products, interiors, training of service delivery staff, software, organisation transformation, and business models. The intangible components often require different design skills than tangible ones. Therefore, Service Design incorporates teamwork involving cross-disciplinary communication. Services continue evolving after the first delivery, thus blurring the boundaries between the conceptualisation, implementation, and use phases. Solutions in service design usually entail a combination of organisation, technology, and people.

MINDSET: Service Design requires thinking in events and scenarios that evolve over time and that involve various stakeholders. In comparison with tangible product design, less attention is given to the material qualities of products in the scenarios.

WHEN? Service Design builds on and integrates earlier design fields such as experience design, interaction design, product design, architectural design, and transformation design. To understand services, you have to examine them over a longer period of time. Business models for services are more complex than the classic 'cash and carry' model for physical products where the designer's job is done before the product hits the shelf. The focus of Service Design is the exchange of value of involved stakeholders. The user experience perspective is usually central – it is the end goal that ties all of the system components together.

HOW? Service Design projects often involve teams of designers and experts with complementary expertise. Service Design requires designers to facilitate the collaboration and bring in new stakeholders and experts along the way.

Step 1: Build a holistic view of the user's context and service possibilities Specify where the service fits in the user's life and which organisations and infrastructures are needed to deliver it. Many designers regard the users as important participants in the design process to gain insight into the users' context of use, their values, routines, skills, and social relations. Accordingly, close collaboration with stakeholders is the key to obtain insight into possible organisation structures to produce the services.

Step 2: Visualise the intangible interactions over time The use over time, encompassing multiple 'touch points' (moments that connect a user with the service), and the way the service fits into the other activities of users involve many intangible and often complex elements to be understood and accounted for in design. This requires appropriate methods, such as Storyboarding, Journey Mapping, Experience Prototyping, Storytelling, and Role-Playing.

Step 3: Develop an interdisciplinary and shared language Services are often conceived as sequences of interactions between users and the service system over time (touch points). Such complexities can be mapped in ways such as journey maps, blueprints, value exchange maps, business model maps, stakeholders' maps, and system maps.

TIPS & CONCERNS:
Service Design uses its own jargon such as:
Customer journey map: *a timeline presentation.*

Front end: *what the user sees.*

Back end: *what happens behind the screens.*

Service blueprint: *a graphic way of describing a concept design.*

Service Design supports users' experiences as an end goal and also the learning processes of users and providers. Therefore, services are often open-ended – meaning that they evolve after implementation – and design iterations are essential.

LIMITATIONS:
Because Service Design is a rather generic approach, it builds upon many other types of design and does not have a single clear set of methods or terms.

REFERENCES & FURTHER READING: Carvalho, L. & Goodyear, P., 2018. Design, learning networks and service innovation. *Design Studies*, 55, pp. 27-53. / Kimbell, L., 2011. Designing for Service as One Way of Designing Services. *International Journal of Design*, 5(2), pp. 41–52. / Sleeswijk Visser, F., 2013. *Service Design by Industrial Designers*. Delft University of Technology. Obtainable through http://lulu.com. / Stickdorn, M., Hormess, M. E., Lawrence, A. & Schneider, J., 2018. *This is service design doing: Applying service design thinking in the real world.* " O'Reilly Media, Inc.".

Defining the transfer effect using one of the oldest and most successful board games in the world. Since its launch by Parker Brothers in 1935, more than 200 million units have been sold. 1. Experience how the economy of money, investment, business and real estate and power work; 2. Learn how investments are linked to business opportunities and making big money; 3. The players make an endless traveling loop passing cities and trainstations where streets and property can be purchased depending on a combination of chance and good luck (dice) and opportunities or bad luck (board positions, cards and jail); 4. Whoever enters a street owned by a competitor must pay him, depending on the amount of property on that street; 5. Whoever owns the most, earns the most, turns the others bankrupt, and wins.

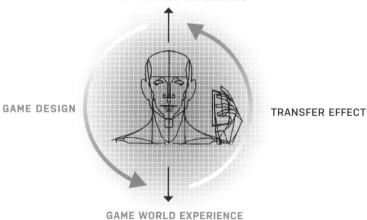

After Visch et al., 2013

Persuasive Game Design

Persuasive Game Design (PGD) is a non-directive approach for designing persuasive games, including practical hand-outs and cards. Designers first consider the game design steps that they should use in creating their game; in each step, they select which components to take into account as well as the tools to use.

WHAT & WHY? Game design has been practiced for a long time despite the lack of standard design methods. In the case of PGD, which aims to facilitate a realisation of the user's goals that go beyond mere entertainment, it can be beneficial to have a method that guides the whole design process for both design practitioners and researchers alike.

The approach is based on the PGD model as well as practical PGD experiences from creative industries and academic design projects. According to the PGD approach, the core of persuasive game design is to 'transport' the user's experience from a real-world experience to an engaging game world experience. The aim is to facilitate the transfer of the intended effects in the real world. The user's experience takes a central position in the approach since it is the essential factor that has to be influenced by design in order to realise the intended effects.

MINDSET: The user experience forms the start and the end of the PGD method. It starts from the belief that a successful game helps a user achieve goals and supports the user's motivation towards achieving these goals. These motivations will guide the designers' creativity and ease the final adaptation of the game by the user. In this way, the PGD method is rooted in psychology, user research, co-creation, and personalisation.

TIPS & CONCERNS
Try to include all ingredients in your design and try to find your personal set of preferred utensils.

LIMITATIONS
The method can be limited in its details, such as the domain specific balance between game elements and serious elements, such as which parts of the serious content (for example, therapy or education material) can be changed by the designer.

71

WHEN? PGD is especially suitable for supporting users in behavioural change processes, such as those with respect to health, lifestyle, or work. When designing and implementing a PGD, the designer is advised to be sensitive and to respond to how problems and solutions are framed, as some users might not welcome the gamification of serious work.

HOW? Focus either on a specific area within the PGD process, such as behavioural change or game mechanic. Or on a specific application domain. To provide enough design freedom on the one hand and enough practical structure on the other, we can apply a 'cookbook' metaphor to increase the usability in research. A meal composed of four dishes represents the overall game design approach. Each dish represents a major step used for designing a persuasive game.

Step 1 - Defining the transfer effect: Clearly define the transfer effect that aims to be delivered by the game experience.

Step 2 - Investigating the user's world: Start from learning more about the context that you are designing for which involves knowing about the user's preferences, needs, values and capabilities. Two extreme positions can be identified: integrate the game in an existing real-world

context with real-world tasks. Or design a game that aims to affect the user within fictional experience.

Step 3 - Game design: First different concepts and game ideas are explored, evaluated, and then refined into an initial game concept. After picking the most promising concept, the various components of the persuasive game are designed, prototyped, tested, and refined. Such components include the narrative, the game experience and user stories. When using digital formats this is done in conjunction with the technical development of the game.

Step 4 - Evaluation of effects: When a playable version is finished, the designer needs to check if his persuasive game is effective. There are three types of values that evaluation can aim to increase: the knowledge level: Can it be made more effective?; At a user-effect level: Does it achieve the transfer effect? and at a commercial level: How will it perform in the commercial market'.

REFERENCES & FURTHER READING: Siriaraya, P., Visch, V., Vermeeren, A. & Bas, M., 2018. A cookbook method for Persuasive Game Design. *International Journal of Serious Games*, 5(1), 37-71. / Visch, V. T., Vegt, N. J. H., Anderiesen, H. & Van der Kooij, K., 2013. *Persuasive Game Design: A model and its definitions*. CHI 2013: Workshop Designing Gamification: Creating Gameful and Playful Experiences, Paris, France. / Green, M., Brock, R. & Kaufman, G., 2004. Understanding media enjoyment: The role of transportation into narrative worlds. *Communication Theory*, 14(4), pp. 311-327. / Woolrych A., Hornbæk, K., Frøkjær, E. & Cockton, G., 2011. Ingredients and meals rather than recipes: A proposal for research that does not treat usability evaluation methods as indivisible wholes. *International Journal of Human-Computer Interaction*, pp. 940-970.

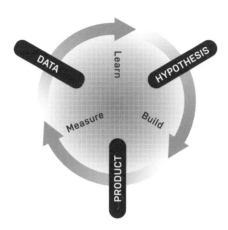

Where a set of posts and a crossbar are unavailable, the nearest bundle of sticks will do. At a loss for a ball, a round fruit or bound rags can suffice. With a modern venue out of the question, dusty streets can instead become a theater of dreams. The very sport itself is an expression of both collective culture and individuality. And for a fair many professionals, it also represents an escape from a life addled by social and economic strife. Playing fast in fierce competion these boys in Egypt explore and develop their talents by learning, testing and sharpening their skills on the go. (Wickimedia, Mohamed Hozyen Ahmed)

Lean Start-up

Lean Start-up is a method for innovating faster, better, and cheaper, just like startups do. The use of compact canvases and the iterative validation of ideas using the 'build, measure, learn' cycle are key to the process.

WHAT & WHY? The Lean Start-up method facilitates rapid, lean project management using pragmatic canvases that can be filled in within the hour; in this way, time can be used to start testing assumptions, rather than putting time in writing detailed plans that may prove to be useless once they are finished.

It is important to know whether ideas or concepts make sense, especially in the early stages of innovation. With Lean Start-up, ideas are therefore formulated as hypotheses that can be tested. Hypotheses are statements that we take as assumptions, for example, 'The consumer is willing to pay 9.95 euros for our product'. Checking the hypotheses against the criteria of desirability, feasibility, or viability in an iterative process – called the Lean Cycle – is the core of Lean Start-up. We test those hypotheses by conducting experiments. These experiments could take several forms, but the challenge is to perform them as cheaply and quickly as possible. Instead of building a full working product, we might simply simulate one.

Desirability is about whether people want a product or service. *Viability* is about whether a business can be built on the product or service. *Feasibility* is about whether product or service can actually be provided.

MINDSET: A key underlying principle is to 'fail fast, fail often'. Accepting assumptions to be true without any validation is risky for innovation. The best mindset is to be willing to kill your darlings and to consider 'abort mission' as a success, rather than a failure.

WHEN? Lean Start-up is typically used in the front end of innovation. The canvases are mostly used in the early phases, for example for identifying what problem to solve and how to build a business on an idea or concept. The validation can be part of any phase in the design process. Of course, the granularity of the validation is increasing when progressing through the design process.

HOW? The Lean Cycle consists of three phases: build, measure, and learn.

First, the idea is formulated as an hypothesis. We then *build* a product that could be a prototype, a probe, or a mock-up. The product is being *measured* in an experiment, for example, an interview, a survey, co-creation, or whatever works to validate it. The experiment delivers research data, from which we *learn* how to proceed. This process could also be depicted as illustrated.

The hypotheses can be gathered in a backlog and then prioritised based on riskiness and effort: the riskiest

assumptions are the ones we prefer to do first. The Lean Cycle has an iterative aspect, in the sense that every learning leads to new known unknowns.

In Agile innovation, the Lean Cycle can best be synced with the Agile rhythm. Next to the development and other tracks, we use a validation track. We call this process Continuous Validation.

When using this method, you'll find that your designs will almost never survive the first contact with consumers or users, but that you'll get all kinds of hints and clues for your next best action.

REFERENCES & FURTHER READING: Ries, E, 2011. *The lean startup: How today's entrepreneurs use continuous innovation to create radically successful businesses.* Crown Books. / Maurya, A., 2012. *Running lean: iterate from plan A to a plan that works.* O'Reilly Media, Inc.

TIPS & CONCERNS
Generating all the relevant hypotheses is essential because those are the ones that we will validate.

Make sure you don't miss important hypotheses. Talking to different experts may help. Having many varied disciplines on board is similarly helpful. Diversity rules!

False positives often appear because designers become too attached to their ideas, leading them to misinterpret the data.

LIMITATIONS
The Lean Start-up method does not deliver a vision on products or services. The starting point for the innovation could either be a vision that is developed beforehand, or an innovation that is more incremental and based on the input from the contact with users.

Artist Jannick Deslauriers uses textiles and threads to weave ghostly, massive sculptures. Whether it's a time-worn car, a white military tank or a cityscape, her works appear as structures that can be passed through. She uses darker threads as her 'pencil outlines,' blending textures and techniques to create pieces that resemble little else. Her hands simultaneously both weave a story and unravel it. Like 'the exploded car' as an icon of our time. (jannickdeslauriers.com)

Jen Keane uses the K rhaeticus bacteria for her project, aptly called 'This is grown'. The bacteria grow a tiny fibre known as nanocellulose. This material is incredibly strong, 8 times stronger than steel and stiffer than Kevlar. In addition, nanocellulose is transparent and incredibly lightweight. The material has already been used for medical applications. If we talk about the work in context to traditional weaving, the designer is weaving the warp, and the bacteria are growing the weft. (jenkeane.com)

Material Driven Design

Material Driven Design (MDD) is a method to facilitate design processes in which materials are the main driver. Grounded on the notion of materials experience, the method adopts a holistic view of materials by emphasising their role in design as something that is simultaneously technical and experiential.

WHAT & WHY? Design can positively contribute to the development of new materials by uncovering the unforeseen potentials of a material. This requires a holistic approach that brings together a technical, experiential, historical, and contextual understanding of materials to the development of materials and products in synergy. The MDD method provides explicit techniques for navigating between these different dimensions as well as to identify and reflect on the material's potential and its possible development directions.

We typically experience materials in products at four experiential levels – sensorial, interpretive, affective, and performative. For instance, salad bags made from PLA have a sharp and loud sound when handled (the sensorial level) that is annoying for some people (the affective level) which can cause them to rip up the bag (the performative level). But the sound can also be perceived as something that echoes crispy freshness (the interpretive level). The MDD method supports designers in understanding these experiential qualities of materials and in bridging them to their technical properties.

MINDSET: MDD requires designers to have an active participation in discovering the novel potentials of a material rather than merely translating known potentials to product applications. It builds on a key premise that material potentials do not present themselves to the designer as something that is already known and ready in their unprocessed form. Rather, they are constructed through situated actions, like tinkering with the material and reflections: Framing the material as a part of a wider context.

WHEN? The method is applicable for designing with conventional or familiar materials such as wood and metal. Or with relatively new materials, including smart materials like shape memory alloys. It can also be used for designing with living organisms, such as fungi, algae, bacteria, and plants. You can try using MDD when there is a resource that can potentially be transformed into a new material.

TIPS & CONCERNS

The suggested sequence and the extent to which activities are implemented must be adopted to the conditions of each project.

Consider factors, such as large- or small-scale, time concerns, limited budget, and the redesign of an existing product.

Start your tinkering by visualising the 'existing' material making process.

Identify the key elements you could play with to alter material performance and experience; such elements can be the ingredients and processing techniques.

Use a logbook. Record your experiments during the steps of material tinkering and testing.

Take high-quality photographs of the samples you create and take videos to record the making processes.

LIMITATIONS

The only limit is your own imagination. You may need some help with technical knowledge on materials.

HOW? *Step 1 - Understanding the material:* The first step involves engaging in extensive *tinkering* to understand the material at hand. You can conduct performance tests such as technical and mechanical tests and user studies to establish a technical and experiential characterisation of the material. To position the material among existing examples and explore the historical development of the material, perform a round of material benchmarking.

Step 2 - Creating materials experience vision: Take the findings from Step 1 and map them to create the materials experience vision. This vision expresses what role the material might play in relation to a product, its user, and the context. This enables you to reflect upon the unique qualities of the

material and then translate them into product offerings.

Step 3 - Manifesting materials experience patterns: In the vision statement, certain experiential qualities become apparent in this step. Examples of such qualities can be descriptive adjectives such as honest, surprising, and playful. These qualities are further explored in Step 3 where you can explore the existing material experience patterns that are prevalent in society.

Step 4: Creating material or product concepts: In this step, the final material and product concepts are created. The vision steers the concept development to ensure an outcome that is grounded in the unique qualities of the material.

REFERENCES & FURTHER READING: Karana E., Barati, B., Rognoli V., Zeeuw Van Der Laan, A., 2015. Material Driven Design (MDD): A Method To Design For Material Experiences. *International Journal of Design*, 9(2), 35-54. / Karana, E. (2009). *Meanings of Materials*, Doctoral Thesis, Delft University of Technology. / Barati, B. (2019). *Design Touch Matters: Bending and stretching the potentials of smart material composites*, Doctoral Thesis, Delft University of Technology. / Giaccardi, E. & Karana, E. 2015. *Foundations of materials experience: An approach for HCI*. In Proceedings of the 33rd SIGCHI Conference on Human Factors in Computing Systems (pp. 2447-2456). New York, NY: ACM. / Karana E., Pedgley O., Rognoli V., 2014. Materials Experience: *Fundamentals of Materials and Design*, 1st Ed., Butterworth-Heinemann: Elsevier, UK.

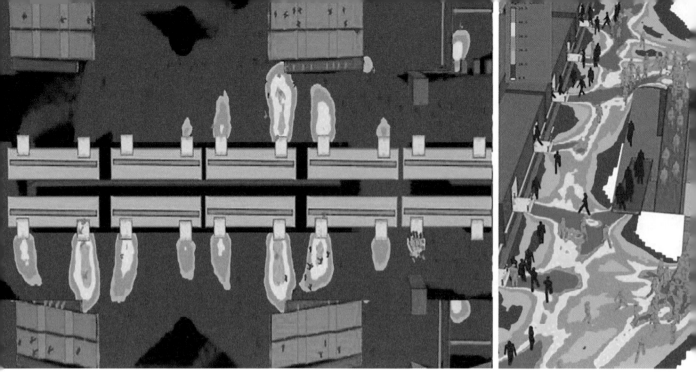

Using eye tracking, virtual reality and crowd simulation are used to support design decision-making for updating overcrowded subway-station. On the right: The images visualise data from subway platform congestion. A crowd walking speed map and a crowd density map.

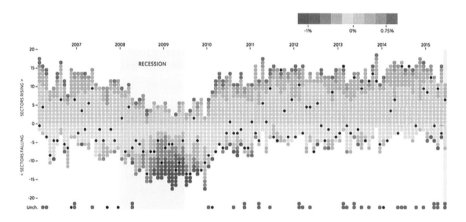

Data Visualization is an increasingly key tool to make sense of the trillions of rows of data generated every day. Data visualization helps to tell stories by curating data into a form easier to understand, highlighting the trends and outliers. A good visualisation tells a story, removing the noise from data and highlighting the useful information. Data can be an ingredient for great design.

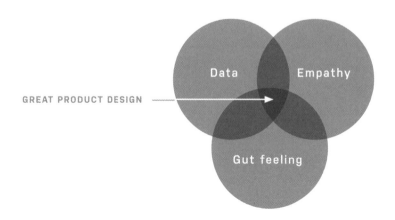

Data-Centric Design

Data-Centric Design is an approach for generating design-relevant insights from quantitative data, and it complements qualitative design and research methods. Quantitative insights can provide designers with a different or more nuanced perspective and can be used to inform the design process, motivate design decisions, and also to evaluate design solutions for products, services, and systems.

WHAT & WHY? Designers develop products, services, and systems in fast-paced and complex societal, technological, and environmental ecosystems. The emergence of digital technologies such as the Internet of Things, machine learning, and image and language processing has enabled designers to collect, process, and analyse large amounts of quantitative data. This data allows them to derive insights about human behaviours, attitudes, perceptions and the context and dynamics of interaction between people and their environment.

Looking at data trails with an ethnographic perspective allows designers to reflect on how people behave online and offline, as well as how they adopt and use products and services, and even how they feel. Data-Centric Design activities can take place at the exploration stage of the design process when you need to develop a perspective on the challenge and solution space; it can also be used at the intervention and evaluation stages for you to measure and reflect on the effect and impact of your design solution.

MINDSET: Designers need to have a critical attitude towards the opportunities and limitations of data representations since these provide no objective representation of the world. It only provides a partial and biased view that needs to be interpreted and thus seek ways to creatively integrate these into design processes. Data collection and use raises ethical issues that require designers to negotiate the often-diverging views on privacy, confidentiality, and transparency; they also need a firm understanding of the legal requirements, such as the General Data Protection Regulation (GDPR).

WHEN? Data-Centric Design is a general approach that can be applied across most phases of the design process – from early conceptual design to product development and testing. Data-Centric Design methods depend on the availability of high-quality data; you would need to marshal existing data resources and use technical means to collect new data.

TIPS & CONCERNS

Avoid common fallacies when working with data such as false causality, McNamara fallacy (relying solely on metrics), cherry picking (selecting data that fits preconceived claims), and sampling bias (drawing conclusions from a set of data that are not representative of the whole).

There is no unbiased data. Always leverage data with reasonable anticipation and consideration of these biases.

You need an understanding of the legal constraints on data collection and use, and ethical concerns. Consult with ethics committees, legal departments, and IT support for advice.

LIMITATIONS:

Available tools are mostly geared towards data scientist, and such tools require a solid knowledge of data techniques.

Data-centric designers should be prepared to creatively adapt and combine the use of these tools to fit their needs..

HOW? Data-Centric Design relies on statistical and computational methods; it involves key activities such as data acquisition, data cleaning, data analysis, and data visualisation. Data is first acquired using software or sensors and then stored in a file or database for further processing. Before data can be analysed, they often need to be cleaned in order to improve their quality. This involves identifying missing data and correcting erroneous data. Cleaned data can be analysed with high-level software tools that allow designers to look at data using a range of standard statistical and machine learning methods. Data visualisation can be used throughout the process to view and inspect data, but it also plays an important role in participatory design and in communicating data insights to external stakeholders.

To design and improve a product or service – such as a website, mobile application, or appliance – designers often collect data on user behaviours to detect significant behavioural patterns (see 'Usage Analytics'). One important method for doing this is A/B testing, which is a controlled experiment for finding statistically relevant differences in the use of two versions of the same product or service.

For communicating data insights to the design team or stakeholders, designers can borrow methods and approaches from data journalism, a new branch of journalism that focuses on the use of data to uncover, explain, and provide context to news stories through a combination of text, graphs, and data visualisations.

REFERENCES & FURTHER READING: Van Kollenburg, J., Bogers, S., Rutjes, H., Deckers, E., Frens, J. & Hummels, C., 2018, April. *Exploring the Value of Parent Tracked Baby Data in Interactions with Healthcare Professionals: A Data-Enabled Design Exploration.* In Proceedings of the 2018 CHI Conference on Human Factors in Computing Systems (p. 297). ACM. King, R., Churchill, E.F. & Tan, C., 2017. *Designing with Data: Improving the User Experience with A/B Testing.* O'Reilly Media, Inc. / Kun, P., Mulder, I., De Götzen, A. & Kortuem, G., 2019. *Creative Data Work in the Design Process.* In Proceedings of the 2019 ACM Sigchi Conference on Creativity and Cognition. ACM.

In retrospect the Design roadmaps for strategic challenges seem obvious. Light bulbs have seen an evolution over the years which has helped the human species in many more ways than we can imagine. From increasing the average workday to being a constant companion in the dark nights, light bulbs have been a driving force for everything we do. In 1835, there was the first sign of a constant electric light and after that, for 40 years scientists worked to develop what today we know as the incandescent light bulb.

TREND RESEARCH

USER VALUE DRIVERS

SYN-CHRONIZE

FUTURE IMAGING

VISON CRAFTING

IDEA SHAPING

TIME PACING

CREATE PATHWAYS

TUNE CONSTRAINTS

FUTURE VISION

TECH SCOUTING

T-MODULE SCOUTING

DESIGN ROADMAP

LINK ACTIVITIES

DESIGN PROGRAM ROADMAP

Another future challenge is reducing the weight and environmental burden of packaging. The first heavy solid glass Coca-Cola bottle was designed in 1915 by the Root Glass Company. In 1994 Coca-Cola introduced the 20oz plastic contour bottle, in 2008 the light weight contour aluminum can and in 2019 the fully recyclable paperboard KeelClip in a move that is projected to save 2,000 tonnes of plastic and 3,000 tonnes of CO_2 annually.

Design Roadmapping

Design Roadmapping is an approach to devise creative responses to future strategic challenges. Guided by future foresight techniques, designers can uncover new trends, scout for new technologies, and map the values and ideas on the roadmap.

WHAT & WHY? Design Roadmapping connects user values to future visions and to an evolutionary pacing of design innovations. A roadmap design of an innovation strategy has three basic characteristics: It presents a visual portrait of the organisation's future innovations; it is outlined by user value, product or service, market, and technology elements, and it is plotted on a timeline. Mapping value propositions and their versions on the future timeline ensures continuous innovation for your organisation in the long run.

MINDSET: The strategic decision making involves the creation, exploration, and convergence of ideas about the future. User values often stick out in a designer's mind. These values drive the design directions and future timing of innovation. The idea can become successful only given several key conditions, namely: When users embrace a new innovation; when there is a close connection between their value wishes, desires, and needs; and when the time has come that a critical majority agrees on the value of the innovation.

WHEN? As part of the strategy development process in organisations, Design Roadmapping can be used for developing the innovation strategy. Through strong visualisation, a design roadmap supports an organisational mindset on user-centred design innovations. In essence, Design Roadmapping offers designers a tactical plan on innovating new value propositions and versions that can turn a future vision into a reality.

HOW? You typically need a team of innovation professionals with diverse backgrounds and roles. Design Roadmapping is a process in which creative conversations and multiple sessions build the common ground for the future plans of innovation. The timeline synchronises the choices and decisions on innovation. It is the bridge in building and discussing the roadmap and in connecting the layers of the roadmap. The roadmapping process is organised in diverging and converging activities:

- **Creative trend research:** Trends provide potential directions of new opportunities of value creation.

- **Future visioning:** This involves creating a roadmap's destination by future imaging and crafting a future vision statement grounded in unique value drivers.

- **Technology scouting:** A modular architecture serves as the radar for the technology scouting activity.

TIPS & CONCERNS

Design Roadmapping is not a job for a lone designer but should be a team endeavour.

Compose the Design Roadmapping team in such a way that you ensure a solid base for creating common ground on the future vision and the design roadmap.

As a general guideline a typical roadmap consists of a future timeline and four layers related to the innovation dimensions, namely user value, markets, product, service, and technology.

LIMITATIONS

Available tools for gathering quantitative data require a solid knowledge of data techniques. Data-centric designers should be prepared to creatively adapt and combine these tools to fit their needs.

A roadmap does not plan the implementation phase of whatever single new product or service.

A roadmap is not a plan for tracking progress on resources or multiple projects on a day-to-day basis.

- **Time pacing strategy:** Three horizons of parallel strategic life cycle evolutions offer a mode of thinking about the future. Ideas are generated and shaped to bridge the connection between the user values and technology application in modules.

- **Synchronise design innovation activities:** The timeline synchronises the choices and decisions on innovation; it is the bridge in building and discussing the roadmap, and it connect the layers of the roadmap.

- **Link activities:** User values are linked to product lines or families of products and services with successive versions of upgraded products and services.

- **Tune constraints:** It is important to know the constraints of the resource investments before creating pathways and before estimating the lead times, resourcing manpower, and initiating financial investment.

REFERENCES & FURTHER READING: Simonse, L.W.L. 2018. *Design Roadmapping: Guidebook for future foresight techniques.* Amsterdam: BIS Publishers. / Simonse, L.W.L., Hultink, E J. & Buijs, J.A. 2015. Innovation roadmapping: Building concepts from practitioners' insights. *Journal of Product Innovation Management,* 32(6), 904-924.

'A bird is an instrument working according to mathematical law, which instrument it is within the capacity of men to reproduce with all it's movements.'

LEONARDO DA VINCI

METHODS DISCOVER

A method offers a specific process for a design activity that is predominantly used within a specific phase of design. In this guide, these methods are categorised into the phases of a design process. However, many methods can be used in several phases, and an overlap occurs in practice. The methods in this section help you to discover, explore, analyse, and understand your design domain.

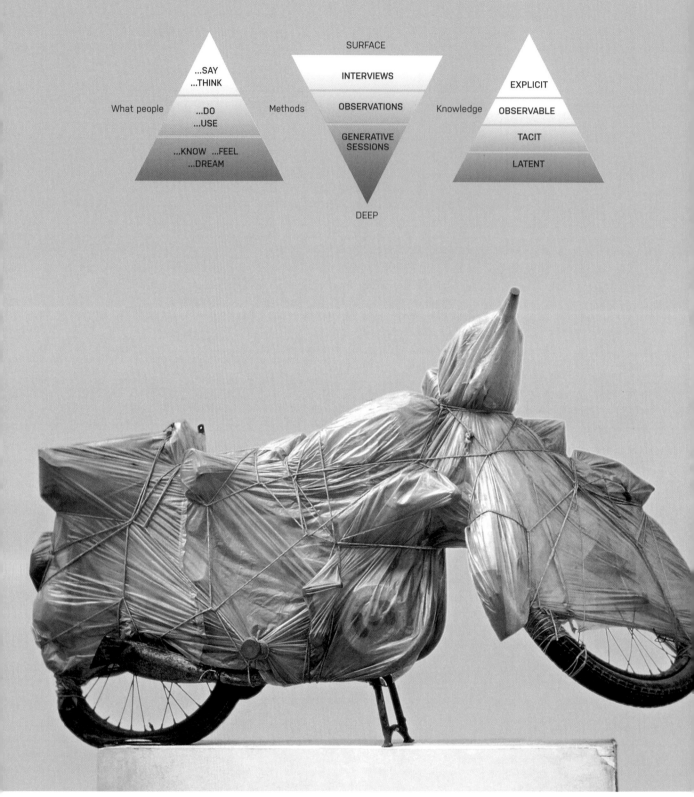

What people / Methods / Knowledge

...SAY
...THINK
...DO
...USE
...KNOW ...FEEL
...DREAM

SURFACE
INTERVIEWS
OBSERVATIONS
GENERATIVE
SESSIONS
DEEP

EXPLICIT
OBSERVABLE
TACIT
LATENT

By wrapping objects, buildings and landscapes, Christo intended to create beauty and the joy of seeing familiar objects and landscapes in a new way – 'revelation through concealment' which is like a reversed version of Contextmapping. Christo and his wife Jeanne-Claude funded projects by selling his preliminary design drawings. (Wrapped Motorcycle, 1962 Photo: Archive, Courtesy Christo

Contextmapping

Contextmapping is a people-centred design method that helps designers learn about people's everyday experiences. The outcomes inform designers and help them to create solutions that fit people's needs. The people involved are usually end users, but they can also include other stakeholders, such as employees and city residents.

WHAT & WHY? Contextmapping involves people sharing personal daily life experiences. In generative sessions, participants are asked to share their own stories. This method uses creative means such as cultural probes that stimulate telling, which aims to bring latent knowledge to the surface. The outcomes help designers to empathize with their intended users. The results can be used in various ways, such as developing Personas, creating strategies for innovation, or generating new views on market segmentation.

MINDSET: Designers are experts in the design process, whereas the people they design for are regarded as experts of their individual experiences in everyday life. The method is based on the belief that everyone is an expert and that designers should take everyone's expertise in a serious way.

WHEN? Contextmapping is most advantageous when a project is in the pre-concept stage where there is still a lot of latitude for finding new design opportunities. It fits well in Co-design or Co-creation processes and with multi-stakeholder projects.

HOW? The Contextmapping process usually consists of a series of activities that are roughly divided into two phases – collecting user insights and communicating user insights. During these phases, designers can use several research methods, such as interviews, observations, generative tools, and certain elements from cultural probes. The number of participating users is usually small; 3 to 20 people.

1. Preparation and sensitising: The design team defines the topic and goal, and they also develop a plan about who to involve, as well as when, how, and why to involve them. In this stage, the team needs to create sensitising materials for the participants; here, sensitising means causing people to be sensitive for a certain matter. With open-ended questions and by using provoking materials as 'homework', people are triggered to map and review their everyday routines around a topic. Furthermore, the design team needs to capture their own preconceptions about the topic in order for them to open up and learn more from the participants' stories.

2. Generative assignments: People are often not consciously aware of their everyday experiences. With interviews, you find out what they think. With observations, you can see what they do and how they use things. With generative techniques, we can have a better idea about what they know and feel – and maybe even what they dream about.

After using the sensitising activity, you can organise home visits, interviews, or group sessions. The sensitising materials serve as a starting point to let the participants tell you their personal stories.

You can then provide exercises with generative tools, which are tools that help participants create artefacts about their experiences. You can do this by firstly asking them what is meaningful for them in the present and in the past, and then you can end the session by asking what might matter to them in the future.

3. Analysis and ideation: Through analysis, you can find patterns and insights for ideation. This step may appear to be quite similar to ethnographic studies, but the purpose is different. In ethnography, the aim is to document the entire situation as detailed as possible, and all insights are relevant. You don't need to gather a complete set of insights; often times simply a few are needed to be taken into the design process to inspire you about design solutions. When presenting a concept, explain and visualise the concept from the user's perspective.

TIPS & CONCERNS
People provide valuable information if they feel recognised. Invite people in their role as an expert and explaining to them how important their contribution from their point of view.

The term 'context' is defined as the situation in which a product or service is used. All aspects that influence the experience of product use are considered valuable. These can be social, cultural, or physical aspects as well as the internal state of the users.

The acquired information should work as a guiding map for the design team. It helps to find their way, structure their insights, as well as recognise barriers and opportunities.

Adapt the participatory session to the participants' own culture by thinking about their selection criteria, materials, and procedure.

LIMITATIONS
Contextmapping can be quite time consuming.

83

REFERENCES & FURTHER READING: Sanders, E.B.N. & Stappers, P.J., 2012. *Convivial Toolbox: Generative research for the front end of design*. Amsterdam: BIS. / Sleeswijk Visser, F., Stappers, P.J., Lugt van der, R. and Sanders, E.B.N., 2005. Contextmapping: Experience from Practice. CoDesign, 29 March, 1(2), pp. 119-149. / Hao, C., van Boeijen, A.G.C. & Stappers, P.J., 2017. *Culture sensitive contextmapping: Discovering the strengths of Eastern and Western participants*. In proceedings Engineering and Product Design Education conference, 7-8 September 2017, Oslo, Norway.

A character is formed through their relationship with other bodies, be they people or objects. In a scene in Wes Andersons film Moonrise Kingdom, each object looks forward to a possible future, possible shared moments, secrets, joys, sadnesses. Suzy opens her suitcase as Sam opens his notebook and jots down: a record player with her favourite record, fantasy- and science fiction books, scissors for cutting hair, rubber bands, extra batteries, a toothbrush and a pair of binoculars. Sam asks her why she uses those binoculars so much and she replies, 'It helps me see things closer, even if they're not far away. I pretend it's my magic power'. (Wes Anderson, Roman Coppola)

Users tend to treat smart products as though they are intelligent and intentional. People's responses show that media are more than just tools. Media are treated politely, they can invade our body space, they can have personalities that match our own, they can be a teammate and they can elicit gender stereotypes. Human interaction is always situated in a context, and it can only be understood by somebody who also understands the context. (Google)

Thing Ethnography

Thing Ethnography helps designers gain access to the social life of connected products, which are also commonly referred to as 'things'. In this way, designers can thus understand their multiple ecosystems of relations and interactions.

WHAT & WHY? Connected products mediate our social, economic, and political interactions. In this mediation, their behaviour is increasingly autonomous and dependent on the actions of one another; for example, one connected product's actions may depend on the autonomous AI interpretations of another product. Understanding their autonomous and interdependent behaviour is critical to designing responsibly in a digital society.

MINDSET: Thing Ethnography is the first step in a More-Than-Human Design research approach that considers connected products as experts of their own experiences, and thus it includes them as participants in the design process.

WHEN? Thing Ethnography is best applied in the initial stages of the design process to explore the boundaries and ethical implications of the design space, and this can be done without a product idea in mind. This is often used in combination with Contextmapping and other types of Co-design methods to complement the understanding of human needs and experiences. Thing Ethnography distinguishes two main phases:

1. *Instrumentation*: The instrumentation phase uses sensors and software to collect data about the multiple ecosystems of a connected product and thus its social life, with the goal to access perspectives that are hidden from human experience and awareness.
2. *Lifeworld analytics:* This phase generates insights into the links among the multiple ecosystems of a connected product; it aims to reveal how the product might become connected to industries and economies that could never have been connected previously. Thing Ethnography can be conducted in two ways. It can be done either by adding sensors and software to objects of everyday use to gain a richer understanding of everyday interactions or by interviewing existing connected products to gain a more nuanced understanding of possible unintended consequences in the future.

TIPS & CONCERNS

Set up your data collection and analysis in a way that will likely give you access to useful data worlds and enable you to find out what you did not already know. For example, you can try instrumenting objects that live in proximity to each other or are used for multiple activities.

The key is not to collect lots of data but to learn how to use data to ask interesting questions. For example, you can also take your data back to people for additional interviews or co-creative activities.

We make things, but things also make us. Spending time and effort to learn from connected products offers different ways of understanding and transforming what we know and what we do.

LIMITATIONS

The use of sensors and software suggests that the result is evidence-based, which is not the case.

HOW? Thing Ethnography offers a flexible set of tools for data collection and analysis from which designers can choose depending on research context, practical constraints, and personal preferences. A growing repository can be found at the Thing-Centred Design toolkit website (www.tcdtoolkit.org/).

Tools for data collection include lifelogging cameras, sensor data, and AI-powered applications. An example of how to collect data from objects of everyday use can be found in the project on protein transition in the Netherlands in collaboration with the Dutch government. In this project, the designer looked at the role of kitchen utensils within the ecosystem of cooking and their impact on particular types of diet. Tools for data analysis include visual timelines, time lapses, and data visualisation tools. In some cases, these may need to be integrated with machine learning algorithms, which are specifically developed in collaboration with an expert.

Step 1: Identify objects that you think are relevant to your research context, and select the ones to be instrumented. Consider whether to instrument an object of everyday use or one that is an existing connected product instead.

Step 2: Choose your tools for data collection and analysis. This will depend on the practical constraints of your research context and your personal preferences (e.g., your context may be too sensitive and thus may not allow for the use of lifelogging cameras).

Step 3: Try repeating the steps again until you are surprised by the results. Make sure you learn something that you did not already know.

REFERENCES & FURTHER READING: Giaccardi, E., Cila, N., Speed, C., and Caldwell, M., 2016. *Thing Ethnography: Doing Design Research with Non-humans.* In Proc. DIS'16 (pp. 377–387). New York: ACM Press. / Giaccardi, E., 2020. Casting Things as Partners in Design: Towards a More-than-Human Design Practice. In H. Wiltse (Ed.) *Relating to Things: Design, Technology and the Artificial.* London: Bloomsbury. / TCD Toolkit: www.tcdtoolkit.org/ Giaccardi, E. & Redström, J. (2020) Technology and More-than-Human Design, *Design Issues*, 36:2.

The LEGO brick crosses cultural and language borders with ease. In the photo, a New Guinean father in a remote settlement on the April Rivers tries his hand at building with a set brought by Danish travellers. The man and his children ignored the pictures on the box and designed their own towers and animal figures on wheels. From Henry Wiencek: The World of LEGO Toys, 1987.

Cultural Probes

Cultural Probes are tailor-made materials that stimulate intended users to reflect on their own cultural context. The probes are used in an inspirational way and are based on self-documentation of daily life experiences.

WHAT & WHY? Probes can be defined as 'packages sent into space'. They help you collect material from a context that you don't know about yet. Moreover, they can give you access to environments that are otherwise difficult for them to observe directly; they also allow you to capture the real-life experiences of your intended users or other people who will be influenced by your design.

MINDSET: For the development of the probes, you need some creativity here. In using the probes, having a healthy dose of curiosity is the key – this means that you won't have any idea about what will be submitted to you and that you need to remain open to all kinds of possibilities. The users' self-documentation will most likely inspire and surprise you. The results of a cultural probe study can help you and your team to become sensitive to the many possibilities of people's experiences.

WHEN? Cultural Probes can be used in the pre-concept stage when there is still a lot of freedom for generating design opportunities.

HOW? The development of the probes starts with a creative session with your design team in order to determine what you want to learn from the intended users. A Cultural Probe package (tnapark.com/cultural-probes) usually entails various elements, such as diaries, postcards, and audio-visual recording devices. In fact, this can be everything that is playful and everything that encourages users to share their personal stories or to express their experiences visually. For instance, participants can be asked to write and draw about their experiences or use premade visuals to express themselves.

Probe packages can typically be sent out to just a few users or up to about 30 people. It is not always necessary to have direct contact with the intended users as long as they are capable to understand your instructions, apply them, and return them back to you.

Probes are often used in sensitising packages for participative sessions (see 'Contextmapping').

Step 1: Organise a creative session with your team members to set your goal.

Step 2: Design the probes.

Step 3: Test the probes with an intended user and adjust the design.

Step 4: Send the probe packages to your selected intended users along with a clear explanation about your expectations. Since the probe works on its own and there is no direct contact between designers and users, the probe assignments and materials should be very inviting and should inspire recipients to use them on their own.

Step 5: If needed, send a reminder for replies or collect the results yourself.

Step 6: Study the results with your team members and use the outcomes in a follow-up session, such as a generative session (see 'Context-mapping').

TIPS & CONCERNS

Make the probes attractive.

Give the probes a somewhat unfinished appearance, otherwise participants may be intimidated to use them.

Personalise the probes for the participants. For example, you can add their photo on the front cover.

Make the assignments fun and interesting to complete.

Clearly explain the goals.

Support improvisation.

Do a pilot test to ensure that your probes will elicit the preferred documentation.

Attune your probes to the cultural background of your participants. This means that you need to consider certain features about your participants, such as their specific values, the kind of materials they have access to, their language, style, and level of education.

LIMITATIONS

Probes will not give you a deep understanding of your intended users since there is no direct contact with them.

Insights are meant to trigger possibilities, not to validate results. A probe may yield insights about someone's daily grooming experiences, but never explain the causes, uniqueness or value.

Probes are not suitable if you are looking for answers to specific questions.

Probes requires open minds; otherwise the material will not be well understood, and some team members may not be satisfied with the results.

87

REFERENCES & FURTHER READING: Gaver, W.W., Boucher, A., Pennington, S. & Walker, B., 2004. Cultural probes and the value of uncertainty. *Interactions*, 11(5), pp. 53-56. / Gaver, W.W., Dunne, T. & Pacenti, E., 1999. Design: Cultural Probes. *Interactions*, 6(1), pp. 21-29. / Mattelmaki, T., 2005. Applying Probes - from inspirational notes to collaborative insights. *CoDesign: International Journal of CoCreation in Design and Arts*, 1(2), pp. 83-102. / Mattelmaki, T., 2006. *Design Probes*. Helsinki: University of Art and Design Helsinki.

The Champa Ling Monastery is home to about 1,200 monks, and more than 700 of them own tablet computers and smartphones. They use social media to read the news, interact with friends and promote Buddhist culture.

In Asian countries umbrellas are used to shield them from the sun. Umbrellas for individual use didn't appear in Europe until the early 18th century, and they were deployed to ward off both the sun and the rain. 20th century mass production turned umbrellas from a status symbol for the wealthy into an everydag rainprotector for the masses.

User Observations

User Observations help designers to study intended users in a specific situation. Specifically, this method enables designers to understand people, the influential variables, as well as other elementary interrelations in real life.

WHAT & WHY? For designers, it is important to understand how and why people relate to our designed world in a certain way. Observing reality can highlight unintended and unexpected scenarios of use which could lead to a better understanding of what makes a good product or service experience. This can turn into food for thought for future ideas and possible improvements.

MINDSET: User Observation encourages you to have an open mind for what people actually do, and you need to remember that there is no wrong way of using an object, but unintended ways. People will stand on chairs, and motorists will exceed speed limits. Any observation can be an eyeopener to you in your journey towards a good solution.

WHEN? There may be different hypotheses and research questions that we need to answer, and we may also have to assess and analyse different kinds of data. Using well-defined indicators can help you describe, analyse, and explain the relations between observable and hidden variables.

When exploring the design problem, it is helpful to articulate the aspects that influence interactions, whether this is between individuals or otherwise. Watching people interact with your prototypes will help you improve your design; this will also provide you vivid and descriptive illustrations when you communicate your design decisions to various stakeholders.

TIPS & CONCERNS

Always carry out a pilot first.

Make sure that the stimuli (such as models and prototypes) are suitable for the observations and are ready in time.

Ask those you wish to observe for their permission if you want to disclose the observations; if they don't, be sure to make them anonymous.

Think about the reliability of your study. It is easier to plan this at the beginning of a study rather than later.

Think about the ways to operationalise the data.

Go through your notes and add impressions as soon as possible after each observation.

Engage stakeholders by doing at least part of the analyses together. Be aware that they might take only one or two impressions as a reference.

LIMITATIONS

When people know that they are being observed, they might behave differently than they would normally.

89

HOW? Observe people in their own setting without intervening or them noticing you too much doing so. Or observe how they react to situations in real practice or in a lab situation. Ask subjects to think out loud. Video is the preferred means for documenting, next to taking photos and jotting down notes. Add further data sources in order to triangulate the analysis and interpretation of the data. Like combining the observations with interviews afterwards. In making analyses, group all data in combinations of pictures, remarks, and quotes and qualitatively analyse these.

Step 1: Determine what, who, and where you want to observe. Map out the whole situation in concrete detail first.

Step 2: Define criteria for the observation, namely the sample size, duration, costs, and the main design criteria.

Step 3: If applicable, select and invite participants. Determine in advance what participants should know and should not know beforehand.

Step 4: Prepare the observation sessions. In particular, check and arrange the ethical aspects involved, such as privacy protection. Especially in the medical domain, ethical procedures need to be strictly followed. Make an observation form that includes a checklist of everything you want to observe.

Step 5: Perform a pilot observation and review your observation plan. Make modifications and improvements afterwards, and test again.

Step 6: Execute the observations with an open mind.

Step 7: Analyse your data. Transcribe video and audio results; identify the themes and cluster them. Afterwards, summarise these insights, and bring them together in a form that can be communicated to other people.

Step 8: Communicate and discuss your findings with your stakeholders.

REFERENCES & FURTHER READING: Abrams, B., 2000. *The observational research handbook: Understanding how consumers live with your product.* Lincolnwood: NTC Business Books. / Daams, B., 2011. *Productergonomie - Ontwerpen voor nut, gebruik en beleving.* Uitgeverij Undesigning. / Suri, F. & IDEO, 2015. *Thoughtless Acts.* San Francisco: Chronicle Books. / Stempfle, J. & Badke-Schaub, P., 2002. Thinking in design teams - an analysis of team communication. *Design Studies*, September, 23(5), pp. 473-496.

Getting to know the customer: before he starts, the barber asks his client about his hairstyle wishes. During the creation of the haircut (the barber's product), some superficial and some in-depth issues are discussed via the mirror. Finally he checks if the end result is satisfactory.

HOLLYWOODIAN

MUTTON CHOPS

A LA SOUVAREV

HANDLEBAR AND CHIN PUFF

VAN DYKE

FRIENDLY MUTTON CHOPS

SHORT BOXED BEARD

GOATEE

CHIN CURTAIN

Interviews

Interviews are face-to-face consultations that can be useful for understanding people's perceptions, opinions, motivation and behaviour concerning any topic, for example experiences with products or services.

WHAT & WHY? Observing intended users or other stakeholders does not give full information on what is going on in their minds. Interviews can give more in-depth understanding of people's opinions, beliefs, needs, and what drives them to choose certain products or services and the way of using them or not using them.

MINDSET: Understanding people's deeper lying motivations helps designers to create better solutions. A curious attitude and an open mind is key to fully understand what people have to say.

WHEN? Interviews can be used in several phases of a design process and for different purposes. In a preliminary phase, they can help you to obtain contextual information about product use and opinions about existing products, or to gain expert input about issues. Interviews can also be used during concept testing of products or services in order to collect detailed consumer feedback. Compared to the focus group method, interviews take more time but provide you with deeper insight, because you can probe further into the answers given by the interviewee.

HOW? Before an interview, make a topic guide to ensure that you will cover all the relevant issues. This guide can be very structured, such as a questionnaire or un- or semi-structured with the questions depending on the answers given. Do a pilot interview to practice first.

Create a safe environment in which people will trust that their stories will be received well. Use open questions, for example, starting with how, what, who, and where. Be careful with the 'why' questions; they are easy to ask, but often difficult to answer. Be sure that you do not ask closed or leading questions such as 'Do you like this colour?' In spoken interviews listen, summarise, and clarify.

The general guideline for the number of interviews is to stop when you feel that an additional interview will not yield new information. Research shows that for the assessment of people's needs, 10 to 15 interviews will reveal about 80% of the needs. Interviews can be combined with collages or sensitising tasks such as keeping a short diary, as in Context-mapping. Possible procedure:

Step 1: Make an interview guide, including a list of topics, based on your research questions. Test this guide in a pilot interview.

Step 2: Invite the interviewees. Depending on your objective you may interview three to eight people.

Step 3: Explain your interviews the goal of your interview and how you will deal with their input. If needed, have them a consent form signed.

Step 4: Carry out the interviews. An inter-view typically takes about one hour and is usually voice recorded.

Step 5: Either make transcripts of what was said or make summarising notes.

Step 6: Analyse your transcripts, draw conclusions and give your interviewees an update if they are interested.

TIPS & CONCERNS:
Check your approach with the support of an ethical committee, if appropriate, for example, in medical projects.
- - - - - - - - - - -
Run a pilot always to test your approach.
- - - - - - - - - - -
Perform the interview in a relaxed atmosphere without distractions.
- - - - - - - - - - -
Start with general topics that are somehow related to your topic and that are not difficult to talk about to put people at ease.
- - - - - - - - - - -
Distribute your interview time among your topics in advance to ensure that you will have enough time left for your final topics.
- - - - - - - - - - -
Check if your interviewees have questions. The quality of your visuals is crucial.
- -

LIMITATIONS: Your interviewees will respond to what they know consciously. Latent or tacit knowledge can be gained by observation or by using generative techniques, such as in Contextmapping.
- - - - - - - - - - -
The quality of the result depends on your own skills and attitude as an interviewer. Are you really curious and motivated to understand the person? People will notice your intentions.
- - - - - - - - - - -
Your interview results are qualitative and from a limited number of respondents. To collect quantitative results from a large number of respondents, you can use questionnaires.
- - - - - - - - - - -
Interviews are most useful when the topic is not new to the interviewees. For innovative topics other methods such as Contextmapping and Observations may be more appropriate.

REFERENCES & FURTHER READING: Byrne, M., 2001. Interviewing as a data collection method. *Association of periOperative Registered Nurses (AORN) Journal*, Augustus, 74(2), pp. 233-235. / Creusen, M.E.H., Hultink, E.J. & Eling, K., 2013. Choice of consumer research methods in the front end of new product development. *International Journal of Market Research*, January, 55(1), pp. 81-104. / Griffin, A., 2005. *Obtaining customer needs for product development.* In K. B. Kahn, S. E. Kay, R. J. Slotegraaf, S. Uban (eds.), The PDMA Handbook of New Product Development. pp. 211–227. Hoboken, NJ: John Wiley & Sons, Inc. Rubin, H. and Rubin I., 2005. Qualitative interviewing, the art of hearing data. Sage, CA: Thousand Oaks.

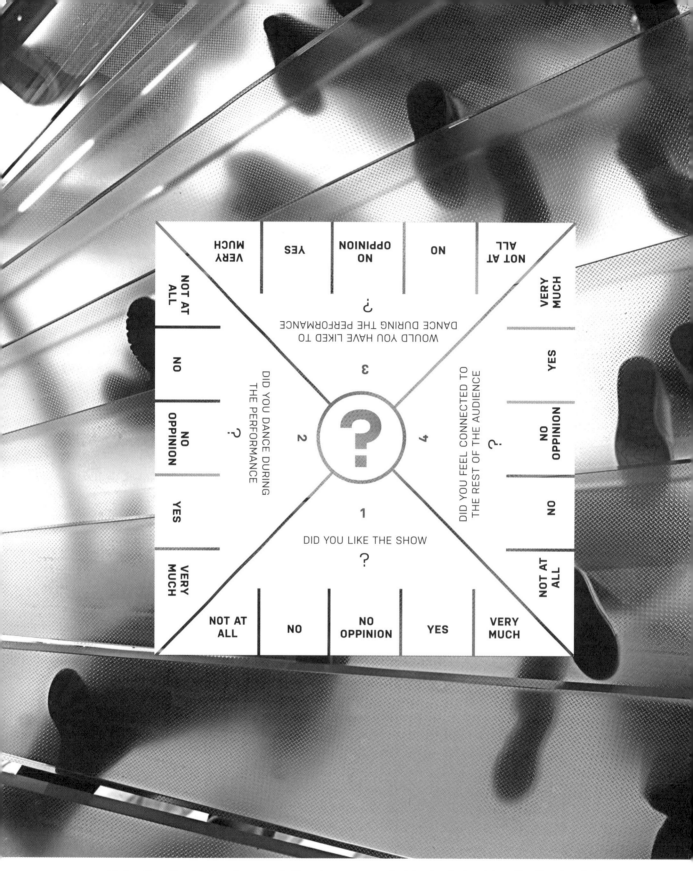

Visitors to a theatrical performance in Copenhagen were asked to give their opinion after the show by tearing this flyer to indicate their answer. Designed by Alessia Cadamuro

Questionnaires

Questionnaires are research tools that consist of a series of questions and other prompts that are intended for gathering information from respondents.

WHAT & WHY? Sometimes quantitative information is needed about people's opinions, beliefs, and needs, as well as what drives them to choose certain products or services. This is considered as vital information for designers working on products, services, and systems that are intended to be used by a great number of people: The success of your design depends on a good understanding of how people make decisions.

MINDSET: For you as a designer, you may choose to follow your own beliefs and develop designs for a limited group of people with a similar mindset. When working in a setting where success depends on reaching a large number of people, qualitative insight into the potential market is important. In politics for instance, candidates often like to know how many voters have a certain opinion about relevant issues at hand.

WHEN? In a preliminary phase, questionnaires are useful for gaining information about the target group, product use, and opinions on existing products. They are also used for concept testing. Questionnaires are helpful when you need to choose one out of several concepts and to assess a consumer's acceptance of your concepts.

Quantitative research methods can be used to gain insight into the frequency with which certain perceptions, opinions, or behaviours occur, as well as the level of interest. Moreover, the method enables you to determine the most interesting target group for the product or service. Questionnaires can be administered face-to-face or by telephone, filled out by the respondents themselves either on paper or via the Internet.

HOW? Of course, the questions in the Questionnaire should help you to answer your main question. However, asking useful questions is more difficult than it seems, and the quality of the Questionnaire determines the usefulness of the outcomes. It is recommended that you read up on Questionnaire construction before using this method.

The end result depends on the goal of the research. Some examples of this include getting an insight into the frequency of certain opinions or behaviours, knowing the frequency of the perceived advantages and disadvantages of existing solutions, or knowing the occurrence of certain needs. Such insights can help you to determine what to focus on in the development and design of a solution.

Step 1: Based on your research questions, determine the topics you want to address.

Step 2: Choose the form of response per question, such as closed response, open response, or categorical.

Step 3: Formulate the questions.

Step 4: Determine the question order; categorise similar questions together and make a clear layout.

Step 5: Pre-test and improve the Questionnaire.

Step 6: Invite the right respondents depending on the topic as random sample or selected respondents, such as those who are knowledgeable about the topic. Be sure the sample varies in age and gender.

Step 7: Present the results by reporting percentages for each answer option or use statistics to report mean results. Be sure also to test relationships between the variables or the questions.

TIPS & CONCERNS
Ask yourself whether the Questionnaire will answer all your research questions and whether all its questions are absolutely necessary.

You can use Questionnaires to collect qualitative data as well. Sometimes the limited numbers of respondents in combination with deep and open-ended questions result in more useful data than large numbers of respondents.

Questionnaires are often boring to fill in, and that can make it difficult to collect enough responses. Make your research more fun, such as by incorporating visuals; online versions provide possibilities for doing this.

When testing one or more concepts with consumers, the presentation of these concepts is crucial, and the concepts should be clear. Test this out before distributing the Questionnaire (see 'Product Concept Evaluation').

LIMITATIONS
Information that is subconscious or more emotional in nature cannot be gathered with Questionnaires.

The quality of the results strongly depends on the quality of the Questionnaire. Longer Questionnaires typically lead to fewer respondents.

Designers often criticise Questionnaire results for being too abstract. Qualitative methods may be better suited for eliciting empathy and deep insights, but for determining whether large groups share certain values and needs, quantitative data are needed and are better suited.

REFERENCES & FURTHER READING: Creusen, M.E.H., Hultink, E.J. & Eling, K., 2013. Choice of consumer research methods in the front end of new product development. *International Journal of Market Research*, January, 55(1), pp. 81-104. / Lietz, P., 2010. Research into questionnaire design - A summary of the literature. *International Journal of Market Research*, 1 September, 52(2), pp. 249-272. / McDaniel, C. Jr. & Gates, R., 2001. Primary Data Collection: Survey Research. In Marketing Research Essentials. pp. 170-208. Cincinnati, Ohio: South-Western College Publishing. / McDaniel, C. Jr. and Gates, R., 2001. Questionnaire Design. In Marketing Research Essentials. pp. 287-324. Cincinnati, Ohio: South-Western College Publishing.

Photographer Ari Versluis and profiler Ellie Uyttenbroek systematically document what they call 'Exactitudes': by selecting subjects in the street and registering them in an identical framework and with similar poses, they provide an almost scientific, anthropological record of people's attempts to distinguish themselves from others by assuming a group identity.

Focus Groups

A Focus Group is a group interview in which several topics concerning a specific product or issue are discussed. Focus Groups often consist of people from the target group of the product or service that is being developed.

WHAT & WHY? People using your products are a valuable source of information. In a group setting, more relevant issues will likely come up than by interviewing users as individuals in one-on-one settings. For example, Tupperware parties are not only organised for the purpose of selling the Tupperware products, but they are also a way to collect essential feedback from users who range from sceptics to life-long fans.

MINDSET: The idea behind Focus Groups is that the social setting creates a critical but also creative debate about which product or brand properties are appreciated and which ones may be not as appreciated.

WHEN? Focus Groups are used in several phases of the development process. In the preliminary phase, they are used for gaining contextual information about product use and also their opinions about existing products. You can also use this approach in the development phase, for example, when testing the usage of the product or the service concepts. A Focus Group can be used when you need to decide on one concept out of several possible options, or when you need to gather recommendations for further development. Focus Groups provide a quick overview of consumers' opinions about a subject. Part of its value lies in the unexpected findings that can come from a free-flowing discussion in the group. When more in-depth and individual information is needed, interviews should be used instead.

HOW? At least three Focus Group sessions should be conducted so that outcomes can be generalised to some extent. A Focus Group usually consists of six to eight participants, a moderator, and someone who is in charge of collecting the data. The moderator has a vital role, so having experience in moderating is very helpful. You should first perform a pilot Focus Group so that you can improve your list of topics. A Focus Group can be combined with making collages or with sensitising tasks such as keeping a short diary (see 'Contextmapping'). Using online Focus Group sessions is a possibility as well.

The end result depends on the goals of the sessions; these goals can include gaining insights into consumer needs within the product area, having ideas for new products, or gaining insights into consumer acceptance and into the perceived advantages/disadvantages of certain product or service concepts.

Step 1: Make a list of topics you want to address in the form of a topic guide; it should contain broad issues or specific questions.

Step 2: Test the topic guide in a pilot Focus Group. Make changes if necessary.

Step 3: Invite the participants – these are people from your target groups.

Step 4: Perform the Focus Groups. A session typically takes 1.5 to 2 hours and is usually recorded for transcription and analysis.

Step 5: Analyse and report the findings by indicating the main opinions and the range in opinions for each topic or issue.

TIPS & CONCERNS

Start with general topics such as product usage and experience. In this way, participants can get into the right context before you ask for their opinions or present new concepts. When testing one or more concepts with consumers, the presentation of these concepts is crucial. The concepts should be clear, so start by asking participants whether they have questions before you ask about their reactions.

Carefully plan how much time to allocate to each topic in order to avoid having to rush through the topics at the end of the session, as these questions at the end are often the most important ones. In your report, illustrate the findings with quotes from the participants, which can make the outcomes engaging.

LIMITATIONS

If participants do not have experience with the product in question, Focus Group sessions may not be that suitable. Group processes might influence the results. For example, dominating participants may push their opinions onto the other participants. For these situations, it is crucial for the moderator to intervene. This is why the quality of the results depends on the quality of the moderator.

A session has a small number of participants. If you want to know to which extent people share the same opinions, you should use quantitative research methods such as Questionnaires.

REFERENCES & FURTHER READING: Bruseberga, A. & McDonagh-Philpb, D., 2001. Focus groups to support the industrial/product designer: a review based on current literature and designers' feedback'. *Applied Ergonomics*, 1 Augustus, 33(1), pp. 27-38. / Creusen, M.E.H., Hultink, E.J. & Eling, K., 2013. Choice of consumer research methods in the front end of new product development. *International Journal of Market Research*, January, 55(1), pp. 81-104. / Malhotra, N. K. & Birks, D. F., 2000. *Marketing Research: An Applied Approach.* Upper Saddle River, NJ: Pearson Education Ltd.

Victor Papanek stated that 'Design has become the most powerful tool with which man shapes society and himself'. He strove to lead by example. In the 1960s he and his student George Seeger designed the Tin Can Radio for isolated and illiterate communities in Third World countries. Made of a used juice can with parafin wax or dried dung to produce voltage across a thermocouple as power source, the simple design could be locally made, repaired and modified. The technology is sustainable at a sociopolitical level and manages to score very well on all axes in the Ecodesign Strategy Wheel.

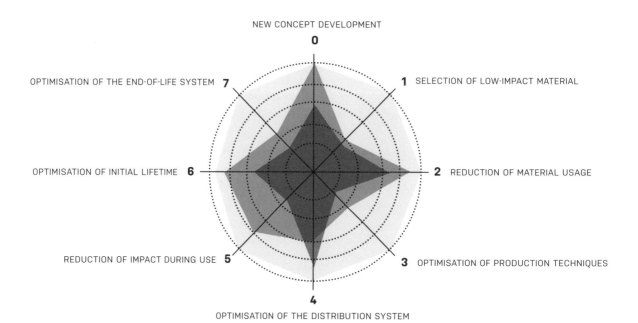

NEW CONCEPT DEVELOPMENT
0

7 OPTIMISATION OF THE END-OF-LIFE SYSTEM

1 SELECTION OF LOW-IMPACT MATERIAL

OPTIMISATION OF INITIAL LIFETIME 6

2 REDUCTION OF MATERIAL USAGE

REDUCTION OF IMPACT DURING USE 5

3 OPTIMISATION OF PRODUCTION TECHNIQUES

4
OPTIMISATION OF THE DISTRIBUTION SYSTEM

Ecodesign Strategy Wheel

The Ecodesign Strategy Wheel – also called Lifecycle Design strategies (LiDs) – helps designers select and communicate strategies to minimise the environmental impact of their design.

WHAT & WHY? The Ecodesign Strategy Wheel is a sustainable design method, and sustainability is a core building block of design. As a designer, you have a responsibility to ensure that the impact of each of your design decisions is positive and not negative.

MINDSET: Sustainability involves complex and sometimes contradictory issues. You need to be willing to make difficult compromises and dig deep to find relevant information. Engaging with sustainable design is also an empowering and enjoyable experience, since it's all about making life better for people on this planet after all.

WHEN? The Ecodesign Strategy Wheel is best applied from the first stage of a product design process onwards – namely the problem analysis or discover phase, possibly with a general product idea in mind. It can be used in conjunction with the Ecodesign Checklist. The Ecodesign Strategy Wheel specifies seven strategies (as defined below) on three product levels and one strategy on a conceptual level.

TIPS & CONCERNS
Use the Ecodesign Strategy Wheel together with the Ecodesign Checklist.

Avoid only considering technical solutions; be sure to also think about psychological ones. How does the design influence the users and their behaviour with respect to energy efficiency, length of the life cycle, and end-of-life?

Be aware that while some Ecodesign strategies may reinforce each other, some can also be in conflict.

LIMITATIONS
The method is based on qualitative data and personal interpretation. The spider diagram may suggest that the result is objective, which is not the case.

97

HOW? The Ecodesign Strategy Wheel is a visual representation of the relevant environmental aspects of a product's life cycle along different axes, which results in a web-like graph. The tool is normally used for comparing different products or design options.

It is a qualitative tool. A set of relevant questions (see Ecodesign Checklist) helps to score each dimension with a low, medium, or high qualitative value. During this scoring process, possible improvement options will become clear, and these can be singled out for further development.

The Ecodesign Strategy Wheel is a useful communication tool. It gives an indication of promising ecodesign strategies and can be used to track progress towards a more sustainable design.

Step 1: Define the product idea, product concept, or existing product to be analysed.

Step 2: Map the current status; score the product on each dimension of the Ecodesign Strategy Wheel. You can use the Ecodesign Checklist to determine a relevant score.

Step 3: Identify improvement options for each of the dimensions, paying special attention to the aspects of the current design with poor scores.

Step 4: After redesign, you can repeat the same procedure to obtain a visual overview of areas where the new design scores better.

0. NEW CONCEPT DEVELOPMENT
- Dematerialisation
- Shared use of the product
- Integration of functions
- Functional optimisation of product (components)

1. SELECTION OF LOW-IMPACT MATERIALS
- Clean materials
- Renewable materials
- Low energy content materials
- Recycled materials
- Recyclable materials

2. REDUCTION OF MATERIAL USAGE
- Reduction in weight
- Reduction in (transport) volume

3. OPTIMISATION OF PRODUCTION TECHNIQUES
- Alternative production techniques
- Fewer production steps
- Lower / cleaner energy consumption
- Less production waste
- Fewer / cleaner production consumables

4. OPTIMISATION OF THE DISTRIBUTION SYSTEM
- Less / cleaner / reusable packaging
- Energy efficient transport mode
- Energy efficient logistics

5. REDUCTION OF IMPACT DURING USE
- Lower energy consumption
- Cleaner energy source
- Fewer consumables needed
- Cleaner consumables
- No waste of energy or consumables

6. OPTIMISATION OF INITIAL LIFETIME
- Reliability and durability
- Easy maintenance and repair
- Modular product structure
- Classic design
- Strong product-user relation

7. OPTIMISATION OF THE END-OF-LIFE SYSTEM
- Reuse of product (components)
- Remanufacturing / refurbishing
- Recycling of materials
- Safer or no incineration

REFERENCES & FURTHER READING: Brezet, H. & Van Hemel, C., 1997. *EcoDesign: A Promising Approach to Sustainable Production and Consumption.* Paris: UNEP. / Remmerswaal, H., 2002. *Milieugerichte Productontwikkeling.* Schoonhoven: Academic Service.

ECODESIGN STRATEGIES (0-7)

CONCEPTUAL LEVEL / NEEDS ANALYSIS

- How does the product system actually fulfil social needs?
- What are the product's main and auxiliary functions?
- Does the product fulfil these functions effectively and efficiently?
- What user needs does the product currently meet?
- Can the product functions be expanded or improved to fulfil users' needs better?
- Will this need change over a period of time?
- Can we anticipate this through (radical) product innovation?

0. NEW CONCEPT DEVELOPMENT
- Dematerialisation
- Shared use of the product
- Integration of functions
- Functional optimisation of product (components)

PRODUCT COMPONENT LEVEL / PRODUCTION AND SUPPLY OF MATERIALS AND COMPONENTS

- What problems arise in the production and supply of materials and components?
- How much and what type of plastic and rubber are used?
- How much and what type additives are used?
- How much and what type of metals are used?
- How much and what other types of materials (glass, ceramics, etc.) are used?
- How much and which type of surface treatment is used?
- What is the environmental profile of the components?
- How much energy is required to transport the materials and components?

1. SELECTION OF LOW-IMPACT MATERIALS
- Clean materials
- Renewable materials
- Low energy content materials
- Recycled materials
- Recyclable materials

2. REDUCTION OF MATERIAL USAGE
- Reduction in weight
- Reduction in (transport) volume

PRODUCT STRUCTURE LEVEL / IN-HOUSE PRODUCTION

- What problems can arise in the production process in your own company?
- How many and what types of production processes are used (including connections, surface treatments, printing and labelling)?
- How much and what type of auxiliary materials are needed?
- How high is the energy consumption?
- How much waste is generated?
- How many products don't meet the required quality norm?

3. OPTIMISATION OF PRODUCTION TECHNIQUES
- Alternative production techniques
- Fewer production steps
- Lower / cleaner energy consumption
- Less production waste
- Fewer / cleaner production consumables

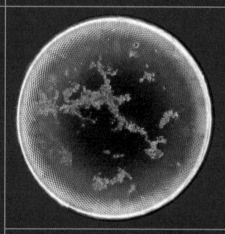

PRODUCT STRUCTURE LEVEL / DISTRIBUTION

- What problems can arise in the distribution of the product to the customer?
- What kind of transport packaging, bulk packaging and retail packaging are used (volumes, weights, materials, reusability)?
- Which means of transport are used?
- Is transport efficiently organised?

4. OPTIMISATION OF THE DISTRIBUTION SYSTEM
- Less / cleaner / reusable packaging
- Energy efficient transport mode
- Energy efficient logistics

PRODUCT STRUCTURE LEVEL / UTILIZATION

- What problems arise when using, operating, servicing and repairing the product?
- How much and what type of energy is required, directly or indirectly?
- How much and what kind of consumables are needed?
- What is the technical lifetime?
- How much maintenance and repairs are needed?
- What and how much auxiliary materials and energy are required for operating, servicing and repair?
- Can the product be disassembled by a layman?
- Are those parts often requiring replacement detachable?
- What is the aesthetic lifetime?

5. REDUCTION OF IMPACT DURING USE
- Lower energy consumption
- Cleaner energy source
- Fewer consumables needed
- Cleaner consumables
- No waste of energy or consumables

PRODUCT SYSTEM LEVEL / RECOVERY AND DISPOSAL

- What problems arise in the recovery and disposal of the product?
- How is the product disposed of?
- Are components or materials being reused?
- What components could be reused?
- Can the components be reassembled without damage?
- What materials are recyclable?
- Are the materials identifiable?
- Can they be detached quickly?
- Are any incompatible inks, surface treatments or stickers used?
- Are any hazardous components easily detachable?
- Do problems occur while incinerating non-reusable product parts?

6. OPTIMISATION OF INITIAL LIFETIME
- Reliability and durability
- Easy maintenance and repair
- Modular product structure
- Classic design
- Strong product-user relation

7. OPTIMISATION OF THE END-OF-LIFE SYSTEM
- Reuse of product (components)
- Remanufacturing / refurbishing
- Recycling of materials
- Safer incineration

Ecodesign Checklist

Whether designers are creating new products and services or redesigning old ones to make them more sustainable, it is necessary to consider the entire life cycle of the product. The Ecodesign Checklist provides a number of key questions for each stage of the product life cycle.

WHAT & WHY? The Ecodesign Checklist is a sustainable design method, much like the Ecodesign Strategy Wheel. Sustainability is essential to our well-being as well as to human survival in the long run. Thus, designers have a responsibility to pay attention to the sustainability impacts that their work can have. The Ecodesign Checklist is a good start that provides you an overview of the field. With this method, you also need to ensure that all your design decisions bring about a positive environmental impact, not a negative one. The drawback of Ecodesign is that it focuses on incremental improvements of existing products.

TIPS & CONCERNS
Use the Ecodesign Checklist together with the Ecodesign Strategy Wheel

----

LIMITATIONS
Checklists aim to be complete but never are. With some common sense, you can adapt the list to your situation.

MINDSET: Sustainability deals with issues that are complex and can sometimes contradict one another; therefore, you need to be willing to make compromises at times and be persistent in identifying relevant information. Remember to enjoy the design process, and remember that your design is for improving the lives of people on the planet, including yourself.

WHEN? The Ecodesign Checklist is best applied in the concept generation phase when you have developed a clear idea of the product. You can also use it to analyse existing products. The Ecodesign Checklist is often used in combination with the Ecodesign Strategy Wheel.

HOW? The starting point for the Ecodesign Checklist is either a product idea, a product concept, or an existing product. The checklist begins with a number of broad and inclusive 'new concept development' questions that you should not skip. It then continues with a more detailed set of questions categorised along the stages of the product life cycle (production, distribution, use, and recovery). The checklist can be used to find options for improvement and to establish a set of product- or service-related environmental goals or priorities that will guide the design.

Step 1: Define the product idea, product concept, or existing product to be analysed.

Step 2: Do research on which materials are commonly used in the products you want to design or redesign and how they are manufactured. Find out how the products are packaged, stored, distributed, and used, and establish what happens to the products at the end of their useful life.

Step 3: Work through the Ecodesign Checklist, answering the questions and brainstorming options for improvement.

Step 4: Describe the options for improvement as clearly as possible. You can use the Strategy Wheel to visualise and prioritize potential improvements.

REFERENCES & FURTHER READING: Brezet, H. & Van Hemel, C., 1997. *Ecodesign: A Promising Approach to Sustainable Production and Consumption.* Paris: UNEP. / Remmerswaal, H., 2002. *Milieugerichte Productontwikkeling.* Schoonhoven: Academic Service.

RENEWABLE MATERIALS

Biological nutrients | **TAKE** | Technical nutrients

MAKE

REGENERATE and capture value at each stage of decomposition

RESTORE
Repair
Reuse
Refurbish
Recycle

CONSUME USE

Minimise lost matter and energy

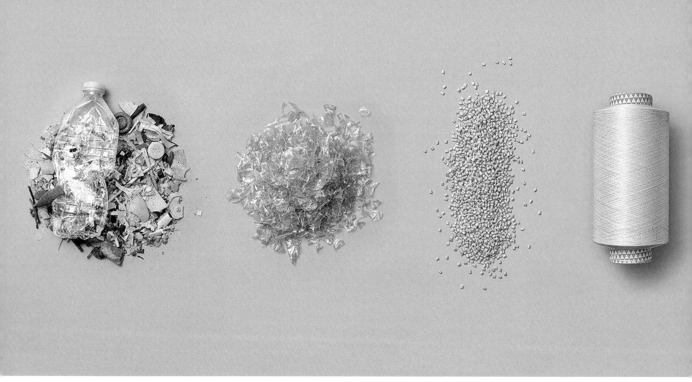

Ocean Plastic® produces a range of premium materials for the sports, fashion and luxury industries made from intercepted and upcycled marine plastic debris. These materials replace virgin materials and allow for the implementation of a long-term strategy: Avoid, Intercept, Redesign

Each model is a simplification of a complex reality and as with all simplifications this means that the reality will be distorted in some way. The challenge for an LCA practitioner is to develop the model in such a way that the simplifications and distortions do not influence the results too much. The best way to deal with this problem is to carefully define the goal and scope of the LCA study.

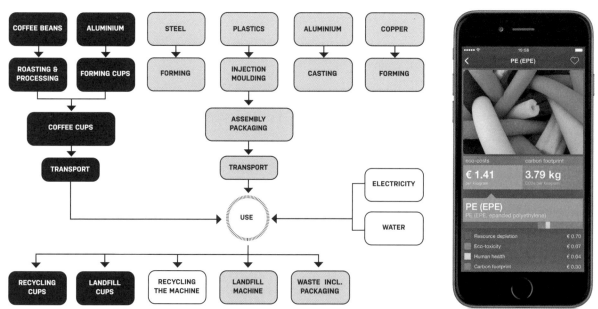

With the Idemat Light app you can make a simple LCA calculation according to the Fast Track method, using the data and the selection method. You can open an LCA, and add materials and processes to it with the required quantities. You can even calculate the eco-costs of products with an Environmental Declaration. (idematapp.com)

Fast Track Life Cycle Analysis

A Fast Track Life Cycle Analysis (Fast Track LCA) is a method for determining the total eco-burden of a product, service, or product-service system over its entire life cycle. A Fast Track LCA can be carried out when there is a limited amount of time.

WHAT & WHY? The Fast Track LCA can give you a thorough and quantitative grasp of your design's environmental impact. This method is a powerful predictor of the environmental impact of different solutions. It helps you to:
• Find the environmental 'hotspots' of a product and lower its overall environmental burden.
• Compare different design and service solutions and thus make a substantiated choice for the product-service system design with the lowest environmental burden.
• Explore both the possibilities for making use of certain materials (such as recycled or renewable materials) and other sustainable options along the product life cycle.

MINDSET: Fast Track LCA is a very powerful tool for determining a product's environmental impact, but it needs to be used with caution. If you do not understand the scientific background of LCAs, you may misinterpret their outcomes, which can lead to misleading or wrong conclusions. Conducting an LCA requires an analytical mindset and a willingness to 'sweat the details'.

WHEN? You can use Fast Track LCA in the beginning of the Develop stage or earlier when analysing existing products.

HOW? You can express the eco-burden – emissions, materials depletion, and land use – in terms of a single-impact indicator using the Idemat database (www.ecocostsvalue.com), which includes over 6000 materials and processes. These tables make LCA comparable to normal cost calculations; it is then a matter of adding up the eco-burden.

Step 1: Establish the scope and the goal of your analysis.

Step 2: Establish a functional unit. Describe the main function or functionality of the product-service and a metric to measure this functionality of the product-service. Validate your metric by evaluating the current solution and an out-of-the-box solution.

Step 3: Establish the system and the system boundaries by describing which part of the life cycle is taken into account.

Step 4: Quantify the materials, and when applicable, quantify the use of energy or other resources during the use phase of the product service system. Collect data such as the weight and material use, energy and resources consumed during use. Determine the accuracy and relevance, and establish allocation rules and cut-off criteria.

Step 5: Quantify the transport involved for the components or for the complete product to be assembled and shipped to the consumer. Determine the routes and means of transport involved 1. for the components to the assembly factory; 2. for the assembled product to the distribution centre,; and 3. for the product's 'last mile' to the consumer.

Step 6: Calculate the total impact, the distribution of the impact over the different life cycle phases (material, production, transport, use, and end-of-life), and the distribution of impact over the different components or material groups.

Step 7: Interpret the results. Which parts of the life cycle are dominant in terms of eco-burden? How can you lower the eco-burden most effectively?

TIPS & CONCERNS:
Doing a Fast Track LCA is a modelling exercise. As with the saying 'garbage in equals garbage out', the same applies for LCA. Make sure you know how an LCA works and understand the significance of the outcomes.

You can also make an LCA from cradle-to-gate where only the production of the product is taken into account. This is when the product does not require any resources during the use phase.

It should always be combined with end-of-life data, since that has an important impact on the total eco-burden of a product life cycle.

If elements are missing, you need to make an educated guess by using comparable materials or production processes or find data from scientific literature. Never leave out a material because of missing data.

LIMITATIONS:
Fast Track LCA is helpful when assessing mature products. New and emerging products and processes may be more difficult to assess because of a lack of data.

An LCA's complexity is difficult to communicate, which may lead to an oversimplification of the results. LCA does not consider rebound and other social effects.

LCA should be applied throughout the design process rather than at the end.

REFERENCES & FURTHER READING: European Commission, Joint Research Centre, Institute for Environment and Sustainability 2010. *International Reference Life Cycle Data System Handbook: General guide for Life Cycle Assessment - Detailed Guidance.* 1st ed. Luxembourg: Publications Office of the European Union. / ISO, 2006. *ISO 14044 Environmental Management – Life cycle assessment – Principles and framework.* 2nd ed. Geneva: ISO. / ISO, 2006. ISO *14044 Environmental Management – Life cycle assessment – Requirements and guidelines.* Geneva: ISO.

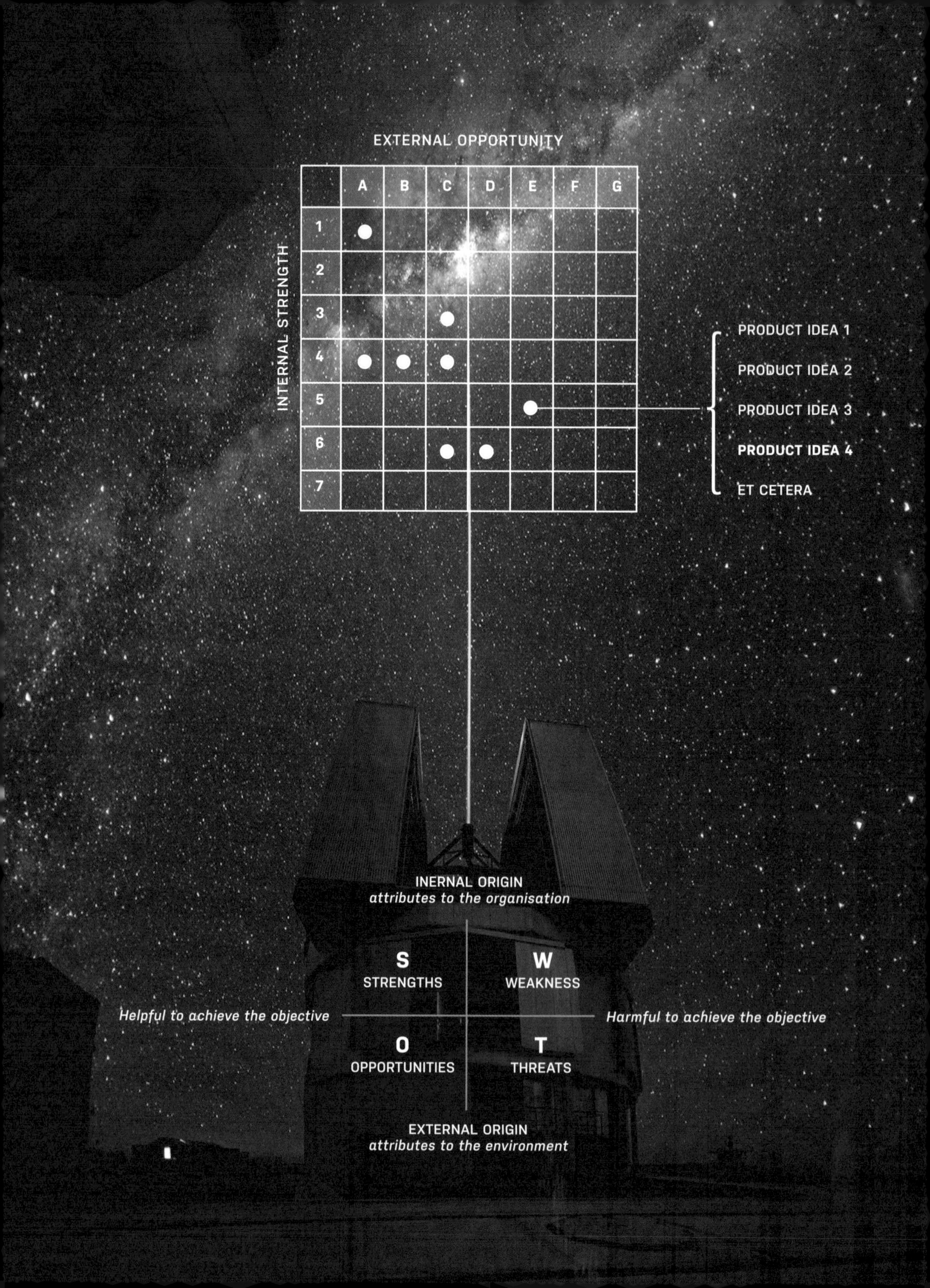

EXTERNAL OPPORTUNITY

INTERNAL STRENGTH

	A	B	C	D	E	F	G
1	●						
2							
3			●				
4	●	●	●				
5					●		
6			●	●			
7							

PRODUCT IDEA 1

PRODUCT IDEA 2

PRODUCT IDEA 3

PRODUCT IDEA 4

ET CETERA

INERNAL ORIGIN
attributes to the organisation

S	**W**
STRENGTHS	WEAKNESS

Helpful to achieve the objective — *Harmful to achieve the objective*

O	**T**
OPPORTUNITIES	THREATS

EXTERNAL ORIGIN
attributes to the environment

SWOT & Search Areas

SWOT & Search Areas is a method to systematically analyse the strategic position of an organisation and, moreover, to find opportunities for new product ideas.

WHAT & WHY? When developing new products or services for a future beyond tomorrow, it is important to firstly know the current position of a company or organisation. SWOT is an acronym for Strengths and Weaknesses – which represent the internal factors of the company (or organisation) – and Opportunities and Threats, which refer to the external factor outside the organisation. The Search Areas are the 'opportunity areas' that are synthesised after a SWOT analysis. They provide a solution space in which you can generate ideas for new product development. The original idea of the method is to help companies position their organisation in order to make strategic decisions and to innovate so that they can be viable.

MINDSET: Originally the method has been developed in a competitive business context, but the method can also be used with a less competitive attitude. For the SWOT analysis, you will need systematic reasoning, while for finding opportunities for new product development, the element of creativity has proven to be a key factor.

WHEN? A SWOT analysis in combination with Search Areas is typically performed at an early stage of the innovation process.

HOW? The quality of SWOT depends on a good understanding of a great variety of factors, and is typically done with a multidisciplinary team. An internal analysis should help to identify if the innovations might fit an organisation's core competences and thus have a higher chance of success. An external analysis should result in a thorough understanding of the current users, competitors, and the competing products and services. Combinations of internal strength (S) with external opportunities (O) should lead to a number of Search Areas in which you will find new opportunities or ideas.

Step 1: Determine the scope of the competitive business environment by asking the question, *Which type of business are we dealing with?*

Step 2: Perform the external analysis by answering questions such as the following: What are important trends in the market environment? What are the needs and frustrations that people have regarding current products? What are the prevailing socio-cultural and economic trends? What are competitors doing and planning to do? Which trends can be seen within the business chain among suppliers, distributors and knowledge institutes? Use checklists such as DESTEP (Demographic, Economic, Social, Technological, Ecological, Political developments) to structure your efforts to and perform a comprehensive analysis.

Step 3: Make an inventory of the organisation's strengths and weaknesses, and evaluate them by benchmarking them against competitors.

Step 4: Summarise findings in a SWOT matrix to allow clear communication with your team members or other stakeholders.

Step 5: Create a large number (about 20 to 60) of Search Areas by combining internal Strengths with Opportunities from the external environment.

Step 6: Select Search Areas using selection criteria such as the newness and originality of the domain as well as the promise of market size.

Step 7: Conduct further contextual user/usage research to check the feasibility and formulate a design brief for the selected search areas.

Step 8: Generate product ideas for each selected Search Area based on the design brief.

TIPS & CONCERNS
Consider the scope of the company's competitive environment carefully. A successful SWOT analysis starts with an appropriate scope, which can be very broad or narrow.

Threats can also sometimes be turned into Opportunities.

The ways in which you define and translate data into worthwhile strategic objectives is a creative process with many possible outcomes.

Seemingly strange combinations of Strengths and Opportunities can be interesting because it could be difficult for a competitor to identify them.

The success of the SWOT & Search Area method depends on how a design team is able to come up with innovative ideas.

To determine the relevance of Search Areas, you can do market research using other methods such as Contextmapping, scientific literature, and experts.

LIMITATIONS
The SO combination is a two-dimensional way to find a Search Area which in reality, is multidimensional. Think of different search matrixes and avoid trying to fit everything in a overarching one.

REFERENCES & FURTHER READING: Ansoff, H.I., 1987. *Corporate Strategy.* Revised ed. London: Penguin Books. / Brooksbank, R., 1996. The BASIC marketing planning process: a practical framework for the smaller business. *Journal of Marketing Intelligence & Planning*, 14(4), pp. 16-23. / Buijs, J.A., 2012. *The Delft Innovation Method; a design thinker's guide to innovation.* The Hague: Eleven International Publishing.

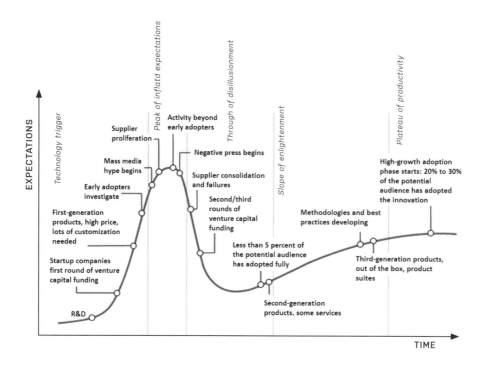

The Gartner Hype Cycle shows that people are notoriously bad at predicting the future since the future tends to introduce the unimaginable. including its unforseen commercial applications and ethical consequences. The first successful transplant of a major organ happened in 1954. Today organ printing is approaching as a potential solution for the global shortage of donor organs. The biggest remaining challenge is creating the fine networks of blood vessels required to keep them alive. Soon we will have companies that exist to process cells, create constructs, tissue. (Image: University of Rochester Medical Center)

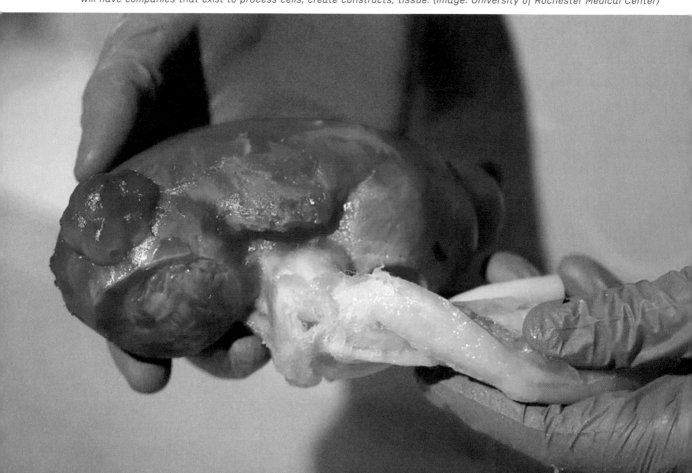

Trend Foresight

Trend Foresight helps designers identify and analyse user needs, user values, and resulting business opportunities in order to develop business strategies, design visions, and new product ideas. Often observed from a few signals that are weak and mostly visual, trends are made by people and uncovered by designers.

WHAT & WHY? With the emergence of strategy in the design discipline, attention to Trend Foresight has increased. Strategic managers have a natural tendency to narrowly scan within the existing market. As a result, they often fail to see opportunities for innovation in the periphery of their current markets. Only broader horizons with respect to innovation objectives and knowledge sources are associated with successful innovation. Trends are changes in society that occur over longer periods of time. They are related not only to people's evolving preferences – such as ones in fashion or music industry – but also to wider-sweeping trends in society. Design research identifies such changes by the early signals of three types of trends:
- *Vogue* is a current style or preference, such as a new fashion trend.
- *Swing* is a social movement, such as the shift towards food truck dining.
- *Drift* is a prevailing direction or inclination and is based on an attitude or preference for one thing over another; for instance, the drift from living in the countryside to the town relates to the trend of urbanisation.

Designers uncover trends through the socio-material nature of trends that can be observed through user-object interactions. Aside from providing insights on new properties of products, trends provide foresights on the user values of the future, referred to as 'user value wishes'.

MINDSET: In sensing early signals of change, it is important to rely on your intuition in detecting clues. In addition, you need to look for confirmation from multiple sources before you call something a trend. To do this, back up your intuition by counting instances of clues you observe over time, and then cross-check your personal observations with other evolving data.

WHEN? Trend foresight is usually performed at the beginning of a design project – not only in projects of strategy development such as Design Roadmapping but also in product and service design projects. These projects may indicate trends that can be the outcome of a deconstruction of a context. Trends can be a rich source of inspiration for vision creation.

TIPS & CONCERNS
Trend foresight strongly relates to communities (including social media communities), and they thrive on three main activities per community mode.

Uncover trends and trend leadership in user communities of interest.

Create trends by attracting creatives towards a creative social media platform or urban area.

Collaborate on trends in collaborative community models of organisations.

LIMITATIONS
One of the major challenges in creating foresight is to scan trends and think beyond the expected. At the same time stay within the limits of understanding the complexity of the environment. To overcome this blind spot, design research might help with scanning beyond the edges.

105

HOW? The Trend Foresight method comes with the Trend Topics technique. This is an opportunity to practice your creative trend research skills.

Step 1: Take a lifestyle magazine or decide to spend around two hours on the Internet to look for images.

Step 2: Formulate a 'radar' to start your trend research. This can be an area of interest, for example, lifestyle activity (dining, sporting), an industry (cars, drones, retail), or a combination of a product, market, or technology (coffee machines, 3D printing).

Step 3: Capture images that are new and innovative and can in some way express a promise for the future. Go for quantity and collect about 80 images.

Step 4: Cluster the images that have similar elements and label these elements. Create larger clusters that connect or unify the image clusters to each other. Propose a term for the trend cluster.

Step 5: Arrange the trend clusters on the decision grid of user impact and innovation. Rank the trends from high to low impact and high to low innovation urgency.

Step 6: Choose the meaningful trends with a significant to high impact on user values for your top 10 list of trend topics.

Step 7: For each trend topic, create an inspirational title, a few sentences of explanation, and one characterising image. Typical outcomes are a list, map, or framework of top-line trends for the next couple years.

REFERENCES & FURTHER READING: Simonse, L.W.L., Stoimenova, N.A. & Snelders, H.M.J,. 2018. *Creative trend research.* In Simonse, (Eds). Design Roadmapping: Guidebook for future foresight techniques. Amsterdam: BIS Publishers. / Kjaer, A., 2014. *The trend management toolkit: a practical guide to the future.* Swiss: Springer. / Raymond, M., 2010. *The trend forecaster's handbook.* London: Laurence King Publications. / Simonse, L.W.L. Simons, D.P. & Skalska, Z., 2020 (expected). *Creative trend foresight drawn from communities: a conceptual framework.* (under review).

BRAND
DNA

PERSONALITY
*5-7 characteristics, not
just archytypes*

POSITIONING
*Target audience, Product
differentiator, Benefits*

World of brands (howmuch.net)

Brand DNA

The Brand DNA method helps designers define the brand of an organisation, product or service. In a world with numerous choices in every category, a brand is an important way to distinguish ourselves or an organisation from competitors and stand out.

WHAT & WHY? Brands are basically webs of associations in the human mind, and they are related to a product, service, or organisation. If we would ask ourselves the question, '*What is the IKEA brand like?*', we can probably come up with various answers to describe the brand, and these answers can be about the founder, the colours, the pricing, the concept, the way they deal with the environmental issues, and so on. If we want to bring a new brand to the market or to manage an existing brand, it helps to understand what the main 'ingredients' of a brand are so they can be designed deliberately.

MINDSET: In order to design a new brand in a world that is already full of brands, you need to have a wide interest to be able to assess the relationship and positioning of your brand in this landscape.

WHEN? The method can be used to construct a new brand. In the same way where products and services are being designed, it is also possible for us to design a brand. This typically happens in the front end of innovation and can inform and inspire development projects.

HOW? The Brand DNA method takes you through the elements of a brand in an iterative process. Each element of the model can be designed in itself by a process of diverging and converging. A design project driven by the DNA of the company or organisation can help the company create outstanding products, services, and systems. The Brand DNA consists of three elements that are in the core definition of a brand: purpose, personality, and positioning. You usually start at the purpose element and move clockwise.

- - - - - - - - - - -

Purpose refers to the beliefs and the values of the brand. It addresses questions such as, What are we striving to do? Why are we here? This element could be expressed in the format of a little story or even a couple of sentences.

Personality refers to the way we do this, and this reflects how we behave as a brand if the brand were a human being. Most of the time this is defined by a shortlist of personality traits. There are numerous interesting models on brand personality that can help to define this, such as the Aaker brand personality model. The typical outcome is a Brand DNA as pictured on the top left.

- - - - - - - - - - -

Positioning is about the offer, and it answers questions as, What do we offer and to whom? In which category is our offer? What are the features, functional benefits, emotional benefits, and self-expression that are connected to this? We capture this in something referred to as the positioning statement.

TIPS & CONCERNS:
The purpose of a brand is about the beliefs of the company. In practise, these can only be partly designed because most of the time this purpose is already anchored in the company from the beginning. We also want the purpose to be *authentic*, since consumers are becoming more critical towards this.

- - - - - - - - - - -

Creating a positioning that stands out is the most challenging aspect of *creating brands* in a world that is already loaded with brands only a mouse-click away. For this, we refer to Contrarian Branding, a book by Roland van der Vorst.

LIMITATIONS:
Brand DNA helps to define the brand in a compact way. The competition, the roots, and the reasons to believe the values are not part of the model, but these could also be considered when creating a brand.

REFERENCES & FURTHER READING: Aaker, J.L, 1997. Dimensions of brand personality. *Journal of Marketing Research*, vol.34, no.2, p.347-356 / van der Vorst, R., 2017. *Contrarian Branding: Stand out by camouflaging the competition*. BIS Publishers.

From The Book to just books. Why? Christianity has been losing 'business' for many decades, resulting in a large number of abandoned churches. Bookshops face difficult times as well. What? People read fewer books as they are spending more time online, and readers now tend to order books online or read them as e-books. Who and how? Merkx+Girod Architects were assigned to convert an abandoned church building into a temple of books. Where? The Dominicanen bookstore in Maastricht.

WWWWWH

WWWWWH is an acronym for Who, What, Where, When, Why, and How. It serves as a checklist of to generate the most important questions to be asked when analysing a design problem. This method entails obtaining a thorough understanding of the problem, its stakeholders, as well as the facts and the values involved.

WHAT & WHY? The WWWWWH is a checklist that helps designers analyse certain important aspects that are involved in a design project. It is typically used when defining your design problem (see 'Problem Definition'). Problems are multifaceted, which means that there is often more than one aspect involved. Checklists help you to recall some important aspects – and always recurring ones. Furthermore, they provide a structure to organise research activities and communication.

MINDSET: The approach is rather analytical. This can be helpful for structuring your thoughts and reporting findings, but you can also use the checklist in a freer way; one example is to use this as stimuli during Brainstorming with other people.

WHEN? Problem analysis is one of the activities you typically perform in an early stage of a design process – usually at a point when you have just read the design brief and want to understand the problem, maybe even to reformulate it. This WWWWWH checklist is also useful in other stages of the design process, such as when you need to prepare user research activities and presentations or write reports.

HOW? An important notion is the deconstruction of the problem. First, define the preliminary problem or draft a design brief. Ask yourself a multitude of questions about the stakeholders and facts. Deconstruct the problem systematically. Consequently, you can review the problem and set priorities. In addition. Expect to gain greater clarity about the problem and its context, as well as a better understanding of the stakeholders, facts, and values of the problem. You will gain greater insight into other problems underlying the initial problem.

Step 1 - Formulating: Write down the initial design problem or task in brief statements.

Step 2 - Diverging: Ask yourself the following WWWWWH questions in order to analyse the initial design problem. Maybe you can come up with more questions yourself!

TIPS & CONCERNS

Who: Mention as many people as possible, particularly the people who are involved in the problem.

What: Think about the problems behind the problem and try to find the essence of the problem.

You can also replace the term 'problem' with 'challenge' to widen the scope. For example, who could be challenged with the innovation? When and in which situation?

You can also ask *'What for?'* instead.

LIMITATIONS

WWWWWH is one of several techniques available for analysing a problem systematically.

Another technique is to break down the original problem into means-ends relationships by asking what the goals are, and with which means are they achieved.

Who are the problem owners? Who have an interest in finding a solution? Who are the stakeholders? What is the problem? What has been done so far to solve it? Where is the problem? Where is a possible solution? When did the problem occur? When should it be solved? Why is it a problem? Why is there no solution? How did the problem come about? How did the stakeholders try to solve the problem?

Step 3 - Reverging: Review the answers to the questions. Indicate where you need more information.

Step 4 - Converging: Prioritise the information. Which is most important, and which is not? Why?

Step 5 - Reflecting: Rewrite your initial design problem (see 'Problem Definition').

REFERENCES & FURTHER READING: Heijne, K.G & J.D. van der Meer, 2019. *Road map for creative problem solving techniques. Organizing and facilitating group sessions.* Amsterdam: Boom. / Tassoul, M., 2006. *Creative Facilitation: a Delft Approach.* Delft: VSSD.

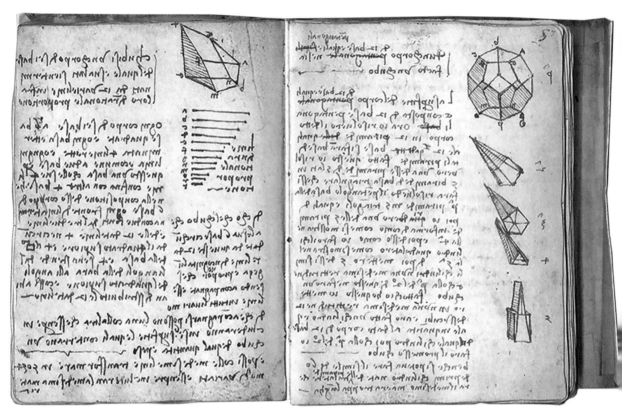

Leonardo da Vinci (1452-1519) was an avid taker of notes in his distinctive mirrored handwriting. He filled thousands of pages with drawings, sketches, equations, and his distinctive mirrored handwriting. As an engineer, Leonardo conceived ideas vastly ahead of his own time, conceptually inventing the parachute, the helicopter, an armored fighting vehicle, the use of concentrated solar power, a calculator, a rudimentary theory of plate tectonics and the double hull.

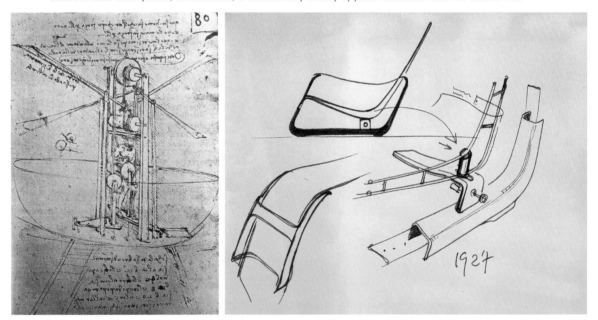

On the left one of Da Vinci's studies for flying machines (15th century). Da Vinci didn't attempt to actually build and test any of these machines, He extensively studied bird behavior and applied its principles to these sketches. On the right a construction study from 1930 by Jean Prouvé for his Cité Armchair with its characteristic coated sheet steel frame and broad leather arm support straps.

Design Drawing to Discover

Design Drawing helps designers analyse and map the design domain to uncover relations between problem factors or to analyse a situation or product. Sketching in this early Discover stage facilitates the development of knowledge and helps refine or redefine the project brief.

WHAT & WHY? From a historic perspective, the human figure drawings by Michelangelo, Raphael, and Da Vinci are well known examples of using sketches for the purpose of analysis and for developing learning. The established image enabled its creator to discover and reflect. The same is true for drawing in today's design context. When starting a project, it is beneficial to start sketching right away as a means to analyse things while visually exploring and trying things out.

Making things visual and consequently more concrete — even though things might still be very abstract — enables you to capture your first thoughts and reflect on them. It can help you gain clarity and it can help to identify problems and even search fields or areas that you were initially unaware of. A visual manifestation enables you to envision your subject's interaction with other parts of the system. In a very tangible fashion, relationships or aspects within the system can be identified in this way, even the less obvious ones.

On a product design level, discovering might entail exploring the context, shape or working principle of an existing object through sketching in order to find provisional areas for improvements. It enables you to uncover structures, details, and underlying principles you would not directly think of. In other words, drawing in this stage helps you discover what the 'real' problem is.

When it concerns an abstract or a non-product design trajectory, you can roughly map and sketch a representation of the factors and elements at play. You can also do this to uncover information, explore an existing use scenario and find opportunities or gaps.

MINDSET: Thinking 'visually' is the key here, which on a system level concerns making use of analogies and metaphors to give a visible manifestation of the system.

WHEN? Although the activity of discovery obviously occurs in the Discover phase, discovery is a continuous process. That is why visual discovery, for example through sketches, is the core of designing throughout the entire design process.

HOW? Sketches like these can contain either 2D or 3D information, and they have a rather informal character, as they are mainly used for internal communication, for yourself or for your team members. Add texts to the images where properties like materials or internal components can't be represented. Sketches made in this stage should focus on what is relevant: for example, if only the working principle needs to be analysed, there is no need for colour or context information.

Sketching in the Discover stage serves to establish a debrief to the client's initial project brief. It helps you to communicate the question: 'Is this what you had in mind?', or you can also highlight issues and potential directions to explore through your analysis.

REFERENCES & FURTHER READING: Eissen, J.J. & Steur, R., 2009. *Sketching*. Amsterdam: Bis Publishers. / Olofsson, E. & Sjölén, K., (2006). *Design Sketching*. KEEOS Design Books. / Robertson, S. & Bertling, T., (2013). *How to Draw*. Design Studio Press. http://www.delftdesigndrawing.com/basics.html

TIPS & CONCERNS
Always have a pen and paper at hand and don't wait for the final definition of a project before starting to sketch. Sketching can help you define the project.

Any drawing tool can be appropriate, as long as it provides clarity for yourself and for others, and that it is comfortable to use.

Pick the canvas you like, but keep in mind the possibility to reproduce and share your work.

LIMITATIONS
Sketching cannot uncover and reveal everything but it helps with thinking and exploring. It facilitates a fast and flexible depiction of thoughts, conclusions, and subsequently reflection.

111

'Mirrors would do well to reflect a little more before sending back images.'

JEAN COCKTEAU

METHODS
DEFINE

The methods in this section help you to define and articulate a design problem, direction or goal. For example, the Persona method helps you to structure and communicate insights into your intended users and define the user group that you want to represent and empathise with during the remainder of a design project.

NAME:
· Manuel Velazquez
· 29 years

WHAT MOTIVATES HIM:
· Wants to solve real problems for the real world

· Single
· Lives in Leiden
· Born in Madrid, Spain

EDUCATION:
· Technical university Madrid

PROFESSION:
· software engineer

KEYWORDS:
· Entrepeneurship
· Philosophy
· music

PREFERENCES:
· Prefers high quality, practicality and utility
· Not likely to use creditcards
· Is concerned about environmental impact
· Likes traveling
· Likes novels, non-fiction, historical books
· Likes arthouse movies
· Likes classical music
· Dislikes social media
· Uses public transport + bicycle

PERSONALITY TRAITS
· Challenging: +++++
· Altruism: ++++
· Self- afficacy: ++++
· Modesty: +++
· Orderliness: +

Personas

Personas are archetypical representations of user groups that describe and visualise their behaviour, values, and needs based on insights into their lives. Personas help you to be aware of and communicate these real-life behaviours, values, and needs in your design work.

WHAT & WHY? The Persona method offers a way to integrate and represent diverse findings about the people you are designing for into a 'story' about one or more individuals. This representation can then be used to empathise with this user group through the Persona story. In other words, a Persona integrates findings about real people into stories, rather than present information about a targeted user group. Representing insights in this way has been shown to be effective in stimulating designers to empathise with the people the Persona represents, rather than to merely reason about them in a rather distant manner. By using Personas you are more likely to deliver a design that is meaningful and valuable to this group of people.

MINDSET: Personas are about empathising with the people you are designing for. It is important to be open to whatever insights the Persona reveals about your user group while being aware of your own biases and preconceptions.

WHEN? A Persona is created using information gathered through various means, such as user research in the Discover phase when you form an understanding of your intended users. The Persona method integrates findings together and can be used to communicate these findings at several stages. In the Define stage it can be used to clarify who the design is intended for; in the Develop phase it can also be used during conceptualisation and when evaluating a design either for yourself or together with your team members and stakeholders involved in your project. Personas help you to have a consistent and shared understanding of the users' values and needs throughout the design process. The development of a Persona starts already in the Discover phase when you form an understanding of your intended users.

HOW? Conduct qualitative research using methods such as Contextmapping techniques, Interviews, and Observations. Based on this information, you can form your understanding of the intended users, namely regarding their behavioural patterns, themes, commonalities, particularities, and differences.

Gather an overview of the characteristics of the members of your target group, including their aspirations, needs, and all kinds of insights.

You can then group the information into clusters according to their similarities and build the archetypes that represent a specific cluster. When the characteristics of the representatives are clear, they can be visualised, named, and described. Usually a limited number of Personas per project (about three to five) is sufficient and still manageable.

Step 1: Collect a rich amount of information and insights about your intended users.

Step 2: Select the characteristics that are most representative of your target group and most relevant to your project.

Step 3: Create three to five Personas:
- Give each Persona a name.
- It is best to use a single piece of paper or other medium per Persona to ensure a good overview.
- Use text and a picture of a person representing the Persona and visual elements of his or her material context, including relevant quotes from user research.
- Add some demographic details such as age, education, job, ethnicity, religious beliefs, and family status.
- Include the major responsibilities and goals of the Persona.

TIPS & CONCERNS:
Use quotes that sum up what matters most to the Persona.

Do not look into the details of your research when creating a Persona.

Make the Personas visually attractive, as this can motivate yourself and others who use the Personas during the design process.

You can use the Personas to make storyboards.

Focus on a specific intended user instead of trying to include everyone.

Make the Persona context specific by including visualisations of his or her material world.

LIMITATIONS:
Personas cannot be used as an independent evaluation tool. You still need real-life individuals to test and evaluate your design.

Individual representations of Personas do not communicate explicitly the fact that your design will be part of a sociocultural context as well. To deal with such contexts, Cultura has been developed, which is meant to represent the characteristics typically shared by groups.

115

REFERENCES & FURTHER READING: Cooper, A., 1988. *The Inmates Are Running the Asylum*. Indianapolis: Sams. / Pruitt, J. & Adlin, T., 2006. *The Persona Lifecycle: Keeping People in Mind Throughout Product Design*. San Francisco: Elsevier science & technology. / Hao, C., 2019. *Cultura - Achieving intercultural empathy through contextual user research in design*. Doctoral Thesis, Delft University of Technology, Delft.

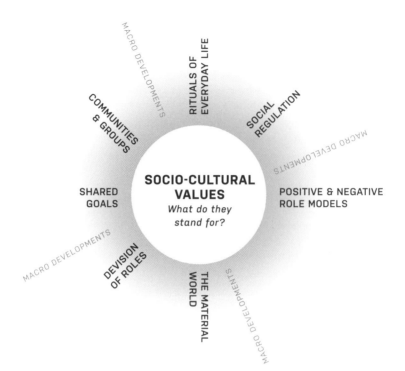

SOCIO-CULTURAL
VALUES
What do they
stand for?

RITUALS OF EVERYDAY LIFE

SOCIAL REGULATION

COMMUNITIES & GROUPS

MACRO DEVELOPMENTS

MACRO DEVELOPMENTS

POSITIVE & NEGATIVE ROLE MODELS

SHARED GOALS

MACRO DEVELOPMENTS

DEVISION OF ROLES

THE MATERIAL WORLD

MACRO DEVELOPMENTS

Getting caught sleeping in public or even on the job is completely acceptable and even admirable in Japan. Known as inemuri, the Japanese believe that sleeping at work means that exhausted employees have been working so hard that they must be totally dedicated to the job. This has lead to the design of special sleeping pods in offices for powernaps.

Cultura

Cultura is a method that helps designers gain an empathic understanding towards end users in cross-cultural situations; it also allows them to communicate these insights to other stakeholders involved. In addition to the Personas method, Cultura is used for developing a more comprehensive view on the cultural context in which the individuals are living.

WHAT & WHY? When we as designers are not familiar with 'the other culture', it is difficult for us to understand the deeper meaning of what individual people do and say. Cultura consists of several components, namely a process, a backbone structure with nine culture-specific themes, and a collection of tools that aim to inspire and inform designers about the everyday lives of their end users in their cultural context. One of these tools is *Cultura Canvas*, which can help you have an overview of how a cultural context is composed using three layers – the shared values of a cultural group, their shared practices, and macro factors. Another tool is the *Cultura Question Card Set*, which contains relevant questions that help you to prepare your field work.

MINDSET: The use of Cultura requires culture sensitivity and the ability to look at people as part of a comprehensive whole. Doing so requires reflecting on your own cultural background. A curious and open mind can 'make the familiar strange and make the strange familiar', and a broad social and cultural interest are the key factors for using Cultura.

WHEN? Cultura is typically used in the discovery stage of the design process to generate culture-specific questions for guiding your contextual user research. It can also be used in the definition stage when you need to structure your findings and communicate them to the design team or with stakeholders in the project.

HOW? Carefully determine the scope of the context. This is not an easy task, and it depends highly on the project. In trying to understand the context of culturally distanced users, it is better to take a wide scope into view and to look at it with a fine-grained detail because many factors are likely to be unfamiliar to you. It is recommended to consider not only what the context is and who are included in the context but also the place and time.

Step 1: Use the *Cultura Question Card Set* as a lens to prepare your field studies.

Step 2: Delineate the context by determining its boundaries and who the 'end users' are. Generate more specific questions for each category and prioritise these questions.

Step 3: Search for answers from sources such as field studies as well as desktop research.

Step 4: Structure findings along the *Cultura Canvas*.

Step 5: Communicate with your project team and other stakeholders; discuss the findings with them using the *Cultura Canvas* as a basis.

TIPS & CONCERNS
The nine culture-specific themes can be helpful not only for formulating questions of sensitising tasks or participatory sessions with users but also for other sources (websites, literature, observations).

They can be used entirely or selectively according to the topic and the scope of the project.

Contextual macro factors provide a broader picture of the cultural context and help explain the gathered user information.

These macro factors can include demographics, economy, infrastructure, composition of the population, geographical characteristics, or politics.

Emphasise the insights and inspiration, not the validation.

Insights are presented mainly for understanding and inspiration rather than proving a truth.

Build a pleasant relationship with your participants so they will be happy to give feedback in a later stage of the design process.

When participants see how designers put effort into understanding their culture, they are more likely to put effort into offering full and informative feedback in return.

LIMITATIONS
Cultura cannot be used as an independent evaluation tool. You need real people in the targeted context to test and evaluate your design.

REFERENCES & FURTHER READING: Hao, C., van Boeijen, A.G.C., & Stappers, P.J. ,2017. *Cultura: A communication toolkit for designers to gain empathic insights across cultural boundaries.* In proceedings of IASDR conference 2017, 31 October-3 November 2017, Cincinnati, Ohio, United States. / Hao, C., 2019. *Cultura: Achieving intercultural empathy through contextual user research in design* (Doctoral dissertation). Delft University of Technology, Delft, Netherlands.

Comedic actor and filmdirector Buster Keaton plays an iceman puzzled by a GE refrigerator. Keaton made numerous brilliant filmscenes of mankind interacting with design and technology, most famously in his film *The Electric House* in which he wires a house with gadgets taking over control, reminscent of our current smart house ambitions a century later. *(General Electric Company 1930, miSci- Museum of Innovation & Science).*

Problem Definition

Designing is often referred to as a kind of problem solving. Before designers start solving anything, they need to be sure that they are working on the right problem. Finding and defining the real problem is a significant step towards a solution.

WHAT & WHY? Working with the right problem is crucial for coming up with innovative and appropriate solutions. The goal of this method is to critically look at identified problems – which can be stated in a project brief – and then analyse them by deconstruction. The outcome of the method should be a formulation of the correct problem that has to be solved through design, and this formulation should include arguments of why this is the right definition of the problem.

MINDSET: Initially, you may be focused on the dissatisfaction or problem of the client and are motivated to support the client. Here, you need a critical and analytical approach so that you can deconstruct the initial problem with the why-question in mind. For what reasons is this the right problem to be solved – and for whom, when, and where? What is the desired situation?

WHEN? A Problem Definition is usually the starting point for ideation. Throughout the entire design process, it is essential to be critical, regardless whether you are still working on the right problem or even sub-problem to be solved.

A problem has to do with dissatisfaction about a certain situation, and a situation only becomes a problem if the problem owner wants to do something about it and has the ability to do so. In such a case, there needs to be a new situation that is more desirable than the present one, and this is what we call the goal situation.

For example, a potential car buyer's main problem appears to be the fact that he or she does not own a car and now needs to own one. But in essence, the real concern is for this potential buyer to get from A to B in a flexible and individual way. Instead of owning a car, the use of a car or other vehicles can be a solution as well. This sharp formulation of the problem steers the possible solution, and this solution could be a car rental service, carsharing, or an e-bike.

TIPS & CONCERNS

There is always a tension between the 'current situation' and the 'desired situation'. By explicitly mentioning these different situations, you are able to discuss their relevance with other people involved in your project.

Make a hierarchy of problems. Start with one big problem and then divide it into smaller ones by thinking about causes and effects.

Use Post-it notes to make a problem tree.

Reformulate a problem as an opportunity, a driver, or a challenge. Doing this may activate ideas and inspire you and your team.

A well formulated problem definition steers the design team and other stakeholders.

LIMITATIONS

Defining the problem does not solve the problem.

HOW? Do not underestimate the work that is required to find and define problems. As a young and ambitious designer, you may be keen to design an innovative products. The real problem might ask for a completely different approach.

Step 1: Start with a problem as formulated by the problem owner, or start from a problem-finding analysis.

Step 2: Deconstruct the problem using open-ended questions (see 'WWWWWH'). For instance, why is this the problem, for whom, when, and where, what are relevant context factors, what is the desired situation, and what are the possible side effects to be avoided?

Step 3: Find the appropriate scope; being too broad is risky because it opens up too many possibilities, and being too narrow may greatly limit your possibilities.

Step 4: Write the problem definition; this is an iterative process. The outcome is a structured description of the design problem, along with a clear description of the desired end situation (or goals) and possibly the direction of idea generation. A well-written problem definition provides a shared understanding between you, your client, and other stakeholders.

REFERENCES & FURTHER READING: Roozenburg, N.F.M. & Eekels, J., 1995. *Product Design: Fundamentals and Methods*. Utrecht: Lemma.

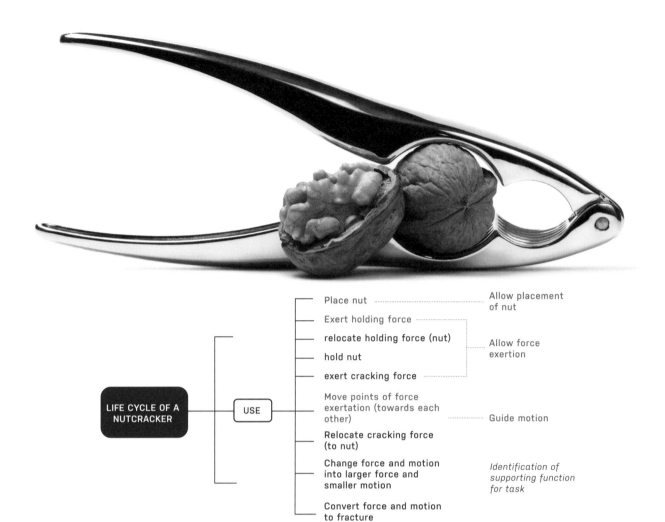

LIFE CYCLE OF A NUTCRACKER → USE

- Place nut ·········· Allow placement of nut
- Exert holding force ··········
- relocate holding force (nut)
- hold nut ··········· Allow force exertion
- exert cracking force
- Move points of force exertion (towards each other) ·········· Guide motion
- Relocate cracking force (to nut)
- Change force and motion into larger force and smaller motion *Identification of supporting function for task*
- Convert force and motion to fracture

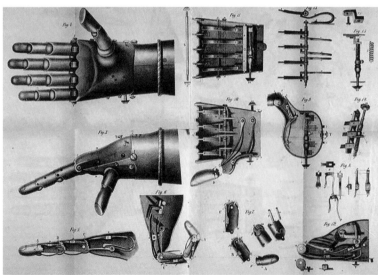

For centuries, humans have invented ingenious devices to replace lost limbs or upgrade their bodies and have new limbs that did more than the old ones. Left: The right arm of Gottfried 'Götz' Von Berlichingen, made of iron, 1500s. Right: Born with a congenitally missing lower left arm, researcher Bertolt Meyer was fitted with his first prosthetic device when he was only three months old. Inspired by the possibilities of Touch Bionics he presented the Channel 4 documentary 'How to Build a Bionic Man'. At the Science Museum in London he is portrayed next to his bionic self.

Function Analysis

Function Analysis is a method for analysing and developing the function structure of an existing product or new product concept. It helps designers to describe the intended functions of the product and to relate these functions to its parts and 'organs'.

WHAT & WHY? Systems, services, products, and their components are there for a reason – their function. Analysing functions and sub-functions can help you find and explore new possibilities to embody them in meaningful ways.

MINDSET: Striving for innovative ideas often requires you to step away from the way an existing product or system manifests itself. To do this, you need an analytical mind to distinguish all the possible functions and sub-functions and to order them in a logical way. You can focus on the purpose or the intended effect of the product – as in 'what the product should do' – rather than on the solution elements such as components, parts, and materials.

WHEN? Function Analysis is typically carried out at the beginning of idea generation. You would usually describe the idea in terms of functions and sub-functions, and you can do this without material features such as shape, dimensions, and materials. The underlying idea is that the function structure can be built up from a limited number of elementary functions on a high level of abstraction. Being forced to think about the product in an abstract way stimulates creativity, and this prevents you from 'jumping to solutions' – meaning to immediately call out and elaborate on the first idea that comes to mind, which is often an obvious idea and may not be the best. In other words, Function Analysis forces you to distance from known products and components by considering this question: *What does the new product intend to do, and how could it do that?*

HOW? Considered a product as a technical-physical system that comprises an overall function and its sub-functions. The principle of Function Analysis entails firstly *specifying* what the product should do and then *inferring* what the parts should do, even though they are yet to be developed. The development of a function structure is an iterative process.

Step 1: Describe the main function of the product in the form of a black box. If you cannot define one main function, go to the next step.

Step 2: Make a list of sub-functions. The use stage of a Product Life Cycle is a good starting point.

Step 3: For a complex product, you may want to develop a function structure.

There are generally three principles of structuring:
- Functions should be put in a chronological order.
- The inputs and outputs of flows between functions (as in matter, energy, and information flows) should be connected to one another.
- Use a clear hierarchy, as in main functions, sub-functions, sub-sub-functions, as so on.

Step 4: Elaborate the function structure:
- Fit in a number of auxiliary functions that were left out, and find variations of the function structure in order to determine the best function structure.
- Variation possibilities include moving the system boundary, changing the sequence of sub-functions, and splitting or combining functions.

TIPS & CONCERNS:
A function or sub-function is always described using a verb and an object; usually a noun. For instance, the function of a mirror is to reflect light, the function of a transformer is to change voltage, and the function of a blender is to cut and mix ingredients. The expression 'drive fast' is not a function of a car; instead, it is something the driver can do with it. A better description of the car's function is 'enable a person to drive fast'.

If you have a function structure, it is recommended that you develop variants of it as well.

Certain sub-functions appear in almost all design problems.

Having a knowledge of the elementary or general functions can help you to seek product-specific functions.

LIMITATIONS:
This analytical approach does not take into account the less rational wishes of users or businesses. Sometimes they are attached to certain features, functions or shapes, even when their function is obsolete. For instance, many modern car grilles no longer have a strict function since air flows in through the bottom of the car, but grilles still help car brands to express their identity and give cars a recognisable face. One could claim this is a function as well, a cultural one.

121

REFERENCES & FURTHER READING: Roozenburg, N.F.M. & Eekels, J., 1995. *Product Design: Fundamentals and Methods.* Utrecht: Lemma. / Van der Vegte, W.F. & Van Breemen, E.J.J., 2009. *Flowchart-assisted function analysis of products to support teaching of the exact sciences.* Proceedings of ICED, Palo Alto, Vol. 10, pp. 101-112.

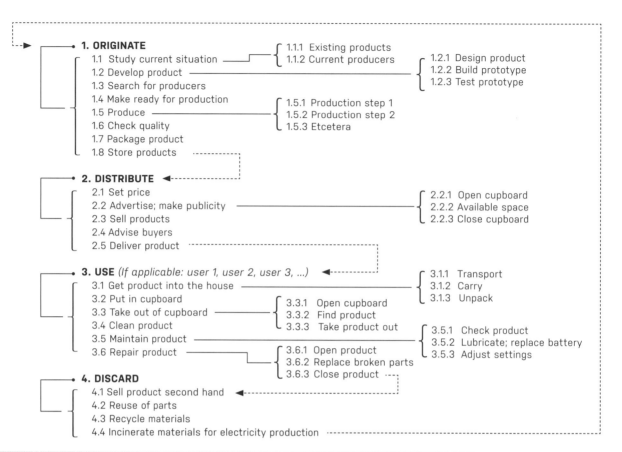

1. ORIGINATE
- 1.1 Study current situation ——— { 1.1.1 Existing products
- { 1.1.2 Current producers
- 1.2 Develop product ——————————— { 1.2.1 Design product
- { 1.2.2 Build prototype
- { 1.2.3 Test prototype
- 1.3 Search for producers
- 1.4 Make ready for production
- 1.5 Produce ——— { 1.5.1 Production step 1
- { 1.5.2 Production step 2
- { 1.5.3 Etcetera
- 1.6 Check quality
- 1.7 Package product
- 1.8 Store products

2. DISTRIBUTE
- 2.1 Set price
- 2.2 Advertise; make publicity ——————— { 2.2.1 Open cupboard
- { 2.2.2 Available space
- { 2.2.3 Close cupboard
- 2.3 Sell products
- 2.4 Advise buyers
- 2.5 Deliver product

3. USE *(If applicable: user 1, user 2, user 3, ...)*
- 3.1 Get product into the house ——— { 3.1.1 Transport
- { 3.1.2 Carry
- { 3.1.3 Unpack
- 3.2 Put in cupboard
- 3.3 Take out of cupboard ——— { 3.3.1 Open cupboard
- { 3.3.2 Find product
- { 3.3.3 Take product out
- 3.4 Clean product
- 3.5 Maintain product ——— { 3.5.1 Check product
- { 3.5.2 Lubricate; replace battery
- { 3.5.3 Adjust settings
- 3.6 Repair product ——— { 3.6.1 Open product
- { 3.6.2 Replace broken parts
- { 3.6.3 Close product

4. DISCARD
- 4.1 Sell product second hand
- 4.2 Reuse of parts
- 4.3 Recycle materials
- 4.4 Incinerate materials for electricity production

Digitally equipped smart packaging not only protects products during transport but also enables checking and tracking throughout the logistics chain, allowing storage conditions and shipment destinations to be dynamically adjusted if and as needed – to create a more efficient, higher value, higher quality delivery. Plus, information is now available to the consumer, not only the supply chain. With smart packaging and automated storage systems, a whole array of benefits emerges: increased product quality, reduced waste, simplified inspections, rerouting alternatives, dynamic repricing, tremendous time and cost savings.

Product Life Cycle

The Product Life Cycle is a schematic diagram of the activities that a product encounters during its life cycle. The method helps designers to focus on the whole product life cycle when defining requirements for product development.

WHAT & WHY? For most designers, their first focus is on the user perspective. Novice designers often have a good view of what it means to be a user of products, and they can imagine design requirements for this phase of the product lifecycle. The Product Life Cycle helps designers identify other important requirements that have to do with manufacturing, distribution, and the end-of-life scenario.

MINDSET: To identify all possible design requirements, you need a complete and systematic way to analyse the entire existence of a product. When designing a chair or a lamp, this might seem exaggerated, but imagine developing an airplane! You don't want to overlook any possible scenario or critical property of the design, as it could be a matter of life or death.

WHEN? A Product Life Cycle is typically used during problem analysis and the conceptual stage of product design. During these stages, you will need to make many decisions that influence the activities of stakeholders in later stages of the product development process. During the product life cycle, each stakeholder process (such as manufacturing, assembly, disposal, and recycling) involves certain requirements and preferences for the new product. For example, the production engineer might want you to use existing manufacturing technology and design simple parts that are easy to manufacture. Making a Product Life Cycle for your concept design forces you to think ahead, particularly with these questions in mind: Which situations, places, and activities will the new product turn up in? Who is doing what with the product in those contexts? What problems can be expected? What requirements do these situations necessitate?

HOW? The starting point of a Product Life Cycle is a product, a product group or service. The outcome of a Product Life Cycle is a structured overview of the important processes and sub-processes that a product encounters. This can be used as a framework and checklist for your List of Requirements.

Step 1: Define the product or product group.

Step 2: Identify the relevant stages in the life cycle of the product. Use the following stages as a start: Originate, Distribute, Use, Discard.

Step 3: Use verbs to describe all the activities that a product goes through, and use the identified stages in Step 2 as a checklist to generate the relevant activities.

Step 4: Write down each activity in the form of a verb-noun combination (such as transport product to store, place product in the store).

Step 5: Visualise the Product Life Cycle and create a table: The column on the left shows the general stages in the product life cycle, while the column on the right represents the activities.

Step 6: After completion, you can use the tree with its list of activities as a checklist to generate criteria.

TIPS & CONCERNS

You will sometimes identify activities that are preceded by a more important activity. It is important to break down this hierarchy into sub-activities until you reach a level where further breakdown is not possible.

Use is typically the stage in which the product fulfils its function. Distinguish between the activities that are performed by the user and the activities or process steps performed by the product.

Ideally, the activities performed by the user are user tasks, and the activities performed by the product are functions of the product.

Distinguish between different types of activities. These can also be forms of unintended use, misuse (such as standing on a chair) as well as malfunction.

For Use, try not to focus on one-to-one product-user interaction, and be sure to incorporate socio-cultural aspects of products.

Usually there are various users. For example, when designing a park bench, you can consider also vandals, park visitors, homeless people, and municipal officials.

When identifying the requirements, ask yourself: *which criteria must the product satisfy during the process of this particular stage?*

LIMITATIONS

Do not overlook certain activities such as the non-intended use of the product. These are your blind spots that cannot be avoided when you are constructing a complete picture of the life cycle.

REFERENCES & FURTHER READING: Roozenburg, N.F.M. & Eekels, J., 1995. *Product Design: Fundamentals and Methods.* Utrecht: Lemma. / Roozenburg, N. F.M. & Eekels, J., 1998. *Product Ontwerpen: Structuur en Methoden.* 2nd ed. Utrecht: Lemma.

123

1. PERFORMANCE *What main functions does the product need to fulfil? What functional properties should it have (speed, power, strength, precision, capacity, etcetera)?*

2. ENVIRONMENT *What kind of environmental influences does the product need to withstand during production, transport and use (temperature, vibrations, moisture, etcetera)? What effects of the product to the environment should be avoided?*

3. LIFE IN SERVICE *With what intensity will the product be used and how long should it last?*

4. MAINTENANCE *Is maintenance necessary and possible? What parts need to be accessible?*

5. TARGET PRODUCT COST *Target Product Cost: What is a realistic price for the product, considering similar products? What margin does it need to deliver?*

6. TRANSPORT *What requirements are set by transport of the product during production and to the location of usage?*

7. PACKAGING *Is packaging needed? Against what should it protect?*

8. QUANTITY *What is the amount of units to be produced? In batches or in continuous production?*

9. PRODUCTION FACILITIES *Should the product be designed for existing production facilities, or is it possible to invest in new production resources? Will (part of) production be outsourced?*

10. SIZE AND WEIGHT *Are there boundaries to the size and weight of the product due to production, transport or use?*

11. AESTHETIC, APPEARANCE AND FINISH *Which preferences do buyers and users have? Should the product fit a house style?*

12. MATERIALS *Should certain materials (not) be used (because of safety or environmental reasons)?*

13. PRODUCT LIFE SPAN *How long is the product expected to be produced and sold?*

14. STANDARDS, RULES AND REGULATIONS *What standards, rules and regulations (nationally and internationally) apply to the product and to the production process? Should standardisation within the company or within the industry be taken into account?*

15. ERGONOMICS *What requirements result from observing, understanding, handling, operating (etcetera) the product?*

16. RELIABILITY *What chance of failure is acceptable? What kind of failure and consequences to the functioning of the product should be avoided at all cost?*

17. STORAGE *Are there long periods of storing time during production, distribution or usage of the product? Does this call for specific storage measures?*

18. TESTING *What quality tests are conducted on the product, both inside and outside the company?*

19. SAFETY *Should specific precautions be taken with regards to the safety of users and non-users?*

20. PRODUCT POLICY *Are there requirements resulting from the company's current product portfolio?*

21. SOCIETAL AND POLITICAL IMPLICATIONS *What opinions are there currently in society concerning the product?*

22. PRODUCT LIABILITY *For what kinds of design, production or usage mistakes can the producer be held accountable?*

23. INSTALLATION AND INITIATION OF USE *What requirements result from assembly outside the factory, installation, connecting to other systems and learning how to handle and operate the product?*

24. REUSE, RECYCLING *Can the material cycle be extended by reuse of parts and materials? Are parts and materials easy to separate for recycling or waste processing?*

List of Requirements

A List of Requirements states the important characteristics that a design must have in order to be successful. With the List of Requirements method, designers describe design goals and design criteria in a concrete way. This can be used for selecting the most promising ideas and design proposals or combinations of proposals.

WHAT & WHY? The List of Requirements is drafted based on an analysis of all the information gathered on the design problem. It helps you set boundaries for your design process. Without this, an infinite number of design proposals can be a valid solution for a given problem, and there would be no justification for choices. It is particularly vital when designing complex products that involve coping with many aspects. In teams, a list is helpful in ensuring that you are all on the same page. This list can even serve as a contract between the client and the designer, whereby both agree on the direction and boundaries for further development.

MINDSET: The method requires designers to think systematically and analytical, rather than an intuitive one.

WHEN? A List of Requirements is created in an early stage of the design process, and evolves during the process in a more detailed one as the design proposals become more concrete.

HOW? Make a structure that helps you to reach completeness. There are several tools for this, such as the Product Life Cycle. At first, the list will simply serve as a checklist. Over time, you need to gather more information to ensure concrete and valid requirements. For example, when designing a playground, you need to know about how children play; you also need to gather information such as ergonomic data and safety regulations.

During a design project, new perspectives on the design problem frequently lead to the identification of new requirements, and they should be constantly updated and changed. The outcome is a structured List of Requirements and standards. Possible procedure:

Step 1: Make a structure based on one of the checklists in order to generate Requirements.

Step 2: Define as many requirements as possible.

Step 3: Identify gaps in your knowledge; this refers to information that needs to be gathered by research.
• Put the requirements into practice: Determine their variables in terms of observable or quantifiable characteristics, such as 'the cost price should be between € 25,- and € 30,-', not 'the price should be as low as possible'.
• Make a distinction between demands and wishes: Demands must be met, whereas wishes are a factor of consideration when choosing between design proposals. An example of a demand can be 'the product weight should not exceed 23 kg because of labour rules'; a wish can be expressed as, 'the product should be considered comfortable by as many test subjects as possible'.

Step 4: Eliminate requirements that either are similar or do not make a distinction between design alternatives. Identify whether or not there is a hierarchy of requirements. Distinguish between lower-level and higher-level requirements.

Step 5: Make sure that your requirements fulfil the following conditions:
• Each requirement must be valid
• Each requirement must be operational
• The list must be non-redundant
• The list must be concise
• The list must be practicable

TIPS & CONCERNS
Make your requirements more concrete, define them in numerical terms. For example, change 'the product should be portable' into 'the product should weigh less than 5 kg'.

Mention the sources in the List of Requirements, such as publications, experts, or your own research.

Give your Requirements a structured numbering so that you can easily refer to them.

Using Product Life Cycle numbering immediately shows the reason for a certain Requirement.

Use more than one checklist; checklists complement each other.

LIMITATIONS
Spending too much time on analysing and defining design requirements can hinder your creative process. ----------
Employ an iterative approach where you switch between sketching and defining criteria.

Do not overly limit the possibilities of your design by defining too many requirements.

REFERENCES & FURTHER READING: Cross, N., 1989. *Engineering Design Methods.* Chichester: Wiley. / Hubka, V. & Eder, W.E., 1988. *Theory of Technical Systems: A Total Concept Theory for Engineering Design.* Berlin: Springer. / Pahl, G. & Beitz, W., 1984. *Engineering Design: A Systematic Approach.* London: Design Council. / Pugh, S., 1990. *Total Design: Integrated Methods for Successful Product Engineering.* Wokingham: Addison Wesley. / Roozenburg, N.F.M. & Eekels, J., 1995. *Product Design: Fundamentals and Methods.* Utrecht: Lemma.

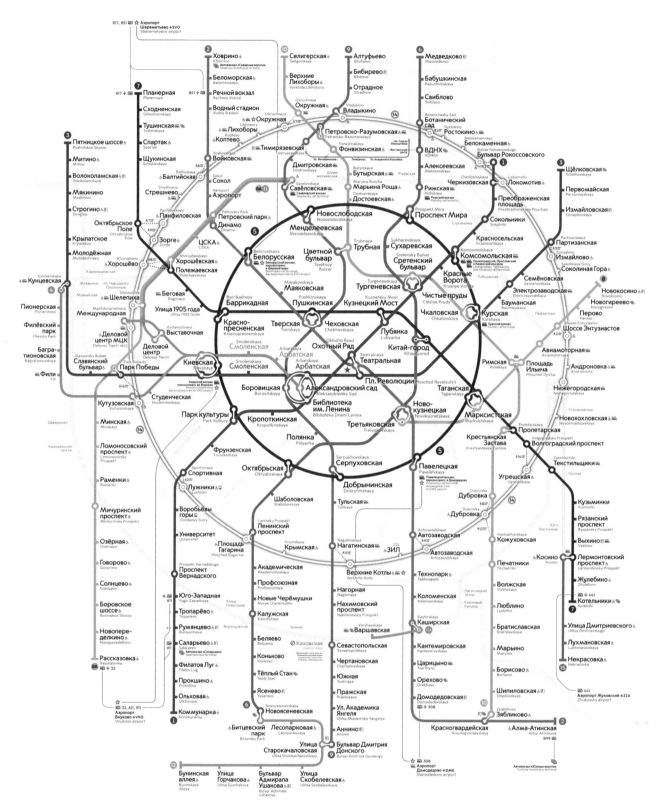

The underground map of a city (in this case Moscow) resembles a mind map structure. This schematic way of representing lines and stations was designed by Harry Beck for the London Underground in 1931. Over the years, the London railway system had become too complex and stretched out to be visualised in a geographically correct map.

Mind Mapping

Mind Mapping is a method for creating an overview. A mind map is a graphical representation of the ideas and aspects that are organised around a central theme, and it shows how these aspects are related to each other.

WHAT & WHY? At the start of a complex project or problem-solving session, you may need an overview of all related subjects, stakeholders, and variables. Putting these on paper can help you empty your mind and make room for new thoughts and ideas. Visualising the relations between the items can give you more insight into how they might influence each other and thus allow you to communicate your point of view.

You can list out all the aspects and ideas that are relevant to a theme, thus bringing structure and clarity to the problem. Mind maps can provide an overview and are especially useful for identifying all the issues and sub-issues related to a problem. They can also be used for generating solutions to a problem and for listing out their advantages and disadvantages.

MINDSET: Mind Mapping requires both an associative and an analytical mindset. The first quality is needed to tap into relevant information that is stored in the brain and the other one to analyse and structure the parameters that might be useful to your project.

WHEN? Mind Mapping can be used in a whole lot of ways and situations. They are often used at the beginning of idea generation. Drafting a mind map helps you structure your thoughts and ideas about the problem and connect them together. It is very useful in the problem analysis phase. And it is an effective method for outlining presentations and reports.

HOW? The main branches of a mind map are the main associations that you have formed with the central subject. Each has sub-branches that present the pros and cons of that particular solution. Making mind maps is a skill that can be trained.
• Do not limit yourself when writing everything down, since the mind map is supposed to help you to analyse the problem.
• Make mind maps separately when working in groups. Then discuss them together after so that you are all on the same page.

Step 1: Write the name or description of the theme in the centre of a piece of paper and draw a circle around it.

Step 2: Brainstorm each major facet of that theme by placing your thoughts on lines drawn in an outward direction from the central thought, just like roads leaving a city.

Step 3: Add branches to the lines when necessary.

Step 4: Use additional visual techniques. For example, try using different colours for major lines of thought, drawing circles around words that appear more than once, and connecting lines between similar thoughts.

Step 5: Study the mind map to see which relationships already exist and what solutions are suggested. Reshape or restructure the mind map if necessary.

TIPS & CONCERNS
You can find software for Mind Mapping on the Internet.

The disadvantages of using computer software are that it slightly limits your freedom compared to working with hand drawings and colours.

Using a computer is also less personal, and it might be less suitable when needing to share the mind map with others.

Make it look good visually. Use drawings, colours, pictures – anything that appeals to the eye.

You can keep adding elements and thoughts to your mind map.

Vary the type and spacing.

Use short descriptions instead of long sentences.

LIMITATIONS
A Mind Map is a subjective view of a project or subject; essentially it is a map of your mind.

It is an effective tool when you are working on your own.

It is also suitable to be used in small teams, although the author may have to provide additional explanations.

127

REFERENCES & FURTHER READING: Buzan, T., 1996. *The Mind Map Book: How to Use Radiant Thinking to Maximize Your Brain's Untapped Potential.* New York, NY: Plume. / Heijne, K.G. & van der Meer, J.D., 2019. *Road map for creative problem solving techniques. Organizing and facilitating group sessions.* Amsterdam: Boom. / Tassoul, M., 2006. *Creative Facilitation: a Delft Approach.* Delft: VSSD.

The Unboxing experience has lead to the phenomenon of the unboxing video's that offer a sneak preview of receiving and unpacking an online ordered product; an emotional high of the customer experience. The Customer Journey Map (CJM) is a basic template that includes a specific persona, the steps beginning-to-end of the customer experience, and the potential emotional highs and lows. Other parts of the journey are optional and depend on your objective.

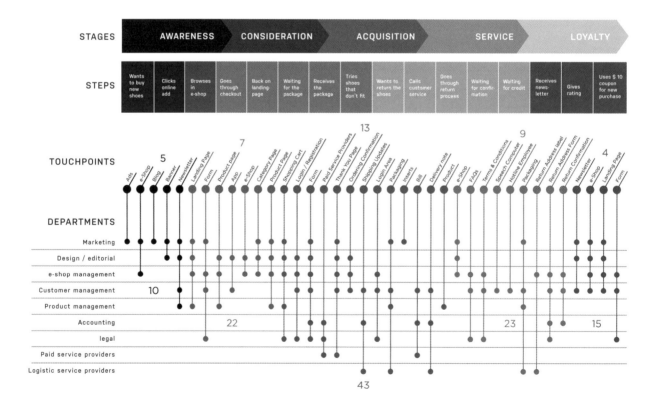

Journey Mapping

Journey Mapping is a method for understanding people's experiences around a specific topic over a certain period of time and place. While creating journey maps, designers can gain insight into different phases of people's experiences.

WHAT & WHY? In designing a product or service, a common challenge is to design touchpoints or features that do not only function properly in isolation but also work in synergy as a whole. The result is a set of journey maps that visualise people's experiences over time and place. Making such maps can allow you to construct your understanding and the resulting visualisations can be useful as you discuss your insights with others, make decisions, and generate ideas.

There are different forms of Journey Mapping like the customer journey for the design of services. Patient Journey mapping is a subset focusing on the patients in their particular experiences, such as when they undergo a treatment process. In the sustainability field, product journey maps can analyse material flows and multiple use phases. In all of these maps, the horizontal axis shows time, while the vertical axis shows a variety of concerns.

MINDSET: Making journey maps requires a broad view on your design task, an interest in human experiences, and an appreciation of the complexity of interacting components. Multi-disciplinary collaboration is often needed.

WHEN? Journey Mapping can be useful in several stages of the design process. In the beginning use them to understand people's experiences with a product or service. Or use them when making decisions on a certain design direction or when ideating new solutions. Crafting the map in a multidisciplinary collaboration and using it as an iterative tool for designing from the user perspective can help to get the team aligned.

HOW? *For understanding the user experience*, make sure your data is based on qualitative research and not on the assumptions of the design team. Use raw data such as quotes and photos to illustrate the journey map.

For the purpose of decision making, add quantitative data to the matrix about customer evaluations and service performance. With such a map, it is possible to make prioritisations of what to improve.

For the purpose of ideation, make iterations of the map. Start with a current journey and then map the ideal journey. Print, sketch, annotate, use Post-it notes, and make many iterations of the map. The map becomes a living document to design with.

When using complex products and services, users have to take several steps across channels or devices. They may have to be done in a certain time span and with several touch points.

Step 1: Determine the type of user. For instance, this can be an end-user, a customer, patient, or a professional. Also, multiple perspectives can be mapped on a journey map if preferred.

Step 2: Along the horizontal axis, map the stages that the user goes through. Take the user's point of view and map the user's activities, as well as what the user tries to achieve in each stage.

Step 3: Choose the themes regarding the user experience for the vertical axis, such as the user's aims, activities, barriers, opportunities, and emotions.

Step 4: Add any other row that might be relevant for the journey map. This depends on the purpose of Journey Mapping; having three to eight of parallel swim lanes usually work well.

TIPS & CONCERNS

Do not only include the touchpoints – that is, when user and service meet – yet also overlook the time in between.

Do not focus on what the user needs to use; focus instead on what the user would like to use.

Use the vertical axis with the themes in a flexible way. Each project may have different ones.

Explore different visual formats. The journey could have a circle shape, or two journeys could meet.

The journey could also be visualised through a metaphor.

Do not hesitate to change the content of cells when new insights emerge.

Use visuals and research data wherever possible.

Choose a title for your journey map that summarises its content. Never use 'Journey Map' as a title. Use descriptive words that both inspires you and summarises its content.

LIMITATIONS:

Journey Mapping is just one means to an end in creating an optimal user experience. There are other methods that contribute to the same goal too (see 'Visualising Interactions').

REFERENCES & FURTHER READING: Roscam Abbing, E., 2010. *Brand Driven Innovation*. Lausanne: AVA Academia. / Stickdorn, M. et. al. 2018. *This is Service Design Thinking*. Amsterdam: BIS Publishing. / Ridder, E. de, Dekkers, T., Porsius, J.T., Kraan, G. & Melles, M., 2018. The perioperative patient experience of hand and wrist surgical patients: An exploratory study using patient journey mapping. *Patient Experience Journal*, 5(3), 97-107.

Before Bugaboo joined the ResCoM project, its products were already designed for circularity in various ways: durable with the potential for multiple use cycles through second hand use, easy to repair, supported by customer services and spare part availability. Bugaboo developed a 'Flex plan', which offers a leasing package for new strollers. In addition, Bugaboo also considers the business case for a scheme where strollers are refurbished as new, certified and sold as a 'Bugaboo approved'. (rescoms.eu)

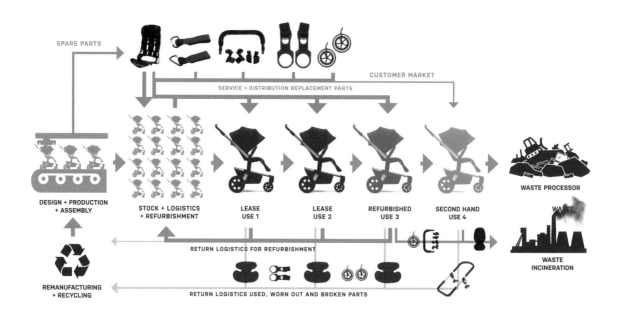

Product Journey Mapping

A Product Journey Mapping (PJM) is a method for mapping and visualising the life cycle of a product over multiple use cycles, and it supports design for circularity. The visualisation provides an overview of the journey of the product, its components, and the stakeholders it meets throughout its lifetime.

WHAT & WHY? The PJM is a circular design method, which corresponds to a circular economy. The circular economy is a world in which reuse through repair, refurbishment, and remanufacturing are the prevailing social and economic models for development and use. The business opportunities are huge. Developing product and service offerings and achieving competitive advantage means rethinking business models. The method helps organisations understand and manage ways to preserve and capture the maximum value from a product over its lifetime and in a circular economy. The goal of PJM is to enhance value capture from a company's products by improving the efficiency and effectiveness of each product use cycle.

MINDSET: PJM requires that you take a long-term view, where you not only focus on one product use cycle but that you ask yourself, what happens after the first use? How can we design products for multiple use cycles? Taking such a long-term perspective to a product's life is new, and it will require courage and lots of creativity to break through many barriers that you will encounter when engaging with this method.

WHEN? PJM is a strategic tool that should be used in the early phases of development. It helps you plan a product's journey over consecutive use cycles and see where potential service touchpoints and opportunities for capturing value may occur. PJM is most useful when applied to durable products that are offered in a product-as-a-service business model.

TIPS & CONCERNS:
Use PJM alongside a Customer Journey Map to find new opportunities that can add value to the customer experience in a Product-as-a-Service model.

It may not always be realistic for companies to integrate multiple cycles in their business models. PJM may help you explore the feasibility of going circular.

Engage all stakeholders in the creation of the product journey map.

LIMITATIONS:
Since PJM is a new method, it has not been validated extensively. Use PJM with care and feel free to adapt it to your personal.

131

HOW? Unlike the customer journey map where the customer experience is at the centre, PJM puts the product on centre stage. In a Product-as-a-Service model, this helps you understand the complexity of the flow of the product, its parts, and its materials over time. In PJM, the service touchpoints are typically depicted along a process timeline.

This method is best used when developing strategies for capturing value over a number of product use cycles. When different stakeholders discuss product journey strategies, visualising these in rough sketches helps you uncover and resolve different interpretations of the scenarios. Later in the process, PJM can be detailed further to provide an accurate representation of the product journey.

Step 1: Analyse the product or product concept and its main components. Define the total number of use cycles the product should or could last and the desired length of the different use cycles.

Step 2: Create a part lifetime overview. For each component of the product, list the number of use cycles the component or part can be expected to last. For example, in the case of a baby stroller, its fabric needs to be replaced before each new use cycle, but the frame can last more use cycles.

Step 3: Map the use cycle stages the product goes through on the horizontal axes to create a timeline.

Step 4: Determine all service touchpoints along the timeline regarding expected in-use repairs, product updates (as in accessories), delivery of consumables (such as detergents), forward and return logistics, and refurbishment activities. Show the flows of products and parts.

Step 5: Include the different stakeholders involved at each touchpoint, including all strategic actions they stand for and the way in which these need to be aligned.

REFERENCES & FURTHER READING: Bakker, C., van Dam, S., de Pauw, I., van der Grinten, B. & Asif, F., 2017. *ResCoM Design Methodology for Multiple Lifecycle Products*, TU Delft. 22 p. / Sumter, Deborah, Bakker, C., Balkenende, R., 2018. The Role of Product Design in Creating Circular Business Models: A Case Study on the Lease and Refurbishment of Baby Strollers. *Sustainability* 10(7).

When it comes down to it, the project value model is really intended to structure the conversation about whether your project is worth it. Should it be started? Is it worth it to continue? The right frame of mind is prerequisite. All terms mentioned need to be defined in advance of departure. The decision to not produce something in a world already overloaded with useless products is an option too often ignored.

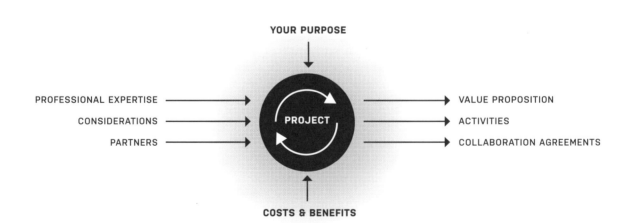

Project Value Modelling

Project Value Modelling helps with discussing how values in design projects can be created and captured. For a particular project, value-related questions are answered in a sequential way that can generate an overview of important relationships, tensions, and opportunities. This allows designers to make well-informed decisions on project selection, contract negotiation, and collaboration.

WHAT & WHY? Project Value Modelling is about reconciling the values (such as saving energy) that are created for users and other stakeholders with the economic and professional values captured by the designer (such as developing expertise). Multiple divergent values need to be created to address the needs of different actors, such as clients, users, governments, and society. Sometimes designers struggle with realising these values for others while they pursue professional ambitions and profitability at the same time. This method helps designers to craft an appropriate value model for a project that facilitates discussion, reflection, and action at the intersection of professionalism and entrepreneurship. It can be used as a guide to make well-informed decisions on project selection, role and fee negotiation, and project execution.

MINDSET: Project Value Modelling requires an open and critical mindset. It is important to look beyond your usual way of working so that there is room for innovation and collaboration. Step by step, you will move from defining relatively abstract values to concrete needs and tasks. Discussion, prioritization, and reflection are vital for bringing your ideas to the next level.

WHEN? Project Value Modelling is specifically of interest before or at the start of a new project that is challenging or highly complex due to the different stakeholders and values involved. It can be used in small groups or individually in the following ways:
- Deciding whether or not to engage in a project.
- Developing a value co-creation and value capture strategy for a project.
- Uncovering, visualising, and communicating the added value of the designer.
- Strengthening collaboration through defining shared goals, aligning roles and facilitating understanding of each other's motivations.

TIPS & CONCERNS
Discuss and think aloud to foster a critical and reflective attitude.

Involve a moderator or critical friend who is not part of the project. This can be someone to help you think outside the box and substantiate your answers.

Focus on the most important aspects and constantly evaluate how your answers are different from those of your partners and competitors.

LIMITATIONS
The tool supporting this method is specifically designed for projects that require actors to reconcile multiple values.

The method can be used to design a value model for a starting firm or a new market approach. It is less suitable for developing firm-level strategies that cover a more diverse range of situations.

133

HOW? This method is supported by a blueprint consisting of eight steps with accompanying questions. The blueprint can be printed on a large sheet of paper and then added with Post-its in the following order. See also the blueprint diagram for each step in detail: (tudelft.nl/valueconflicts)
Step 1: Determine the goal of your exercise.
Step 2: Choose a case or project and write it down in the middle of the paper.
Step 3: Identify the most important values that need to be created and captured by answering the questions of Step 1 (values for others) and Step 2 (values for yourself).
Step 4: Prioritize these values by answering the questions of Step 3 and 4 about expertise and risks.

Step 5: Take a look at the entire blueprint; remove answers that are less important and add or specify answers if needed.
Step 6: Determine how you can secure these values by answering the questions of Steps 5–8 about partners, activities, collaboration agreements, and the revenue model.
Step 7: Reflect on how your answers relate to each other and make changes if needed.
Step 8: To wrap up, identify which opportunities or challenges you consider most important for reaching your determined goal, and think of concrete actions to take.
Step 9: Check the intended outcome, namely having a better idea of what to go for, what to look out for, and how to achieve this.

REFERENCES & FURTHER READING: Bos-de Vos, M., 2018. A toolkit for developing project-specific value capture strategies. In Bos-de Vos, M., *Open for Business: Project-Specific Value Capture Strategies of Architectural Firms* (pp. 161-194). PhD thesis, Delft University of Technology. Delft: A+ BE| Architecture and the Built Environment. / Bos-de Vos, M., Volker, L., & Wamelink, J.W.F., 2019. Enhancing value capture by managing risks of value slippage in and across projects. *International Journal of Project Management*, 37(5), 767-783. / Wikström, K., Artto, K., Kujala, J., & Söderlund, J., 2010. Business models in project business. *International Journal of Project Management*, 28(8), 832-841.

KEY PARTNERS

- bicycle shop
- sponsors
- webprovider
- mobile phone provider

KEY ACTIVITIES

- delivering packages on bicycles
- maintenance
- acquisition
- administration
- planning

KEY RESOURCES

- workspace
- personnel
- smartphones
- website
- laptops
- bicycles (+ trailers)
- bags
- cycling clothes
- good physical condition

VALUE PROPOSITION

- saving the customer's time by offering an ecofriendly, fast, cost-effective and reliable bicycle courier service
- taking care of: internal mail, PO-box delivery, express delivery and one-day service

CUSTOMER RELATIONSHIPS

- face-to-face
- telephone
- e-mail
- newsletter,
- website

CHANNELS

- Mouth-to-mouth
- (social) media
- telephone
- pay online
- couriers

CUSTOMER SEGMENTS

- anyone who needs packages and letters (max. 1 x 0.5 x 0.5 m and up to 50 kg) to be delivered quickly within a 15 km radius.

COST STRUCTURE

- Workspace
- personnel
- bicycles + equipment
- insurance
- maintenance
- laptops
- smartphones
- website

REVENUE STREAMS

- paying customers
- shirt sponsoring

Example of a business model canvas filled in for a bicycle courier service. (After Osterwalder & Pigneur, 2010)

Business Modelling

Business Modelling is a method for developing the reason to exist of our designs from a business point of view. The Business Model Canvas serves as a checklist to generate business ideas; it also structures, discusses, and evaluates these ideas on a conceptual level.

WHAT & WHY? Business Modelling enables you to see the economic relevance and context of the product or service that you are developing: What exactly is the added value of the product or service and for whom and how can you generate a revenue?

MINDSET: Business Modelling requires both an analytical and creative mindset, as well as an interest in how organisations 'get things done'. Discussion with other stakeholders, prioritisation, and reflection are needed to fill in the blank spots.

WHEN? Business Modelling with the Business Model Canvas as a tool can be used in various stages of the development process. In the idea generation phase, it can help you in completing ideas or in evaluating them. The same goes for the conceptual phase where you need to choose between several business concepts: Which concept can be expected to generate the required turnover or profit? Which concept will strengthen the company's competitive position? Making a perfectly detailed lamp might be your dream as a designer, but if it turns out to be affordable for a handful of buyers only, it might not make a lot of sense from a business point of view, even if it has a high profit margin.

HOW? The canvas, divided into nine areas, supports the method. Each area should be defined, and the relationship between these areas can be described using arrows and drawings. Preferably, the template should be printed on a large sheet of paper (minimum A3) so you can work on it with a team in a brainstorm-type setting. This stimulates analysis, discussion, and creativity in the group.

These nine key elements of the canvas should finally be 'aligned' so that you can create a well-defined product-service proposal, though not necessarily in this order. The nine key elements can be structured in four clusters:

Group 1 – Offering (reason to exist):
What do you offer and how is that different from the offers of competitors?
• Value Propositions

Group 2 – Infrastructure (internal):
What tasks and assets are important to deliver your Value Proposition?
• Key Activities
• Key Resources
• Key Partners

Group 3 – Customers (external):
• Customer segments
• Customer Relationship
• Channels:
  - Awareness: How do we raise awareness about our company's products and services?
  - Evaluation: How do we help customers evaluate our company's Value Proposition?
  - Purchase: How do we allow customers to purchase specific products and services?
  - Delivery: How do we deliver the product or service to customers?
  - After sales: How do we provide post-purchase customer support?

Group 4 – Finances (input-output):
What are the major costs and how are they covered?
• Cost Structure
• Revenue Streams

In a further stage, the external context of the business idea can be drawn up around the Canvas and more Canvases can be drafted to communicate the development of the new business over time.

TIPS & CONCERNS
Postpone criticism. New ideas and approaches should be welcomed, and if needed, adapt them in order to improve them.

If an idea is not realistic, change it. Or add a new idea to make it realistic. Often the trick is to turn the problem into a possibility.

When a business concept is chosen for further elaboration, draw a more detailed business plan.

This method focuses on the economic interest of organisations. You can also use it to identify social and environmental interests by adding categories to the canvas that you think are relevant, such as societal- or the environmental costs and benefits.

LIMITATIONS
Compared to a classic business plan, this Business Modelling method using the canvas represents a more conceptual level of thinking about new business development.

Ensure that the order and magnitude of the numbers are realistic enough. This could be a first step in working out several business ideas.

Do not try to put in exact numbers, such as the estimated turnover or running costs.

135

REFERENCES & FURTHER READING: Osterwalder, A. & Pigneur, Y., 2010. *Business Model Generation*. New Jersey: John Wiley & Sons Inc.

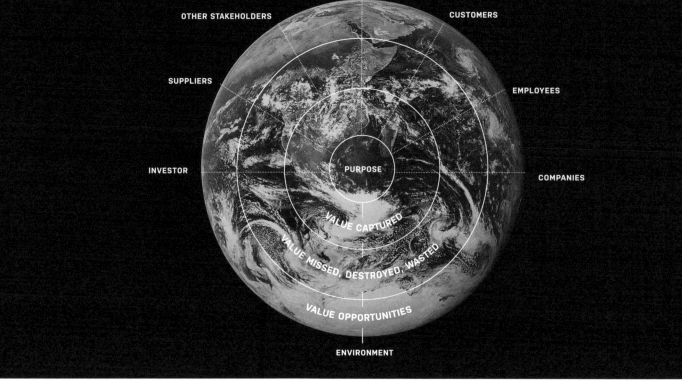

The sustainable business model is closely linked to the concept of the Circular Economy; a system of closed loops in which raw materials, components and products lose their value as little as possible, renewable energy sources are used, and systems thinking is at the core. Social inclusiveness is also a necessary part of this model.

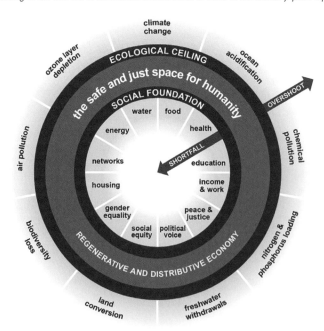

Economist Kate Raworth advocates 'Doughnut' Economics where economic growth is never a goal in itself. Humanity's 21st century challenge is to meet the needs of all within the means of the planet. The Doughnut of social and planetary boundaries is a playfully serious approach to framing that challenge, and it acts as a compass for human progress this century. The environmental ceiling consists of nine planetary boundaries. The twelve dimensions of the social foundation are derived from internationally agreed minimum social standards. Between social and planetary boundaries lies an environmentally safe and socially just space in which humanity can thrive.

Sustainable Business Modelling

Sustainable Business Modelling is a method to develop new sustainable business model ideas. The Value Mapping Tool assists in this process.

WHAT & WHY? A classic business model is typically described according to the value proposition, value creation, and value capture mechanisms. By contrast, a sustainable business model considers more stakeholders than just customers and owners/investors, and it explicitly recognises 'society' and 'environment' as stakeholders. The result is a more systemic view on doing business through the mitigation of negative impacts and the increase in positive impacts.

Designers are challenged to design product service systems that not only serve the customer but also the wider societal good. The Value Mapping Tool supports the design of your sustainable business model by understanding the positive and negative aspects of value in a network of stakeholders related to the business model. Identify conflicting values where one stakeholder benefit creates a negative for another. And Identify opportunities for business model redesign, thereby improving the overall positive impact for all stakeholders.

MINDSET: The method requires designers to understand the values missed and destroyed. The method assumes that society and environment must be equally considered as business benefits.

WHEN? Sustainable Business Modelling should be used early on in the design process.

TIPS & CONCERNS
Involve some of the actual stakeholders in the brainstorm, for example, NGOs as environment and society stakeholders, or find representations from the company, such as sustainability officers.

If the company has conducted a Life Cycle Assessment (LCA) or other sustainability assessment, this approach can help to identify important issues.

LIMITATIONS
The tool chiefly focuses on idea generation and less on implementation. Thus, it should be complemented by other tools.

137

HOW? Each ring in the value map is populated in steps through Brainstorming sessions. During each, all stakeholders need to be considered: Customers; investors and shareholders; Employees; Suppliers and partners; Environment, and Society.

Step 1: Discuss the purpose of the business. Why is the business here in the first place? What is the product or service offered by the company or business unit? What is the primary reason for the existence of the business? The motive should not be primarily financial.

Step 2: Explain the nature of the value. What value is created for the different types of stakeholders? What positive value is created and what negative value do all the stakeholders mitigate?

Step 3: Identify the consequences of the value. What is the value destroyed or missed or a negative outcome for any of the stakeholders? For example, what are the effects of waste in landfills or the loss of employment caused by automation? Are there contradicting impacts at a global and local level? Is the business missing an opportunity to capture value, or squandering value in its existing operations?

Step 4: Conduct a Brainstorming session. The brainstorm is intentionally put at the end of the process and is about blue-sky thinking. The focus is on turning the negatives into positives. What new positive value might the network create for its stakeholders through the introduction of activities and collaborations? What can you learn from competitors, suppliers, customers or even other industries?

REFERENCES & FURTHER READING: Bocken, N., Short, S., Rana, P., & Evans, S. 2013. A value mapping tool for sustainable business modelling. *Corporate Governance*, 13(5), 482-497.[NB1] / Bocken, N. M. P., Rana, P., & Short, S. W. 2015. Value mapping for sustainable business thinking. *Journal of Industrial and Production Engineering*, 32(1), 67-81. / Bocken, N. M., Schuit, C. S., & Kraaijenhagen, C. 2018. Experimenting with a circular business model: Lessons from eight cases. *Environmental innovation and societal transitions*, 28, 79-95. [NB2]. / Osterwalder, A., & Pigneur, Y. 2010. *Business model generation: a handbook for visionaries, game changers, and challengers.* John Wiley & Sons.

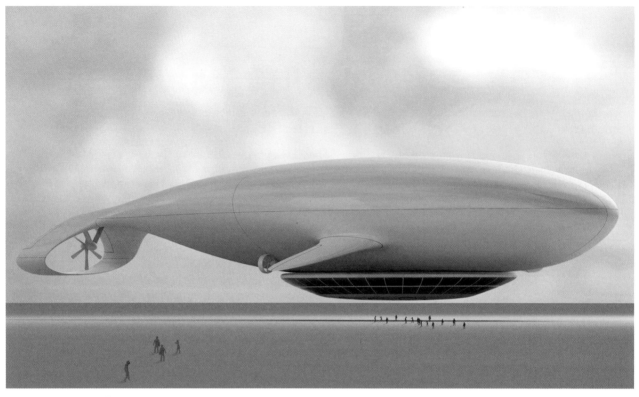

Manned Cloud is a flying hotel proposed by French designer Jean-Marie Massaud. With a capacity of 40 passengers and staffed with 15 persons, it permits people to explore the world without a trace on a 3-day cruise in 170 km/h.

From eccentric inventions to fears of invasion; from social degeneration to visions of apocalypse; literary depictions of the future reflect contemporary fears of social, technological and political change. Discouraged that modern societies are increasingly disconnected from the sources of their food, Precht Designers encourage sky-high agriculture with gardens that can be used by residents to grow their own food.

Future Visioning

Future visioning is a method used for expressing a desired future that serves as a strategic reference point and motivates innovators in an organisation. Unlike a strategic goal, a vision aims to establish a tension between 'what is' and 'what could be', so as to provide long term direction for innovations.

WHAT & WHY? To inspire an organisation, a strong future vision includes four distinguished properties: 1. *Clarity of the desired user experience:* The experience of the future innovation in a desired end state is explicitly expressed. 2. *Value drivers:* These drivers capture the unmet needs of user or the unsolved dilemmas of a user target group in the future. 3. *Artefacts:* The imagined value wishes are materialised through concrete images. 4. *Magnetism:* This entails 'the thing' that vision designers are truly passionate about and is expressed in a way that can energize others to direct their actions towards it. The art of visioning lies in capturing people's wishes for the future. People's passions, desires, and aspirations can be framed as future visions.

MINDSET: For imagining desired user experiences, it is important to listen carefully to people's wishes and to articulate these explicitly. Often times the topmost thought on a designer's mind are the imaginations and dreams about the future. These can only take root through true leaps of inspiration, which are sometimes based on observed trends and identified opportunities, and sometimes on personal inspiration or intuition.

WHEN? Future visioning is typically used in the innovation strategy development of an organisation. In principle, this is done at the start of a new organisation after the formulation of a first proposition. In most cases, the method is used again after a couple of years.

TIPS & CONCERNS

Future visions entail a specific call to action. According to Ruud van der Helm (2009), 'Dreamers dream about things being different. Visionaries envision themselves making the difference.'

The team does not only imagine what needs to be different in the future, but they also express a specific and achievable end state to make the difference.

Take the creative lead and organise a team of innovation professionals to create a vision together.

LIMITATIONS

A future vision is not a personal vision on the direction of the solution nor a vision statement for a corporate strategy.

HOW? The Future Visioning method has three main steps:

Step 1 - Turn trends into value drivers: To learn what is happening in the direct environment, this first step consists of sharing creative trend research results with a series of short presentations or talks. The group members capture user wishes of unmet needs or unsolved dilemmas by listening carefully and writing on sticky notes.

Step 2 - Create vision statements on the desired future experience:
1. In subgroups of 3 to 5 people, consider these inputs in a more in-depth way and envision desirable futures.
2. Start the conversation about a future vision by telling each other which values and desires you are interested in, and which you consider to directly affect your organisation. One by one, ask each person to go around the room and capture perceptions, ideas, sketches, and stories on sticky notes. Be open to each other's reactions and interpretations. Encourage the association of ideas on how users and organisations are, or could be responding to these values and desires.

3. Generate a bunch of ideas on strategic value opportunities in the future. These may include new user experiences, new technology interactions, or new services. If there is an idea that does not resonate, drop it and move on to the next.
4. Put those value opportunities that resonate in the team on a big sheet. Move the most compelling, common, and inspiring values together and sort them into categories.
5. Look for patterns and relationships between categories and move the sticky notes around as you continue grouping. Arrange and rearrange the sticky notes as you discuss, debate, and talk through what is unique. Do not stop until everyone is satisfied with the clusters that represent rich value drivers.
6. Take the value drivers that you identified and place them on a wall. Now, take three to a maximum of five value drivers and rephrase them in the form of short statements.

Step 3: Express the future vision for your organisation Sketch an image that illustrates the vision statement by focusing on the value drivers. From this rough image, you can materialise the future vision later on.

REFERENCES & FURTHER READING: Simonse, L.W.L., 2018. *Future visioning.* Chapter 3, p.76-83. In: Design Roadmapping: Guidebook for future foresight techniques. Amsterdam: BIS Publishers. / Mejia Sarmiento, R. & Simonse, L.W.L., 2018. *Vision Concept.* p.84-87 In: Design roadmapping: Guidebook for future foresight techniques. Amsterdam: BIS Publishers. / Van der Helm, R., 2009. The vision phenomenon: Towards a theoretical underpinning of visions of the future and the process of envisioning. *Futures,* 41(2), 96-104. .

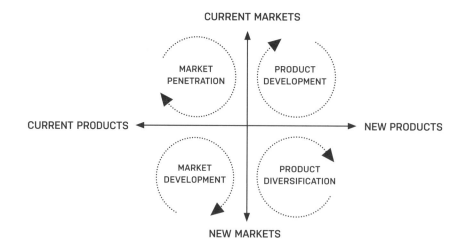

CURRENT MARKETS

MARKET
PENETRATION

PRODUCT
DEVELOPMENT

CURRENT PRODUCTS

NEW PRODUCTS

MARKET
DEVELOPMENT

PRODUCT
DIVERSIFICATION

NEW MARKETS

Ansoff Growth Matrix

The Ansoff Growth Matrix is a strategic marketing tool that specifies four alternative strategies for corporate growth, and it is based on different product-market combinations. Its basic premise is that a company's attempts to grow depend on whether it markets new or existing products in new or existing markets.

WHAT & WHY? The application of the Ansoff Growth Matrix can help you evaluate alternative growth strategies and assess which ones are likely to result in the best possible return. The matrix can also support you in making informed decisions regarding the company's product portfolio and its market position. These decisions set the direction for the company's business strategy, and they have important implications for what kinds of new products you develop. The Ansoff Growth Matrix is a two-by-two matrix with four quadrants. Each quadrant identifies generic strategies for corporate growth, as listed below:
1. *Market penetration:* The company sells existing products to existing customers.
2. *Market development:* The company sells existing products to new customers.
3. *Product development:* The company sells new products to existing customers.
4. *Diversification:* The company sells new products to new customers.

Each strategy is associated with a different level of risk, and this increases as the company moves into a new quadrant, whether vertically or horizontally. Accordingly, market development carries the lowest risk and diversification the highest risk.

MINDSET: The usage of this method requires some analytical thinking but also creativity, since it is used to generate new opportunities. The method is typically used in a team and in collaboration with stakeholders.

WHEN? In design, the Ansoff Growth Matrix is typically used for defining a company's strategic objectives in the early stages of product innovation.

HOW? Decisions about the company's growth strategy precede business and marketing strategies, and are typically made by senior innovation managers. Novice designers are unlikely to use the Ansoff Growth Matrix, yet a thorough understanding of its basic principles is valuable because growth is one of the key objectives of companies.

From a designer's standpoint, the method can best be viewed as a means of goal setting because the design, development, and marketing of a company's new products are guided by its overall growth strategy. Be reminded of the risks associated with the predetermined growth strategy.

Step 1: Define the company's current products and markets.

Step 2: Identify which quadrant best describes the company's current growth strategy.

Step 3: Define the new products and markets that the company can feasibly venture into.

Step 4: Plot each product or market combination on the two-by-two matrix.

Step 5: Assess the risks and opportunities associated with each product-market combination.

Step 6: Choose a growth strategy in consideration of the company's ambitions and ability to mitigate the risks, and exploit the opportunities associated with each option.

TIPS & CONCERNS
The Ansoff Growth Matrix does not identify the most ideal strategy; it merely provides an outline of alternative methods of achieving growth.

Ultimately it is the decision maker's responsibility to evaluate these methods while keeping in mind the company's capabilities and external conditions when making the final choice.

A constructive use of the Ansoff Growth Matrix relies heavily on a clear definition of 'new' product or market. First establish what the current products and markets are.

The four strategies carry different levels of risk, which doesn't mean that you should stick to the least risky strategy. The risks should be assessed not in isolation but in conjunction with the potential returns.

LIMITATIONS
This method is particularly useful for multi-product organisations or organisations that plan to increase their market share. The method is less applicable for small businesses with a single division or for entrepreneurial start-ups.

In practice, cases do not fall neatly into one of the four alternative strategies. For instance, an organisation may use a product development growth strategy, but might follow a market penetration strategy in certain markets.

141

REFERENCES & FURTHER READING: Ansoff, H. I., 1957. Strategies for diversification. *Harvard Business Review,* September-October, 35(5), pp. 113-124. / Johnson, G. and Scholes, K., 2002. *Exploring Corporate Strategy: Text and Cases.* 6th ed. London: Prentice Hall.

SEGMENTATION

TARGETING

POSITIONING

1. **Identifiable**: Can the organisation identify customers in each segment and to measure their characteristics?
2. **Substantial:** Are the segments large enough for the organisation to serve profitably?

3. **Accessible**: Can the organisation reach the segments through communication and distribution channels?
4. **Stable:** Are the segments likely to be stable over a long enough period of time that any marketing effort would be successful and profitable.

5. **Differentiable**: Do the needs in one segment differ meaningfully from the needs of consumers in the other segments?
6. **Actionable**: Can the organisation create products and marketing programs for attracting and serving customers in the segments identified?

Prada Marfa is an art installation by American artists Elmgreen and Dragset (2005) near Marfa, Texas. It was intended to be not repaired or maintained so it would slowly degrade. Prada provided 14 right-footed shoes and six bags, but they were stolen three days after the opening. The artists decided to restore and repair the installation. Photo: Marshall Astor, Creative Commons.

Segmentation-Targeting-Positioning

Through the processes of segmentation, targeting, and positioning, organisations can identify their potential customers, select customer groups to pursue, and formulate a value proposition that appeals to the groups.

WHAT & WHY? Segmentation-Targeting-Positioning sets the foundation for the marketing plan and the marketing mix decisions that are needed before the company launches a product or service into the market. A thorough analysis can also inform companies about new opportunities in the form of unmet needs or about underserved customer groups that companies can target by designing new offerings or revising existing ones. There is no correct way to segment a market, and many organisations often segment the same market differently based on how they view the customers.

MINDSET: Adopt a user-oriented mindset and develop a segmentation scheme based on the behaviour, needs, and preferences of users, even though the scheme can also address demographic characteristics.

WHEN? Segmentation and Targeting are useful in the opportunity identification stage to help designers refine their initial ideas based on what the target group needs and wants. Positioning is useful in the commercialisation stage, as it sets the stage for subsequent marketing mix decisions.

TIPS & CONCERNS

Positioning based on benefits and values (*What can the product or service do for me?*) resonates more with consumers than positioning on features or attributes (*What does this product or service have?*).

Keep your positioning simple and to-the-point. Do not emphasise everything that is great about your service – this will confuse your audience and dilute the message.

The positioning statement is not a slogan aimed at customers. It is used by the firm internally to guide the subsequent marketing mix decisions.

LIMITATIONS

Segmentation, targeting, and positioning are not one-off tasks. Market and competitive conditions change, as do the firm capabilities and resources, making it necessary for firms to rethink their targets and reposition their products or services.

HOW?

Step 1: Select the segmentation base you will use for dividing the market into groups:
- *Demographics, geographics, and psychographics:* Who are the customers? Where do they live? What is their lifestyle?
- *Behavioural characteristics:* How do customers behave in relation to the product or service the organisation is offering?
- *Needs and preferences:* Why do customers buy the sort of product or service offered by the organisation? What do they look for? What are their priorities? What sort of decision process do they follow?

The choice of a segmentation base depends on the characteristics of the market itself as well as the product or service in question. Whichever base you choose, the resulting segments should be identifiable, substantial, accessible, stable, differentiable, and actionable.

Step 2: Identify the most attractive segment(s) based on your assessment of each segment:
- *Worthwhile to pursue:* Are there unmet needs in the segment? What is its size, growth rate, and profit potential?
- *Suitability:* Does the segment fit the organisation's goals? Does the organisation have the resources and capabilities to serve the segment?

- *Competition in the segment:* How intense is the competition in the segment? Are there already strong, established competitors?

Step 3: Choose the targeting strategy. For small organisations with limited resources or organisations with a specialised product or service offering, the logical choice is to follow a niche strategy, which involves serving a single, narrowly defined segment. Other organisations may opt to serve all of the segments they identified as attractive, or they may even cover the entire market.

Step 4: Determine the positioning base which involves getting your product or service to occupy a distinctive place in the minds of your target groups relative to what they value and how they view existing offerings. Positioning can be based on features/attributes, benefits provided, or customer values met. Perceptual maps and value curves are helpful.

Step 5: Formulate the positioning statement. Ask yourself: why should people buy your product? The answer to this question is encapsulated in the value proposition, which is a succinct statement that specifies (a) the target market, (b) the category in which your product or service competes, (c) the unique value claim promised by the product or service, and (d) a logical, evidence-based argument for supporting the value claim.

REFERENCES & FURTHER READING: Kotler, P., & Keller, K.L., 2012. *Marketing Management* (14th ed.) Upper Saddle River, New Jersey: Prentice Hall. / Lei, N., & Moon, S.K., 2015. A Decision Support System for market-driven product positioning and design. *Decision Support Systems*, 69, 82-91. / Mullins, J.W. & Walker Jr., O.C., 2013. *Marketing management: A strategic decision-making approach* (8th ed. international). Singapore: McGraw-Hill/Irwin.

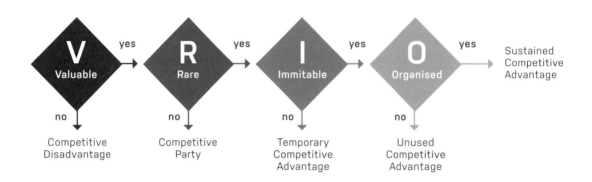

V	yes	R	yes	I	yes	O	yes	Sustained Competitive Advantage
Valuable		Rare		Immitable		Organised		

no ↓ Competitive Disadvantage

no ↓ Competitive Party

no ↓ Temporary Competitive Advantage

no ↓ Unused Competitive Advantage

The first game mastered by a computer was tic-tac-toe in 1952. In 1997 Deep Blue famously beat Garry Kasparov at chess. In a game c chess, a player typically has about 35 possible moves to choose from in a given turn. In Go, the number is closer to 200. Over an entire game, that's a whole other level of complexity. This is what makes Go an irresistible challenge to artificial intelligence (AI) researchers AlphaGo neural networks were trained on 30 million moves from games played by human experts. Then it was set learning to discover new strategies for itself, by playing thousands of games between its neural networks, and adjusting the connections using a trial-and- error process known as reinforcement learning. From october 2015 Alpha Go started beating professional Go champions.

VRIO Analysis

VRIO Analysis is a method for determining the competitive potential of an organisation's resources and capabilities, that is, what the organisation has and what it can do. Such an analysis helps you to identify the specific resources and capabilities that the organisation excels in, thereby setting it apart from competitors.

WHAT & WHY? VRIO Analysis pinpoints the internal strengths of an organisation, which can be used for exploiting opportunities and neutralising threats. Knowing which resources or capabilities the organisation excels in is vital. If the project demands a resource or a capability that the organisation does not have, managers need to take the necessary actions to nurture it, or obtain it via other means, for example by outsourcing. If these activities are out of the question, the resource requirements of the project may need rethinking.

MINDSET: With the VRIO method, you typically look inwards while simultaneously exploring the external (competitive) factors of the organisation. This method requires analytical, critical, realistic thinking and the motivation to work in teams.

WHEN? VRIO Analysis is a part of internal assessment, and it should be conducted during the planning stage of product innovation. However, VRIO Analysis can be used for evaluating an organisation at any time. The value of a resource can change over time, or new technological developments may make it easier for competitors to imitate a resource. Consequently, what used to be a source of competitive advantage may now yield only normal returns.

HOW? Assessing how imitable a resource is demands a thorough understanding of how this resource is cultivated which can take many different forms. As VRIO Analysis is fairly structured, it does not allow for substantial flexibility. It is also linear, meaning that it does not require iteration unless errors have occurred.

Step 1: Involves identifying the organisation's resources and capabilities.

Step 2: Entails assessing each resource with respect to these criteria, in the following order: value, rarity, imitability, and organisation.
• Value: Does this resource/capability add value? Value can take the form of increased efficiency, better quality, improved customer responsiveness, and greater innovation capacity.
• Rarity: Do many other organisations also possess this resource or capability?
• Imitability: Is it easy for other organisations that currently do not possess this resource or capability to acquire or develop it?
• Organisation: Do the current organisational structure and practices allow this resource or capability to be used to its full potential?

Step 3: Requires determining the competitive and economic implications of each resource based on this evaluation. Resources that are valuable, rare, inimitable, and organised are sources of sustainable competitive advantage for the organisation.

TIPS & CONCERNS

To evaluate an organisation, use the VRIO Analysis in combination with other methods such as SWOT and DESTEP analyses.

Develop an exhaustive list of resources before embarking on the analysis.

Consider all the resources of the company – tangible and intangible as well as organisational capabilities.

Individually perform VRIO Analysis for each resource or capability. The analysis should not be conducted on the organisation as a whole.

Purposefully arrange the different criteria for VRIO Analysis in a specific order. If a resource is not valuable it is not relevant if it is rare, inimitable, or organised.

As soon as one resource is negatively evaluated on a criterion, you can stop further analysis of that resource.

Regularly update the VRIO Analysis.

A resource or capability that is not valuable can hinder the development of other resources or capabilities.

LIMITATIONS

VRIO Analysis requires individual judgement and, to a certain extent, expertise on the part of the user.

VRIO Analysis merely facilitates the identification of the current sources of competitive advantage for the organisation. It does not say anything about how the new sources of competitive advantage can be fostered.

REFERENCES & FURTHER READING: Barney, J.B., 1991. Firm resources and sustained competitive advantage. *Journal of Management*, March, 17(1), pp. 99-120. / Johnson, G. & Scholes, K., 2002. *Exploring Corporate Strategy: Text and Cases*. 6th ed. London: Prentice Hall. / Mullins, J.W. & Walker, O.C., 2013. *Marketing Management, A Strategic Decision-Making Approach*. 8th ed. Singapore: McGraw-Hill/Irwin. / Wernerfelt, B., 1984. A resource-based view of the firm. *Strategic Management Journal*, April-June, 5(2), pp. 171-180.

1.
Threat of
NEW
ENTRANTS
2.
Bargaining
power of
SUPPLIERS
5.
INDUSTRY
COMPETITORS
Rivalry among
existing companies
3.
Bargaining
power of
BUYERS
4.
Threat of
SUBSTITUTE
products or
services

Roadcycling is not only about muscle power. To beat about 150 competitors at the finish line is a process that involves strategic calculation while balancing forces in ever changing circumstances. Among the many forces to deal with are wind resistance, gravity, unpredictable road- and weather conditions, forging alliances and strong opponents. Unexpected breakouts, crashes and punctures ask for fast adaptation of tactics. Cycling is probably the only athletic sport that is invented as a result of technical innovations: The chaindriven bicyle and the pneumatic tire. Like in innovative design, taking the lead in competition is beneficial if you manage to break away. At the same time this can also be a disadvantage, as you have to invest extra energy and take risks to stay ahead. Champions come and go as they both inspire and challenge young competitors.

Porter's Five Forces

Porter's Five Forces is a method that helps designers assess the attractiveness or profitability of a business environment and subsequently decide how the organisation they work for should position itself and compete in that environment.

WHAT & WHY? The method helps you to understand the forces in the organisation's environment that can affect its viability. If you know these forces, you are able to adjust your development strategy accordingly. Take advantage of a strong position or improve a weak one to help you avoid taking wrong steps in the future. The method sheds light on five competitive forces that either constrain or create strategic opportunities.

This method also helps organisations deciding the most appropriate entry- and competitive strategies when considering to pursue a partnership with key players. Or to what degree the organisation needs to differentiate its products or services from current competitors.

MINDSET: The underlying belief is that a company can sustain only if it is profitable, that is, based on financial and market growth. Whether it is a company, foundation, or non-governmental organisation, it needs to be viable – meaning that it needs to have a reason to exist. Since the method is developed in the 1970s in the Harvard Business School, the main drivers for application have been the profitability and the financial and market growth.

WHEN? When organisations are deciding whether to enter a competitive environment. Compare the attractiveness of different options such as search fields or design directions. The framework is used before starting the idea generation.

HOW? The method is based on the assessment of five competitive forces:
- *Threat of new entrants:* The extent to which it is easy to enter an industry or competitive environment, measured in terms of required knowledge, investments, and capabilities.
- *Bargaining power of suppliers:* The extent to which key suppliers influence competitive dynamics.
- *Bargaining power of buyers:* The extent to which key buyers influence competitive dynamics.
- *Threat of substitute products or services*: The numbers of products or services that meet the same basic needs in a different way.
- *Rivalry among existing competitors:* The number of competitors and the intensity of competition.

Step 1: Define the relevant competitive environment: What products or services does it include? Which ones belong to another competitive environment? Geographical scope: Is the competition national, regional, or global?

Step 2: Identify the competitive environment players: Who are the buyers? Who are the suppliers? Who are the competitors? Who are the potential entrants? What are the substitute products?

Step 3: Assess the drivers of each competitive force: Which forces are strong (unfavourable) and which ones are weak (favourable)? Why?

Step 4: Consider the combined effect of the five forces: What is the overall attractiveness of the competitive environment? What are the most important forces that determine attractiveness? How are competitors positioned in relation to the five forces?

Step 5: Analyse recent and likely future changes for each force: Which forces are stable? And which are likely to change in your favour or against your favour?

Step 6: Position your company in relation to the five forces: Can you use your company's strengths, capabilities, and resources to position them where the forces are weakest?; Can you use them to reshape the structure in your favour?

TIPS & CONCERNS
Do not define the competitive environment either too broadly or too narrowly.

Assess each force from the perspective of the organisations that are already in the competitive environment.

The competitive environment structure is dynamic, so do not limit your analysis to the current situation. Instead, try to consider trends in the strength and favourability of the five forces.

Porter's Five Forces is primarily for making strategic choices on how to position an organisation by leveraging favourable forces and protecting it against unfavourable ones. So do not stop at Step 4.

LIMITATIONS
Additional forces affect the attractiveness of a certain competitive environments. The method does not take into account the role of complementary products, strategic alliances, and governmental regulations reshaping the competitive environment.

The presence of increased globalisation and technology has significantly altered the dynamics of economic growth and competition since the model's inception in 1979.

147

REFERENCES & FURTHER READING: Kotler, P., & Keller, K. L., 2012. *Marketing Management* (14[th ed.]) Upper Saddle River, New Jersey: Prentice Hall. / Lei, N., & Moon, S. K., 2015. A Decision Support System for market-driven product positioning and design. *Decision Support Systems*, 69, 82-91. / Mullins, J.W. & Walker Jr., O.C., 2013. *Marketing management: A strategic decision-making approach* (8th ed. international). Singapore: McGraw-Hill/Irwin.

Defining the attributes to register perceptions can include feateres such as price, level of innovation, ease of use, ease of maintenance, flexibility, weight, modularity, sustainability, fair trade, et cetera. People's preferences will also be based on highly subjective criteria such as brand identity, status, conventions or favourite colours.

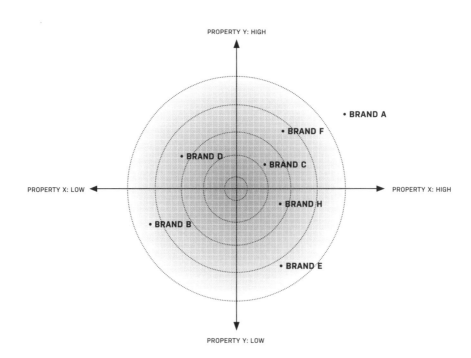

Perceptual Map

Perceptual Map, sometimes called positioning grid, is a visual representation of what consumers think about products or brands. It helps designers to assess how consumers view the company's products or brands in relation to those of competitors.

WHAT & WHY? Perceptual Maps are useful tools for building an effective marketing strategy. They provide you with valuable input for segmentation, differentiation, positioning, and the subsequent decisions on marketing mix elements. For potential new brands or products, Perceptual Maps can help you to identify market opportunities. This is typically the case when there are no current offerings that come close to customers' ideal points. Whether the product in question is existing or new, it is very important for you as a designer to know how customers perceive products and what they would like in an ideal product. You can then use this information in the actual design process.

MINDSET: Perceptual mapping typically requires analytical, critical, and realistic thinking. The method is used in teams, in collaboration with stakeholders, or both.

WHEN? Perceptual Maps can be used for existing products or brands as well as potential new ones. For existing products, this method helps you evaluate the strengths and weaknesses of competing offerings with respect to criteria that customers find important. It can also help you identify sources of competitive advantage. Perceptual Maps can reveal a need to reposition a brand or product, and they can show the dimensions along which a repositioning needs to take place.

HOW? Putting together a Perceptual Map does not require a lot of expertise and experience. While more advanced forms require the use of statistical methods, having basic Excel skills should suffice for creating a simple map. It would be helpful to do some reading on how questions should be worded and which response formats should be used; this can help prevent you from needing to collect the data all over again if the original data is unusable due to misleading wording or the use of inappropriate response formats. Doing a pilot run is advisable for refining the data collection instrument. The basic steps of creating a Perceptual Map are as follows:

Step 1: Identify the attributes (such as price and innovativeness) that potential customers are most likely to be aware of, and find the most important ones, referred to as determinant attributes.

Step 2: Identify the competing products or brands, the competitive set.

Step 3: Ask potential customers to rate each product/brand with respect to the most important attributes.

Step 4: Ask potential customers to rate how important these attributes are.

Step 5: If you received ratings for more than two attributes, select two of them, and it would be a good idea to start with the two most important ones. After this, plot the findings from Steps 3 and 4 on the map. Repeat with other attribute combinations.

TIPS & CONCERNS

Areas on the Perceptual Map where products or brands are located very closely together often indicate intense competition between them. When they are further apart, this means competition between them is low.

Areas on the Perceptual Map where there are no products or brands indicate competitive gaps.

These gaps can be considered opportunities only if customers want that particular combination of attributes.

A cluster of ideal points indicates a segment within the target market, such as a group of people with similar preferences in relation to the product of interest. The more ideal points in the cluster, the bigger the segment.

LIMITATIONS

Only two attributes at a time can be represented on a Perceptual Map. When there are more than two, multiple Perceptual Maps or a Value Curve should be used.

A Perceptual Map represents the perceived position of brands at a specific point in time. They must be updated regularly, particularly when the market is changing rapidly.

A Perceptual Map can indicate market opportunities, but it says nothing about how long the window of opportunity is or whether the organisation has the internal resources and capabilities to realise it.

REFERENCES & FURTHER READING: Mohr, J.J., Sengupta, S. 7 Slater, S.F., 2010. *Marketing of High-Technology Products and Innovations.* New Jersey: Prentice Hall. / Mullins, J.W. & Walker, O.C., 2013. *Marketing Management, A Strategic Decision-Making Approach.* 8th ed. Singapore: McGraw-Hill/Irwin. / O'Shaughnessy, J., 1995. *Competitive Marketing: A Strategic Approach.* New York: Routledge.

As well as professing a love of photocopiers, Richard Hamilton was one of the first artists to make good use of digital capabilities and sampling techniques. In reaction to Claude Shannon's 1948 essay 'A Mathematical Theory of Communication,' he enthused that it 'revealed the mind-blowing notion that electrical currents switching on and off could articulate everything—the digital era was born.' Using the collage technique he was able to bring his message accross.
(Richard Hamilton, Interior study, 1964)

Collage

A Collage is a visual representation of the context or products. It is something that designers can use for their own inspiration, as it helps them to analyse and develop visual design criteria. They can also use a Collage to inspire and communicate their ideas regarding form to stakeholders.

WHAT & WHY? Using the Collage method can brings you into the right visual mood. This is because saying a firm 'yes' or 'no' to images helps to give form to a desired meaning such as 'playful' or 'elegant' or moods such as 'satisfaction' or 'boredom'. Collages also support the generation and communication of an image of your desired context. The term *collage* derives from the French word *coller*, meaning 'glue'. This term was coined by both Georges Braque and Pablo Picasso at the beginning of the 20th century when this technique became a distinctive part of modern art. However, a design collage is not an art collage, since a design collage serves another purpose.

MINDSET: You need both a creative and analytical mind. You can use multiple ways to explore visual materials – in magazines, on the Internet, the world around you, pictures, and movies. This exploration helps you develop a sensitive eye and a feeling for form; it is a rather intuitive process and needs time for reflection.

WHEN? The need for the Collage method comes during different stages in the design process. In the problem analysis phase, it is useful to decide on the context in which your new design will intervene. In an early stage of your project, the Collage method is a very suitable means for analysing the current context. In the ideation phase, the method can help you think 'outside the box' and explore all kinds of solutions. In the concept phase, a collage can provide insights into the possibilities and restrictions for the looks of the final product.

HOW? First, determine its purpose, for example, is it instrumental in the design project as a means to generate criteria, or will it be used to communicate a design vision? Analysing collages helps you determine the criteria that needs to be fulfilled by the solution. These criteria can consist of a lifestyle of a target group, the visual appearance of a product, a context of the use and the interaction with a product, or a product position in the market.

Step 1: Determine the most suitable materials (either 2D and 3D). Allow your intuition to guide you and gather as much raw imagery as possible.

Step 2: Group together the imagery that concerns everything related, such as target group, environment, handling, actions, products, colour, and material.

Step 3: Decide on the function and meaning of the background, such as the orientation (landscape or portrait), colours, texture, and size.

Step 4: Experiment by drawing small sketches to set down the structure of the composition. Be sure to pay attention to the creation of lines and axes.

Step 5: Think about which imagery should be placed in the foreground and which in the background. Consider the size of the imagery and its relationship with the background.

Step 6: Make a provisional composition of the collage with the means at your disposal.

Step 7: Assess the overall picture: Are most of the characteristics represented?

Step 8: Once the picture meets your expectations, paste the collage.

TIPS & CONCERNS:
Make sure the collage is not too literal: If you use stereotypes, it will not inspire you or other people.

The collage should not be lacking in aesthetic qualities. As with any design, expression and aesthetics are crucial. It should be engaging and should be convincing for your clients and other stakeholders.

Your collage may only be a collection of images. Inexperienced collage makers often use simple and linear layouts by simply placing components next to each other without creating new meaning by combining components.

Novice designers tend to include too many elements. Try to make a stance with your collage, otherwise it will not help to steer the design direction.

Consider the use of zoomed-in details of pictures and scale them up or down according to your needs.

LIMITATIONS:
A collage is personal, and therefore you might find it hard to communicate its meaning to others.
It takes a lot of time to find the right imagery for a collage.

Working from a computer screen and using digital images only limits your freedom and originality.

151

REFERENCES & FURTHER READING: Wormgoor, R. & Desmet, P.M.A., 2018. *Collage for designers: invent, involve, inspire.* Delft, Delft University of Technology. / Bruens, G., 2007. *Form/Color Anatomy.* Utrecht: Lemma. / Muller, W., 2001. *Order and Meaning in Design.* Utrecht: Lemma.

Shot 18, cont. 1

Shot 19 (Shot 5 passenger?)

Walt pulls power cord.

Coffee maker falls over, pot falls, bounces. Doesn't break.

Shot 19, cont. 1 (Shot 5?)

Shot 19, cont. 2 (Shot 5?)

Walt disappointed.

Walt shuts off power strip.

Shot 20

Shot 20, cont. 1

Walt chews on power cord. Mouth bleeds.

Walt separates the two bare wires.

Shot 20, cont. 2

Shot 20, cont. 3

Power strip back on.

Walt puts wires on either side of zip cuff, moves them closer.

Storyboard by Ted Slampyak

Two styles of storyboards represent scenes from Vince Gilligan's 'Breaking Bad': 'There are many ways to entertain people; you can make them feel good; you make them feel bad.' (illustrated by Ted Slampyak and Erika Lee)

Storyboarding

Storyboarding uses visual representations of stories or narratives about designs in their context of use over a certain period of time. Storyboarding helps designers understand the existing or future context, product use, and interactions of the intended users or user groups.

WHAT & WHY? Storyboards have their origins in the movie industry, where they have been used by directors, engineers, stage managers, and even actors in planning the shooting of a movie. They consist of a sequence of pictures to tell the story; each picture is complemented by an annotation to explain the whys and whens of the actors in the story. Storyboarding in design exploits the powerful aspects of visualisation. The whole setting can be shown at a glance – where and when the interaction happens, which actions take place, how a product is used, how it behaves, and what are the lifestyles, motivations, and goals of the users. Storyboards allow you to literally (and physically) point your finger at elements during a discussion with team members and other stakeholders.

MINDSET: For Storyboarding, you need both an analytical and intuitive mindset, and you need to be motivated to work with others to enrich the story. Because Storyboarding can carry so many aspects. This method is especially suited for collaborative activities, such as Co-design.

WHEN? Storyboards can be used throughout the design process. Readers of a storyboard will experience the intended interactions, and they may also reflect on these interactions. In each phase of the process, the storyboard serves a different purpose; it can express different ideas and should have an appropriate format. At the beginning of the process, the storyboard will appear to be a rough sketch and might evoke comments and suggestions. But throughout the process, the storyboard will become more detailed, and eventually it can help you in making decisions and exploring ideas. In the final stage of the design, you can use Storyboarding to reflect on the product's form, values, and qualities.

HOW? When you use Storyboarding to develop ideas, you can start making one based on your first idea about the interaction between the product and its user. The outcome is a good conceptual idea about the interaction, as well as visualisations or written descriptions of the interaction. Both visualisations and written descriptions can be used for communication and evaluation purposes.

Step 1: Start from the following elements: subject; setting; time; development; characters, et cetera.

Step 2: Define a story and a message: What do you want the storyboard to express? Limit your story to a clear message and try to limit the number of panels you use, roughly 5 to 12 will do.

Step 3: Sketch out storylines. Place steps on the timeline before adding details; for emphasis and expression, use variations in panel sizes, white space, frames, and captions.

Step 4: Create a complete storyboard. Use short captions to complement the images instead of merely describing the content. Do not make all the panels the same – try to use a hierarchy.

TIPS & CONCERNS

Comics and movies are great sources of expressive techniques that can be applied to product design scenarios and storyboards.

Think about visual and plot elements such as camera position (close-up versus wide shot), sequence, and the style in which you visualise the storyboards.

The Visualising Interaction approach in this guide describes how to combine this method with other methods, such as Journey Mapping and Written Scenarios.

Start with an 'establishing shot' to convey where and when the story takes place. The later images can zoom in while retaining that context.

Give each storyboard a clear title that summarises the key message, especially if you make multiple storyboards.

A storyboard could lead to a video clip highlighting the unique qualities and selling points of the design.

Storyboards help you communicate with your stakeholders.

LIMITATIONS

Sketchy visualisations evoke unclarity whereas very sleek and detailed ones could be overwhelming, holding back discussion.

REFERENCES & FURTHER READING: Wormgoor, R. & Desmet, P.M.A., 2018. *Collage for designers: invent, involve, inspire.* Delft, Delft University of Technology. / Bruens, G., 2007. *Form/Color Anatomy.* Utrecht: Lemma. / Muller, W., 2001. *Order and Meaning in Design.* Utrecht: Lemma.

Jacques Tati was a French screenwriter, film director and actor. In his movies, Tati's characters are often in conflict with infrastructure, modern architecture, products and modernity in general. In 'Jour de Fête', postman François is inspired by a movie about mail delivery by airplane in America. Teased by his fellow villagers, he tries to achieve the same speed of delivery on his bicycle, but of course everything does not go as planned. In his films, Tati shows how people lose track of the changing world around them due to so-called improvements that are often driven by a combination of commerce, overconfidence in technology and wrong assumptions. (Photo by Robert Doisneau, 1949)

Written Scenario

A Written Scenario tells a story about your intended users' experiences in a specific situation. Depending on your aim, the story depicts either existing product–user interactions or possible interactions in a future situation that creates certain experiences.

WHAT & WHY? User experiences are comprehensive. Many different factors evoke our experiences. A Written Scenario is ideally suited for communicating comprehensive information. Written Scenarios read as stories or narratives that help you to bring alive existing or intended user experiences. For example, you can write a story about all the possible interactions a mother could have with your designed object and her child and between the moment she wakes up until the moment she leaves her house. You may want to describe a realistic, state-of-the-art scenario, but you can also depict a new, more futuristic and desired one.

MINDSET: The mind set is similar to the one when designing a product, that is, you iteratively rewrite your scenario, harnessing both your analytical and creative mind. However, relatively more attention is paid to time; tempo, rhythm, duration, and linear or cyclic pattern, and with or without a beginning and an end.

WHEN? Similar to storyboards, Written Scenarios can be used in the early stage of the design process to develop user criteria for interaction with a product or service, and in a later stage to generate ideas. You can also employ Written Scenarios to reflect on a developed concept, present and communicate ideas and concepts to your stakeholders, and perform concept evaluations and usability testing. Written Scenarios can be used for designing to ensure that all the participants understand and agree on the design parameters and specify the precise interactions that the system must support. Furthermore, you can use Written Scenarios to envision future scenarios, describing a desired and imagined new context with new interactions.

HOW? Before you start, you need to have a basic understanding of your intended user(s) and the interactions within a specific and imagined/intended or real context of use. Scenarios can be derived from data gathered during contextual enquiry activities. You then describe, in simple language, the interaction that needs to take place. Stakeholders can review your scenario to ensure that it accurately represents the real world or that they agree on the intended world you propose in your scenario.

- - - - - - - - - - -

Step 1: Determine the *aim of* your scenario and the required number of scenarios and length. Gather *insights* and define the *context* in which the interactions transpire.

- - - - - - - - - - -

Step 2: Determine the *actors*, your intended users, and the *goals* that the main actors have to complete. The actor has an active role in the scenario. If you have several actors,

you should establish more scenarios. Determine the starting points of the scenario, which can be a trigger or an event.

- - - - - - - - - - -

Step 3: Choose the writing style of your scenario, for example, a neutral sequence of steps or a moving and epic narrative. Start drafting the scenario.

- - - - - - - - - - -

Step 4: Bring scenario to life by writing dialogues between actors. Give your scenario an inspiring title.

- - - - - - - - - - -

Step 5: Focus on or select the most promising and successful scenario. Test it with stakeholders such as clients or intended users.

- - - - - - - - - - -

Step 6: Iterate and rewrite your scenario until you achieve your aim.

TIPS & CONCERNS
Books, comics, movies, and commercials are some means of telling a story. They can be enormous sources of inspiration for your Written Scenario.

- - - - - - - - - - -

Adding a variation to your scenario is beneficial, but do not strive to include everything in the narrative; otherwise, your message will get lost.

155

LIMITATIONS
Don't expect others to be grasped by your scenario naturally. Presenting a convincing story is difficult.

- - - - - - - - - - -

A scenario cannot cover all the possible realities.

REFERENCES & FURTHER READING: Carroll, J.M., 2000. Five reasons for scenario-based design. *Interacting with Computers*, September, 13(1), pp. 43-60. / Jacko, J.A. and Sears, A., 2002. *The Human-Computer Interaction Handbook: Fundamentals, Evolving Technologies and Emerging Applications*. New York, NY: Erlbaum and Associates.

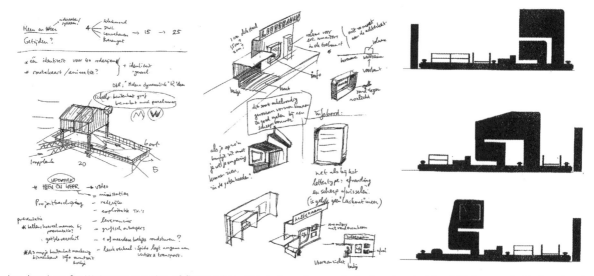

Design drawings for Waternet, a series of floating boardingstations for a watertaxis network. After initial concepts that explored the concept of boathouses it developed into a concept in line with shipping architecture. An important aspect of the study was the defintion of the silhouette, which is the main characteristic of objects floating on water.

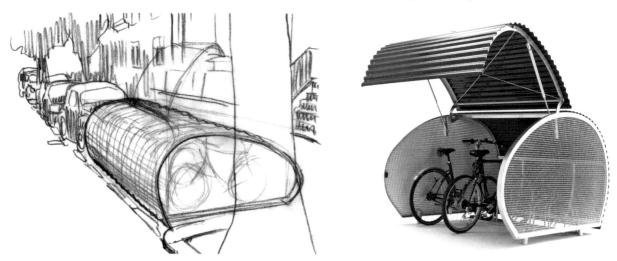

Design Drawing to define the dimensions for the development of a concept with the aim to recapter space in the public domain for parking bicycles in inner cities where people often have to park their bicycles outside. Drawing different solutions projected in between parked cars helped define and fine tune a concept of a lockable 'Fietshangar' that can be shared by neighbours to store and protect 5 bicycles. Below: documenting design elements.

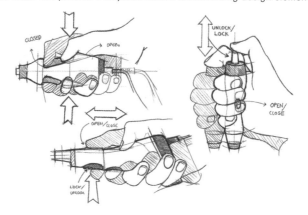

Design Drawing to Define

In the Define stage, all relevant conclusions from the previous stage are taken as part of a new brief. Sketches and other visualisations for this definition stage typically involve components such as a customer journey, a collage, or preliminary sketches of a design direction, all of which then serve as a starting point for the next stage.

WHAT & WHY? The definition of a project is mostly about 'freezing' some of the starting points and defining its boundaries. A List of Requirements as well as agreements on the process such as budgets, planning, and project goals represent a rather formal part of the assignment. Other starting points that may be rather visual could focus on the contents of the project. These can be realised as an envisioned use scenario, a patient journey or a collage that visualises the style elements agreed upon.

It can also be a visual depiction of an envisioned direction concerning structure, aesthetics, interaction, proportions, size, or use. Abstract types of visual depictions that complement the design brief can be drawings concerning the design vision or the design strategy; examples include process schemes or visual storytelling canvases. Infographics and data visualisation could be helpful in this stage for communicating design goals or potential opportunities.

Drawings and other forms of visual depiction are helpful to get you and all stakeholders on the same page. They can help to align staff, departments, and different management levels of the client company.

MINDSET: Focus on capturing the design space. Visualisations and sketches in this stage are used for documenting the design elements agreed upon by the stakeholders, and these can be seen as part of the contract. Since this stage occurs early on in the project, it is important to identify and concretise what is fixed and more importantly, to leave open what is yet to be designed: no solutions, no details.

WHEN? The Define phase of a project mostly includes 'freezing' some of the starting points and defining the boundaries. This is done as a preparation for the Develop phase.

HOW? The frozen design brief, with all relevant elements, would need to be presentable enough to share them with all stakeholders. For this reason, sketches in this stage should have a rather formal character and should be properly articulated to a presentable state. Often these drawings are made with pen and paper (analogue form) and can be finished digitally using a drawing tablet. These drawings often include an elaborate use of colour and graphic aspects, such as backgrounds, frames, and layout.

REFERENCES & FURTHER READING: Fissen, J. J., & Steur, R., 2009. *Sketching.* Amsterdam: Bis Publishers. / Olofsson, E., & Sjölén, K., 2006. *Design Sketching.* KEEOS Design Books. / Robertson, S., & Bertling, T., 2013. *How to Draw.* Design Studio Press. / Hoftijzer, J. W., Sypesteyn, M., et al., 2019. *The Visionary Purpose of Visualization; A study of the 'Quinny Hubb' Design Case.* Paper presented at the E&PDE, Glasgow. / http://www.delftdesigndrawing.com/basics.html

TIPS & CONCERNS
Manage expectations. In this early communication stage, it is important to find a balance between the following tips and concerns.

Imagine future options for your client, inspire them and invite them to trust your creativity and professionalism in finding new directions.

Do not try to solve the problem right away.

Do not promise what you can't deliver.

LIMITATIONS
Sketching cannot define everything in the design brief, but it does help with the communication to diverse stakeholders.

157

'It is
important to
use your hands, that
is what distinguishes
you from a cow or a
computer operator.'

PAUL RAND

METHODS DEVELOP & DELIVER

The methods in this section help you to develop ideas and concepts and deliver them to stakeholders. For example, Brainstorming is a well-known method for generating ideas and weighted objectives to select ideas or concepts. Several methods for evaluating designs are available. For example, PrEmo assists in the evaluation of the emotional effect of a design.

159

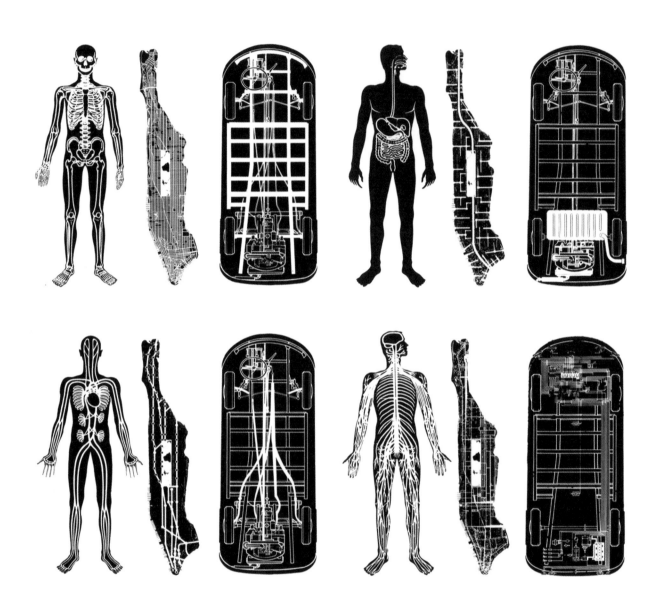

First published in 1982, German architect Oswald Mathias Ungers' City Metaphors juxtaposes more than 100 various city maps throughout history with images of flora and fauna and other images from science and nature. Ungers assigns each a title; a single descriptive word printed in both English and German. In Ungers' vision, the divisions of Venice are transformed into a handshake and the 1809 plan of St Gallen becomes a womb. Ungers writes in his foreword: 'Without a comprehensive vision reality will appear as a mass of unrelated phenomenon and meaningless facts, in other words, totally chaotic. In such a world it would be like living in a vacuum; everything would be of equal importance; nothing could attract our attention; and there would be no possibility to utilize the mind.' A classic of creative cartography and visual thinking, City Metaphors is also an experiment in conscious vision-building.

Analogies & Metaphors

Analogies & Metaphors help designers to find inspiration for the development and communication of a design direction. They can also help designers identify new solutions that are derived from a mapping process between inspirational sources and a target domain, which is the problem to be solved.

WHAT & WHY? When using Analogies, inspirational sources can be either closely or distantly related to the current problem. For example, a close analogy for a new office air conditioning system might be air conditioning systems in cars, hotels, or airplanes. A distant analogy might be a self-cooling termite mound.

Metaphors, on the other hand, are mainly helpful for communicating particular messages to users. They typically do not help in solving practical problems, but they represent the meaning a product evokes. For example, you can attribute a certain personality description such as adventurous, feminine, or trustworthy to a solution concept, and you can then use that description to evoke particular emotions. When using metaphors, the source of inspiration should be from distantly related domains.

MINDSET: For Analogies, use your analytical skills to understand the compared artefact. For both Analogies and Metaphors, you need an open and creative mind to find the ones that inspire you. For technology-oriented individuals, metaphors might be too vague and confusing.

WHEN? Metaphors are useful when framing a problem and defining a design goal, whereas Analogies are typically used for ideation and conceptualisation. Analogies are typically used for conceptualisation, starting from a clear problem definition, while Metaphors can be used for early problem framing and analyses.

HOW? Start by searching for inspirational material. If you want to come up with more creative and innovative thoughts, try searching in distant domains. When finding workable material, ask yourself why you associate that particular inspirational source with your design. You can then decide whether to implement Analogies or Metaphors by asking yourself how you will employ it in the new design solution.

When using Analogies, be careful not to simply copy the physical attributes of a given source to your problem. You need to identify relevant relationships in the remote domain and turn them into potential solutions through abstraction and transformation. The better you abstract from the relationships you observe, the more inspiration you are likely to receive. Possible procedure:

Step 1: Framing For Analogies: Frame the design problem to be solved.

For Metaphors: Frame the qualities of the experience you want to provide to users through the new design solution.

Step 2: Searching For Analogies: Search for situations where the problem has already been successfully solved. *For Metaphors:* Search for a distinct concrete entity that already has the quality you intend to convey.

Step 3: Applying For Analogies: Retrieve the relationships from the existing components and processes in the inspirational domain. Abstract from what you see, and capture the essence of that relationship. Transform and transfer the abstracted relationships to fit your new problem situation. *For Metaphors:* Retrieve the physical properties of the inspirational domain. Abstract the essence of these properties. Transform them to match the inherent constraints of the product or service at hand.

TIPS & CONCERNS

When using analogies it is important to play with both close and distant domains.

With only close domains, you risk finding obvious and unoriginal solutions.

Your success depends partly on how you abstract and transform inspiration into innovative solutions.

When applying metaphors it is a good idea to look for qualities and meanings that you want to emphasise in your concept, and then find the metaphors that encapsulate these.

Try to establish subtle yet identifiable references to the original entity.

Avoid the obvious and stereotypes that easily lead to 'kitsch' products.

LIMITATIONS

Do not waste time in trying to identify an appropriate source domain without any guarantee of arriving at a useful search.

Don't get stuck when the inspirational material does not help you find a solution. Develop a good knowledge about the source domain you are exploring to recognise such situations early on.

REFERENCES & FURTHER READING: Casakin, H. & Goldschmidt, G., 1999. Expertise and the use of visual analogy: Implications for design education. *Design Studies*, 1 March, 20(2), pp. 153-175. / Hey, J., Linsey, J., Agogino, A.M. & Wood, K.L., 2008. Analogies and metaphors in creative design. *International Journal of Engineering Education*, March, 24(2), pp. 283-294. / Madsen, K.H., 1994. A Guide to Metaphorical Design. *Communications of the ACM,* December, 37 (12), pp. 57-62. / Van Rompay, T.J.L., 2008. *Product expression: Bridging the gap between the symbolic and the concrete.* In H.N.J. Schifferstein & P. Hekkert (eds.), Product experience, pp. 333-352. Amsterdam: Elsevier.

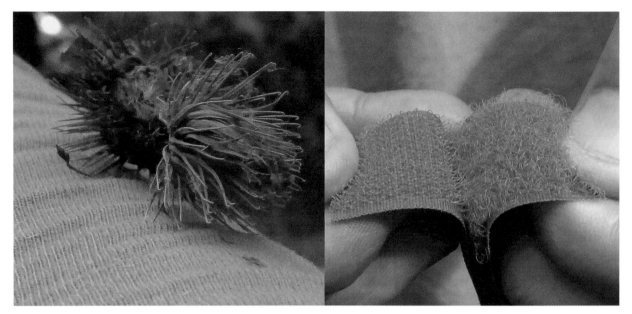

The original hook-and-loop fastener was conceived in 1941 by Swiss engineer George de Mestral. The idea came to him after a hunting trip with his dog in the Alps. He took a close look at the burs of burdock that kept sticking to his clothes and his dog's fur. It took ten years to create a mechanized process that worked.

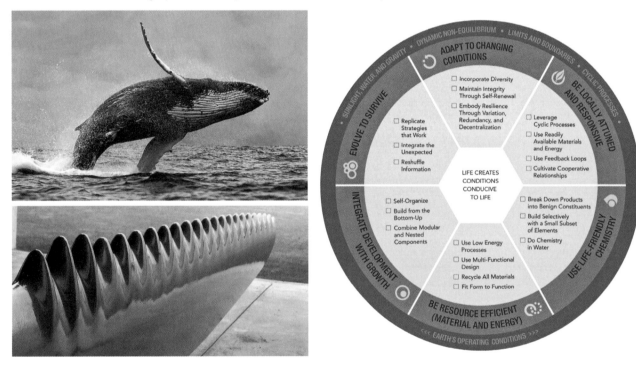

The company Whale Power from Toronto, Canada produces biomimetic blades for windturbines that generate the same amount of power at 10 miles per hour as conventional turbines generate at 17 miles per hour. These biomimetic fins reduced drag by nearly a third and improved lift by eight percent overall. (scheme: Biomimicry.net/AskNature.org)

Biomimicry

Biomimicry is an approach for sustainable innovation that is 'inspired by nature'. Nature offers a wealth of knowledge on solutions that are both effective and enhancing for the ecosystem of which they are a part, instead of harming it. By learning from biology, designers and engineers can integrate this knowledge to tackle design challenges.

WHAT & WHY? Biomimicry is about looking at nature from a different perspective, namely as a source of knowledge and inspiration for sustainable design. This approach is useful for design challenges that have no easy solution and require out-of-the-box thinking. You may already know of bio-inspired products that mimic specific natural forms, like Velcro. Biomimicry is more-encompassing – it includes knowledge of natural processes and natural systems. The system level is what makes Biomimicry an approach for Design for Sustainability and the circular economy.

The premise of Biomimicry is that in the past 3.8 billion years of evolution, nature has come up with many effective solutions to specific challenges in a way that is beneficial for the ecosystem. The rationale is that to endure in the long run, organisms need an ecosystem they can thrive in, while organisms that destroy their habitat run the risk of going extinct.

MINDSET: The core concept behind Biomimicry is that designers can apply knowledge and inspiration from biology to develop solutions. The method requires curiosity, an open and critical mindset, as well as sufficient perseverance to truly understand and integrate biological knowledge at a systems level.

WHEN? Biomimicry can be used across different stages of the design process, such as during ideation, concept development, and embodiment design. You can use it to find inspiration and insight in design principles, or to obtain detailed knowledge about specific organisms and ecosystem functions.

HOW? The Biomimicry design cycle shows much resemblance to the basic design cycle and is also used iteratively. In comparison, more emphasis is placed on the 'translation' of design challenges into biological language and on the integration of knowledge from biology. Here are the basic steps in the Biomimicry design cycle:
- *Evaluate:* Analyse your current system using ecosystem principles.
- *Scope:* Define context, identify function, and translate them to biology.
- *Discover:* Search for examples and role models.

- *Create:* Brainstorm, emulate, and select solutions.
- *Evaluate:* Evaluate your new solution using ecosystem principles.

One of the core tools in Biomimicry are the ecosystem principles. They describe generic strategies that can be found in biological systems of any size – from single celled bacteria to entire rain forests. But you can find many different examples in books on biology, ecology, and bio-inspired design.

TIPS & CONCERNS

For sustainable design, integrate the system level with ecosystem principles.

Involve biologists or ecologists. You can use Biomimicry without them, but their insights are usually highly valued by designers.

Check the websites asknature.org and eol.org to find biological information.

Know when to stop. If you study an organism long enough and have yet to understand the solution you wish to derive from your exploration, you run the risk of turning your design project into a research project that takes way too much time.

LIMITATIONS

Although Biomimicry is already being applied to design social practices, we still lack specific methods and tools for integrating social sustainability in the design process.

To date, Biomimicry offers only qualitative assessment and evaluation tools.

This method is not suited for time-constrained projects that aim to realise short-term economic benefits. It is more useful for strategic, out-of-the-box innovations.

163

REFERENCES & FURTHER READING: Benyus, J., 1997. *Biomimicry: innovation inspired by nature.* New York, William Morrow & Co. / Baumeister, D., R. Tocke, J. Dwyer, S. Ritter & J. Benyus, 2013. *Biomimicry Resource Handbook: A Seed Bank of Best Practices.* Missoula, Biomimicry 3.8. / Tempelman, E., B. van der Grinten, E.J. Mul & I. de Pauw, 2015. *Nature inspired design: a practical guide towards positive impact products.* Boekengilde, Enschede, the Netherlands.

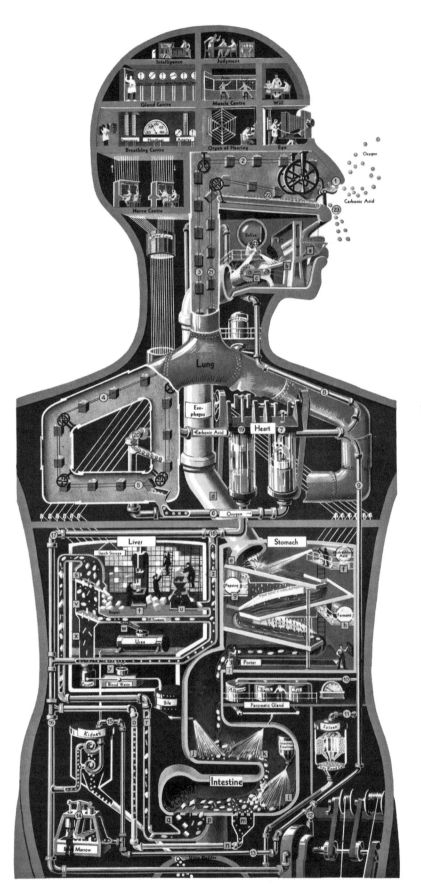
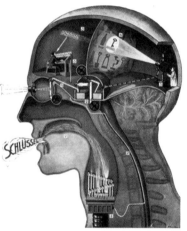

Fritz Kahn: The Man as Industrial Body. Fritz Kahn (1888-1968) is considered by many to be the founder of conceptual medical illustration. Kahn produced a series of books during the 1920s on the inner workings of the human body using analogies of modern industrial life. His modernist visualisation was fitting since he was writing during a time of great industrial and technological change, especially in Germany.

Synectics

Synectics is a comprehensive method consisting of a series of techniques. The essence of the technique lies in joining together different and apparently irrelevant elements. By making the familiar strange and the strange familiar, designers may generate surprisingly high-quality ideas.

WHAT & WHY? The Synectics method requires you to use Analogies to come up with design ideas because Analogies help you move away from the original problem statement and existing solutions. The 'clues' found in the context of the analogy should be force-fitted to the problem statement. This allows you to develop ideas based on the analogy instead of solely based on the problem definition.

MINDSET: Synectics is based on the belief that the existing world is rich in ideas that can be utilised for new solution. Similar to other creativity methods it requires an analytical mind as well as a creative one.

WHEN? The starting point for using Synectics could be a preliminary problem statement. Synectics is best applied for complex and intricate problems because the procedure is systematic and requires a relatively large investment of time and effort. Synectics can be used in teams and also individually. The method contains guidelines for a problem analysis, idea generation, and selection of alternative solutions.

HOW? Synectics can be divided into several phases, such as *problem finding and purge, excursion* (stepping aside from the normal or traditional way of doing things), *force-fitting* (the core of Synectics), and *converging.* The key here is the use of Analogies that can make the strange familiar and the familiar strange.

Start with a problem statement or briefing. Based on this, Synectics users will go through an extensive problem analysis phase, in which they can include discussion between participants if possible. This should lead to a single concrete target, which is seen to be 'the problem as understood'. In a next 'shredding the known' phase known and immediate ideas are collected and recorded. Use Analogies to estrange yourself from the original problem statement to generate inspirations for new solutions and approaches. Gordon (1962) suggested using four types of Analogies in the following sequence:

• *Personal:* Imagine that you are the product yourself.
• *Direct:* Use something from nature.
• *Symbolic:* Use art forms (such as poetry, novels, and movies) to explore how an object elicits certain traits, such as 'the humour of a bicycle'.
• *Fantasy:* Use something that is imagined and does not exist in real life yet.

TIPS & CONCERNS

Visual and auditory Synectics is a variation of the common Synectics procedure.

Introduce soothing images and music to induce an incubation phase in which the participants can daydream in a relaxed state.

After some time, switch to more active music and images so that your participants are stimulated to generate ideas.

LIMITATIONS

With an untrained group, the facilitator needs to work in one small step at a time and have enough experience to inspire the group.

Synectics can be quite demanding for inexperienced participants.

165

For the converging stage, various methods can be used, such as Itemised Response and vALUe.

Step 1: Start with the original problem statement. Invite the problem owner to present and discuss the problem briefly.

Step 2: Analyse the problem. Restate the problem, and formulate the problem as a single concrete target.

Purging - Step 3: Generate, collect, and record the first ideas that come to your mind. Be sure to shred the known.

Excursion - Step 4: Find a relevant analogy.

Step 5: Ask yourself these questions in order to explore the analogy: What types of problems occur in the analogous situation? What types of solutions are there to be found?

Force-fitting - Step 6: Force-fit various solutions to the reformulated problem statement. After this, generate, collect, and record the ideas.

Converging - Step 7: Test and evaluate the ideas. Use the Itemised Response method or another evaluation method to select ideas for further conceptualisation.

REFERENCES & FURTHER READING: Gordon, W., 1976. *Synectics, the Development of Creative Capacity.* New York, NY: Collier. / Heijne, K.G & J.D. van der Meer, 2019. *Road map for creative problem solving techniques. Organizing and facilitating group sessions.* Amsterdam: Boom. / Tassoul, M., 2006. *Creative Facilitation:* a Delft Approach. Delft: VSSD. / Wallas, G., 1926. *The art of thought.* In P.E. Vernon (eds.), Creativity. Penguin.

Brainstorming & Brainwriting

Brainstorming and Brainwriting prescribe a specific approach with rules and procedures for generating a great number of ideas. It is one of many methods used in creative thinking and is based on the assumption that quantity leads to quality.

WHAT & WHY? Brainstorming is an oral exchange of ideas, whereas Brainwriting starts with individuals writing down their ideas on their own. Both are developed with the notion that good solutions can be found when they are generated at a high quantity and when people share their thoughts with each other. Brainwriting is developed to speed up the idea generation and is much easier to facilitate than Brainstorming.

MINDSET: The methods are based on the belief that sharing thoughts between people can help with generating many ideas leading to good quality concepts. As with all diverging techniques, the overall mindset while practicing the methods is to postpone judgment.

WHEN? Brainstorming and Brainwriting can be useful during each phase of the design process, especially when initiating the generation of ideas after defining the design problem and the first set of design requirements. Because speed is encouraged, they are most effective for problems that are clearly defined as opposed to ones that are complex and ill-defined.

HOW? Work with between 4 to 15 people. Several strict rules must be followed during a Brainstorming session:
- *Postpone judgment:* During the session, try not to think about utility, importance, feasibility, and the like. Just try not to make any remarks of evaluation.
- *Be receptive to freewheeling:* You can express any idea you can think of; the wilder, the better. The session needs to allow participants to feel safe and secure.
- *Encourage 'hitchhiking':* Endeavour to come up with more ideas by making combinations and building upon the ideas of others.
- *Emphasise quantity:* The underlying idea is that quantity breeds quality. Due to the rapid succession of associations, there is little opportunity and room for judgment.

Step 1 - Task appraisal: Start with a single concrete target in the form of a 'How To?' question (see: How Tos). Write down a clearly visible problem statement. Let the problem owner explain the task and allow them to ask questions for clarification. Explain the four rules of diverging, and a warm-up exercise to get the group in the right mindset.

Step 2 - Diverge: For Brainstorming: Ask the group to share out loud all ideas that pop into their heads. Nominate someone to be the facilitator, whose job is to capture all the ideas on a flip chart.

For Brainwriting: Ask the group to write all their ideas in silence on Post-it notes and hand them to the facilitator, who places them on a flipchart.

For both methods: If the idea generation slows down, either repeat the problem statement, encourage the group or ask provocative questions to encourage 'hitchhiking'. Continue until the target number of ideas is reached.

Step 3 - Reverge: Revisit all generated ideas by inventorying and clustering them. Once an overview is created, the team can decide to repeat Step 2 (diverging) or proceed to Step 4 (converging). An example of a reverging technique is C-Box.

Step 4 - Converge: Once many ideas have been generated, the group selects the most promising and interesting ones as input for the next phase of the design process. Define criteria to be used in this selection process. Examples of converging techniques include Itemised Response and PMI.

Step 5 - Reflect: Reflect on the process to see whether the method has provided the expected results.

TIPS & CONCERNS

See Braindrawing for an alternative method.

In case a combination of Brainstorming and Brainwriting is used all participants are allowed to share their written ideas aloud. This may encourage hitchhiking, but may hinder some people from generating ideas.

Although the term 'brainstorming' is widely known, only a few know how to carry it out effectively.

LIMITATIONS

Extrovert people may dominate a setting where ideas are shared out loud.

For more complex problems work with sub-problems without loosing sight of the problem as a whole.

Brainstorming is not suited for problems that require highly specialised knowledge.

REFERENCES & FURTHER READING: Gordon, W., 1976. *Synectics, the Development of Creative Capacity.* New York, NY: Collier. / Heijne, K.G & J.D. van der Meer, 2019. *Road map for creative problem solving techniques. Organizing and facilitating group sessions.* Amsterdam: Boom. / Tassoul, M., 2006. *Creative Facilitation*: a Delft Approach. Delft: VSSD. / Wallas, G., 1926. *The art of thought.* In P.E. Vernon (eds.), Creativity. Penguin.

What is portable? This can be interpreted in many different ways beyond preassumped features such as 'small' and 'lightweight'. When radio-cassette players became smaller, lighter and more portable in the 1980s, a subculture developed where youngsters would carry around large ghettoblasters, heavily packed with batteries. In the streets they shared their musical tastes and showed off dance moves. Also known as boom boxes, special models were designed by JVC, Hitachi, Panasonic and others. The trend eventually disappeared during the 1990s.

Braindrawing

Braindrawing is an alternative for Brainstorming where participants draw their ideas on a sheet of paper. During the session, there are several rounds where they pass the papers to each other so that they can all build upon one another's ideas. The quantity of ideas is typically lower than in Brainwriting, although the sketched ideas are more rich and elaborated.

WHAT & WHY? Drawing an idea can be powerful in communicating technical problems. Also, thoughts that are very abstract are often difficult to put into words, and such thoughts can be captured more easily in a sketch than in a verbal discussion. When drawing together, ideas can be readily communicated to one another, which is conducive to on-topic discussions and building consensus.

MINDSET: Braindrawing is pre-eminently a method that assumes participants can encourage each other as they explore one another's ideas and build upon them.

WHEN? Once initial ideas are generated – such as those in a Brainstorming session – Braindrawing can be used to elaborate on selected ideas, since ideas in words can be interpreted in many different ways by participants. For example, a tricycle can be interpreted as a kid's bike, while it could also be a speedy sports bike. Some tricycles have two wheels at the back, while others may have two wheels in the front. Once this tricycle is drawn on paper, others can either add their thoughts or draw a variant on a new sheet.

TIPS & CONCERNS

Add a catchy title to each drawing so that the ideas or concepts can be more memorable to people.

The starting point of Braindrawing can also be a set of ideas from a brainstorm.

Use A3 paper instead of A4 for an optimal expression of ideas.

Use dark coloured markers to make them legible.

Do not try to make the drawings too polished. It's all about what you draw in the content; not the quality of the drawing itself.

LIMITATIONS

Some people feel reluctant to draw and need some exercise or must be reassured.

169

HOW? It is in the nature of designers to sketch when they need to organise their thoughts, communicate ideas, or try out ideas by letting their sketch 'speak' for itself. The Braindrawing method as described here is carried out in a group of four to eight people. During the session, the same four rules in the Brainstorming and Brainwriting methods must be followed (see 'Brainstorming & Brainwriting' for the four rules).

Step 1 - Task appraisal: As in Brainstorming and Brainwriting, start with a single concrete target, for example: 'how to make something portable'. Write down the problem statement clearly and visibly for all participants, and ask the problem owner to explain the task while allowing questions for clarification. Explain the four rules of diverging and if needed, use a warm-up exercise to get the group in the right mindset.

Step 2 - Diverge: Each participant draws one idea on a sheet of A3 paper. After a few minutes, have each person pass their paper to the next team member, who needs to either add their own drawings to the initial one or start a new sketch on a new sheet of paper. This can be a variant or a completely new idea. Repeat the process several times.

Step 3 - Reverge: Revisit all generated ideas. This may be done by pitching the ideas and adding a catchy title to each drawing. In this way, a shared understanding of all generated ideas is built within the group; this is useful prior to the next step, which is converging.

Step 4 - Converge: Ask the group to select the most promising and interesting sketches to take along to the next phase of the design process. Some criteria are usually used in this selection process. Up to 10 sketches can be used when applying converging techniques such as Itemised Response, PMI, and vALUe.

REFERENCES & FURTHER READING: Heijne, K.G. & van der Meer, J.D., 2019. *Road map for creative problem solving techniques. Organizing and facilitating group sessions.*Amsterdam: Boom. / Roozenburg, N.F.M. & Eekels, J., 1995. *Product Design: Fundamentals and Methods*. Chichester: John Wiley & Sons. / Van der Lugt, R., 2001. *Sketching in design idea generation meetings*. Doctoral dissertation, Delft University of Technology.

Morphology is the study of the evolution of form. Morphology originates from the biological study of animals and their functional body parts. In the design process it is used to deconstruct an overall function in sub-functions and to generate innovative combinations.

SUPPORT KART	4 wheels A	4 wheels B	3 wheels A	3 wheels B	3 wheels C	
PUT KART INTO MOTION	Direct drive	Chain drive	Belt drive	Drive shaft	Crankshaft	
STOP KART	Disk brakes	Rim breaks	Tire breaks	Feet	Parachute	Anchor
CONTROL DIRECTION	Central axis	Ackermann				
SUPPORT DRIVER'S BODY	Saddle	Chair	Plank	Cloth		

SUB-FUNCTIONS

Example of of a morphological chart for a pedal kart. In the left column the main functions are listed. On the right for each function all possible solutions are listed. The most promising combinations are selected to be used as starting points for further development.

Morphological Chart

The Morphological Chart helps designers generate solutions in an analytical and systematic way. It is based on the deconstruction of the overall function of a product or service into sub-functions.

WHAT & WHY? The Morphological Chart is a matrix of sub-functions and solutions – also referred to as parameters and components. While functions are abstract, solutions are concrete, but they do not need to have a definite shape or size yet. The matrix enables to describe possible principal solutions by combining solutions for each sub-function.

MINDSET: Similar to methods such as Problem Definition, this approach is rather analytic, in that the deconstruction requires you to have a systematic and analytical way of working. Solutions for sub-functions need idea generation, so you also need a creative and free minds for this process.

WHEN? The Morphological Chart is useful at the beginning of the idea generation phase after some ideas have been sketched. A Function Analysis is used as a starting point to break down the overall product function into sub-functions. In most cases, a number of solutions to these sub-functions are already known, while others still need to be generated.

HOW? Start with a well-defined main function of the product or service and its sub-functions. These describe all the product characteristics needed to fulfill its function. Express these by an active verb and a measurable noun. For example, a teapot: receives water; it contains tea, and allows for holding and pouring tea in a cup. In a Morphological Chart, functions and sub-functions are independent and have no reference to material features. Through a careful selection and combination of a set of solutions, a 'principal solution' is formed.

Step 1: Formulate the main function of the product or service.

Step 2: Identify all the functions and sub-functions that are needed in the solution.

Step 3: Construct a matrix with these sub-functions as rows. For example, in designing a pedal cart, its sub-functions could be: put cart into motion; stop cart; control the direction and support the driver's body.

Step 4: Fill the rows with solutions for a particular parameter. Solutions can be found by analysing similar products or by thinking up new principles for these sub-functions. Use evaluation strategies to limit the number of principal solutions.

Step 5: Create solutions by combining one solution per row for each sub-function.

Step 6: Carefully analyse and evaluate all solutions with regard to the design requirements, and choose at least three principal solutions.

Step 7: Sketch possible ideas for the whole product based on each solution.

Step 8: Elaborate on a selection of the ideas by turning them into design proposals with more detail. For services, use methods such as roadmapping and scenarios to further detail the best service ideas.

TIPS & CONCERNS

A 10 x 10 matrix yields 10,000,000,000 solutions! To limit the number of options, analyse the rows critically and group the solutions together before making the combinations.

Use the design requirements to rank the solutions per sub-function in order of first and second preference.

Group the sub-functions in groups of decreasing importance. At first only evaluate the most important ones.

Choose one or more combinations of solutions for evaluation.

Draw all the solutions or components when you develop an idea or design proposal.

Challenge yourself by making counterintuitive combinations of solutions.

LIMITATIONS

This method is initially developed for design problems in the field of engineering design, but can also be applied to other design problems.

For service design, you need to have a very clear goal and a main function. Otherwise use less systematic methods.

171

REFERENCES & FURTHER READING: Heijne, K.G. & van der Meer, J.D., 2019. *Road map for creative problem solving techniques. Organizing and facilitating group sessions.* Amsterdam: Boom / Roozenburg, N.F.M. & Eekels, J., 1995. *Product Design: Fundamentals and Methods.* Utrecht: Lemma. / Cross, N., 1989. *Engineering Design Methods.* Chichester: Wiley. / Steen, M. Manschot, M. & Koning, N. (2011) Benefits of co-design in service design projects, *International Journal of Design*, Vol. 5(2) August 2011

Pablo Picasso: Bull's Head, 1942

SCAMPER

SCAMPER is a creativity method that can help designers improve ideas and concepts through the application of seven heuristics: substitute, combine, adapt, modify, put to another use, eliminate, and reverse.

WHAT & WHY? SCAMPER helps to create possibilities for unexpected ideas or form stepping stones to new ideas and concepts without considering feasibility or relevance at first. Each letter in the method name stands for a topic with related questions to be answered.

MINDSET: Since some of the SCAMPER questions may seem difficult or even ridiculous to be applied to a certain idea or concept, having a divergent mindset of postponing judgment is key.

WHEN? The SCAMPER method can be used in a later stage of idea generation when initial ideas or concepts already exist. The method is typically used after you have run out of ideas. SCAMPER is often used as part of a creative session to elicit a new range of ideas based on what is already on the table, which can even be a competitor's product.

HOW? When using the SCAMPER method, you will typically confront each product idea or concept with the seven heuristics by asking a number of questions per heuristic. After you have generated a satisfying number of new ideas (diverging), you can proceed by clustering the ideas (reverging) just like you would in a creative session, and then you can select the most promising ones for further detailing (converging).

Step 1
- What can be *substituted* in the idea in order to improve it?
- What materials or resources can you substitute or swap?
- What other product or process could you use to achieve the same outcome?

Step 2
- What can be *combined* to improve the idea?
- What would happen if you combined a product with another to create something new?
- What if you combine the purposes or objectives of the ideas?

Step 3
- What aspects of the idea can you *adapt* to improve it?
- How would you adapt or adjust the product so that it can serve another purpose or use?
- What else can you adapt another product which is similar to your product?

Step 4
- How could you *modify* your idea or concept to improve it?
- How could you change the shape, look, or feel of your idea?
- What would happen if you magnify or minimise the size?

Step 5
- How can the idea be *put* to another use?
- Can you use the idea somewhere else, perhaps in another industry?
- How would the product behave differently in another setting?
- Could you recycle the waste to make something new?

Step 6
- What aspects of the idea or concept can be *eliminated*?
- How would you streamline or simplify the idea?
- What features, parts, or rules could you eliminate?

Step 7
- Which part of the idea can be reversed?
- What would happen if you reversed the use process, or if you change the sequence of use?
- What if you were to try to do the exact opposite of what you are trying to do now with the idea?

TIPS & CONCERNS
The heuristics of SCAMPER is at the core of creative thinking, and these kinds of questions should occur again and again in the mind of a designer.

Ask radical questions, such as: 'What does this idea look like from the perspective of a fly?'

To reap the greatest benefits be willing to challenge your own creativity.

Avoid criticism and try not to discard seemingly unrealistic ideas.

Evaluate ideas, cluster them, select promising ideas, and proceed with detailing them. It might take a few rounds until successful results are achieved.

LIMITATIONS
It is tempting to think that success is guaranteed just by applying these seven steps. All depends on the designer's competences and experience. Therefore, SCAMPER is not very suitable for untrained designers.

173

REFERENCES & FURTHER READING: Eberle, B., 1996. *Scamper On: More Creative Games and Activities for Imagination Development*. Waco: Prufrock Press Inc. / Heijne, K.G & J.D. van der Meer, 2019. *Road map for creative problem solving techniques. Organizing and facilitating group sessions*. Amsterdam: Boom. / Osborn, A., 2007. *Your Creative Power*. Meyers Press.

The 'Egg of Columbus' refers to a brilliant idea or discovery that seems simple or easy after the fact. Christopher Columbus, having been told that finding a new trade route was inevitable and no great accomplishment, challengend his critics to make an egg stand on its tip. After his challengers gave up, Columbus did it himself by tapping the egg on the table to flatten its tip. Inventions consists of the capacity of seizing on the capabilities of a subject, and in the power of moulding and fashioning ideas suggested to it.

How to expand your mind? Olafur Eliasson (1967) is a Danish-Icelandic artist known for his sculptures and large-scale installation art employing elemental phenomena such as light, water and air temperature to enhance the viewer's experience. Photo: Pedestrian Vibes Study (2004).

How-Tos

How-Tos are problem statements written in the form of questions that support Brainstorming and idea generation. How-To questions reflect the different life phases and the stakeholders of a product-to-be.

WHAT & WHY? With How-Tos, you can formulate the hands-on design problem in various different ways to stimulate you or your team to come up with ideas. In other words, How-Tos questions deal with 'how to do something,' and the action verb is the key to forming this question. You can ask problem-questions such as, 'How can families save energy at home?' or 'How to make a thermostat attractive to each family member, young and old?'

MINDSET: Since How-Tos are typically used in brainstorm sessions, a free and open-minded attitude is important. For this, you need to try postponing your judgment about the possible outcomes of the How-To questions. However, the exact formulation of the How-Tos needs a more analytical approach.

WHEN? How-Tos are most helpful at the start of idea generation. The How-To way of phrasing is dynamic and inviting, and this method is very suitable for groups to use. The idea is to create a wide variety of design problem descriptions. In this way, different perspectives on the design problem will become clear to everyone involved. When using the How-To method, it is important to follow the rules for divergent thinking, such as postponing judgment. How-Tos are open-ended questions that are intended to stimulate your creativity almost immediately. Asking a wide variety of How-To questions help you gain a comprehensive overview of the problem that you are working on.

HOW? The starting point is a problem formulation. It is typically a short description of the problem or a problem statement. By formulating many different How-To questions, you can quickly generate many different design ideas. Each question is typically associated with a certain stakeholder or life phase of your product-to-be. For example, if you expect transportation to be a crucial issue in the product's life, you might ask, '*How can I fit as many products as possible in a standard shipping container?*'

Step 1 - Task appraisal: Provide a short description of the problem. After this, invite the group to name all the important stakeholders and aspects of the problem that are associated with the different life phases of a product-to-be. Use a mind map if needed.

Step 2 - Diverge: Invite the group to formulate as many How-To questions as possible from the different points of view of the stakeholders and concerning different life phases. You can use a flip chart or Post-it notes to write down the questions.

Step 3 - Reverge: Revisit all the How-Tos by using methods such as clustering. Identify common elements of the How-Tos.

Step 4 - Converge: Select a number of How-Tos that cover the different points of view, reagarding different stakeholders and product life phases.

Step 5 - Diverge: Start generating ideas with the whole group, based on How-To question until no new ideas emerge. Skip to the next How-To question until you have covered all the selected questions.

TIPS & CONCERNS
Change your How-To formulation by being either more precise or more abstract If you do not find it easy to come up with ideas.

To make questions more precise, distinguish more concrete sub-problems within your design problem and work on those.

If you need more holistic or integrated ideas, you could try to formulate your problem in more abstract ways!

Instead of using different How-Tos to come up with design ideas (Step 5), the selected How-Tos can be used to merge the ideas into one single concrete target.

LIMITATIONS
The How-To method is suitable for idea generation in the early conceptual design stage but can also be used in later stages of the design process up until detailing.

The How-To method requires participants who are familiar with the design problem at hand, preferably the ones who know about some of its stakeholders or life phases.

175

REFERENCES & FURTHER READING: Heijne, K.G. & van der Meer, J.D., 2019. *Road map for creative problem solving techniques. Organizing and facilitating group sessions.*Amsterdam: Boom / Tassoul, M., 2006. *Creative Facilitation*: a Delft Approach. Delft: VSSD.

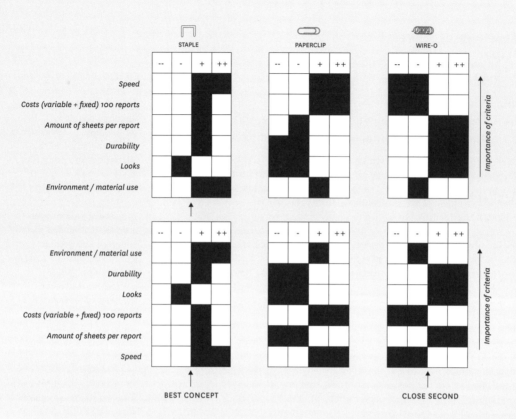

	STAPLE					PAPERCLIP					WIRE-O			
	--	-	+	++		--	-	+	++		--	-	+	++
Speed														
Costs (variable + fixed) 100 reports														
Amount of sheets per report														
Durability														
Looks														
Environment / material use														

Importance of criteria

	STAPLE					PAPERCLIP					WIRE-O			
	--	-	+	++		--	-	+	++		--	-	+	++
Environment / material use														
Durability														
Looks														
Costs (variable + fixed) 100 reports														
Amount of sheets per report														
Speed														

Importance of criteria

BEST CONCEPT   CLOSE SECOND

In a Harris profile, the main design requirements are ranked in order of importance with the most important one on top. An even number of possible scores are used to prevent neutral scoring. This way of evaluating is helpful when ideas and designs are still conceptual and not worked out in detail: imagine the black squares are building blocks of a tower. By viewing 'which way the tower of blocks would fall', a choice can be made. Colours should not be used and scores can not be added up. In general, all decision making methods are meant to initiate discussion within the development team and to structure the process of chosing. In the lower example, another design prevails because the design requirements are listed in another order. It shows how another team could have a different view on what is important.

Harris Profile

A Harris Profile is a graphic representation of the strengths and weaknesses of design concepts with respect to predefined design requirements. It is used to evaluate design concepts and facilitate decisions regarding which concepts designers should continue exploring within a design process.

WHAT & WHY? John S. Harris created this visual method in 1961 to enable fast decision making in product development. This method allows a team of developers to quickly rate the properties of several design proposals, choose a 'best' proposal, and make new combinations of high scoring properties.

A Harris Profile is based on the design requirements for your design. Whenever a number of alternative product concepts need to be compared and evaluated, you can use the Harris Profile to make your evaluation explicit. As a designer, you may often make your evaluations intuitively, and the Harris Profile can be helpful in making those intuitions more explicit so that you can discuss them with other stakeholders.

MINDSET: The method is visual and does not claim to be precise; it also does not involve calculations. This is conducive in a design setting where many iterations are made and where exact properties of design proposals might be not defined yet.

WHEN? A Harris Profile can be useful during each phase of the design process, but typically it is used after an idea generation phase when certain ideas or concepts need to be eliminated.

HOW? First, create a Harris Profile for each alternative design concept. A Harris Profile consists of an assessment of how the concept meets each of the listed design requirements. The evaluations are relative; you can compare the different concepts in terms of their performance in each criterion. A four-point scale is typically used for scoring the concepts. You should interpret the meaning of the scale positions (such as −2 = bad, −1 = moderate). Thanks to visual representation, decision-makers can quickly view the overall score of each design alternative for all the criteria and compare them easily. An important role of the Harris Profile is to make your evaluation explicit and easy to understand. The method can help you stimulate discussion with your project's stakeholders in the early phases of design, where design requirements typically change as the concepts evolve and you can thereby gain a greater shared understanding of the design problem.

Step 1: List the design requirements as fully as possible and rank them according to their importance for the design project.

Step 2: Create a four-point scale matrix next to each requirement (coded as −2, −1, +1, and +2).

Step 3: Create a Harris Profile for each of the design alternatives by evaluating the relative performance of each alternative with respect to the requirements.

Step 4: Draw the profile by marking the scores in the four-point scale matrix for all the criteria.

Step 5: Present the profiles next to each other to allow for discussion with stakeholders and to determine which design concept has the best overall score.

TIPS & CONCERNS

Use drawings to represent concepts in each profile as this will enhance the communicability of your profiles.

Cluster the criteria if possible.

Design is not a linear process, and so it is possible that you discover new design requirements while evaluating the concepts.

You can add those requirements to your Harris Profile and enhance the accuracy of your evaluation.

When attributing the −2 or +2 values to a criterion, be sure to colour all the blocks in the Harris Profile to create a quick visual overview of the overall scores.

The primary function is to communicate evaluations made after careful discussions and deliberations.

Open up discussions to sharpen the definitions of the requirements or to improve design concepts.

LIMITATIONS:

Each requirement on the four-point scales should be interpreted differently. They are not necessarily comparable.

The performance assessment of design concepts is typically an intuitive prediction and not a 'true' representations of the performance of design alternatives.

177

REFERENCES & FURTHER READING: Harris, J.S., 1961. New Product Profile Chart. *Chemical and Engineering News*, 17 April, 39(16), pp.110-118. Roozenburg, N.F.M. & Eekels, J., 1995. *Product Design: Fundamentals and Methods*. Utrecht: Lemma.

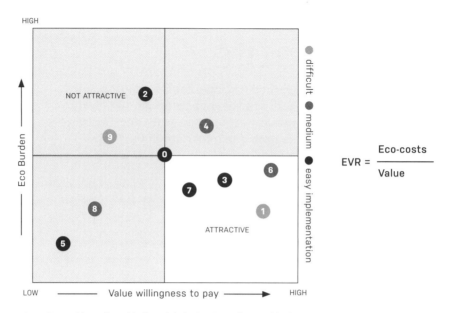

HIGH

NOT ATTRACTIVE

2

9

4

0

3

6

7

8

1

5

ATTRACTIVE

Eco Burden

LOW ——— Value willingness to pay ——→ HIGH

difficult ● medium ● easy implementation

$$EVR = \frac{Eco\text{-}costs}{Value}$$

70 years ago French designer Jean Prouvé introduced industrial design into the world of architecture with prefab elements and demountable houses that could be assembled in as little as a day. Prefab constructions can be built much cheaper and faster than traditional building methods. Prouvé started using Cross Laminated Timber (CLT) constructions that today set a new standard because they do not cause emissions, but instead store CO_2. Even high-rise buildings can be constructed in CLT. Prouvé's groundbreaking work also lives on in the new trend of prefab tiny houses that are both eco-friendly, energy efficient, affordable, and mobile.

EVR Decision Matrix

EVR refers to the expression Eco-costs / Value Ratio. The EVR Decision Matrix is a decision tool for selecting the most promising sustainable solution from a number of design alternatives on the basis of the eco-costs and the expected market value of the product. EVR is a quick method used for discussing and selecting the most promising designs.

WHAT & WHY? The EVR Decision Matrix was developed to make designers aware of this basic parameter when considering the ecological impact of product and system designs. Simply put, a dollar spent by a consumer cannot be spent again on something that burdens the planet. In Circular Design, the best scenario is one where an upcycling of products, materials, and resources can take place, as this gives them a higher value than they had originally. Examples include vintage fashion made from used clothes and high-end PVC bags made from discarded truck tarp by Freitag bags.

MINDSET: It would be beneficial for the planet Earth to create the maximum amount of value with a minimum amount of material and energy resources. With this view in mind, you can rate design proposals according to their Eco-cost to Value Ratio.

WHEN? The EVR Decision Matrix is typically used in the fuzzy front end of the design during the concept development stage, especially when the selection of materials is an issue. You may consider this in other stages of product development as well in order to structure team-based decision taking.

HOW? The basis of the tool is the product portfolio matrix, which is used to position design alternatives in terms of eco-cost and value:
- The eco-burden, such as the eco-costs or carbon footprint of a product, is on the y-axis.
- The value Willingness To Pay (WTP) is on the x-axis.

The matrix has four quadrants with a reference product in the middle. The reference product can be an existing product that the new design will compete with. The design objective is to obtain a high value with a low eco-burden. Your team assesses the value of each solution. The eco-burden can be based on intuition, but it is better to make a quick and rough assessment of the eco-cost based on the materials used, the manufacturing processes, and the end-of-life scenario. Possible procedure:

TIPS & CONCERNS:
Use either the Idemat app (idematapp.com), the LCA data book or the Excel lookup tables of the Idemat database at ecocostsvalue.com.

Each solution has a position in the matrix.

Sometimes it is handy to provide a further indication of the characteristics of the solutions by labelling each solution with a colour to indicate how difficult these are to implement.

LIMITATIONS:
The method is not applicable for assessing the most profitable design solution, since costs are not known at the fuzzy front end.

The method should not be used for benchmarking products with a major energy demand in the use phase.

Step 1: Rank the product solutions in order of relative value.

Step 2: Rank the product solutions in order of relative eco-burden such as relative eco-costs.

Step 3: Characterise the product solutions with relation to an important issue, such as the expected market volume, the ease of implementation, ease of production, and costs.

Step 4: Draw the EVR Decision Matrix on a white board or flip chart; after this, draw a red, green, or blue dot at the right spot for each product solution, and label each solution.

Step 5: Discuss the result and decide on the most attractive solutions.

REFERENCES & FURTHER READING: Vogtländer, J.G., 2011. *A quick reference guide to LCA DATA and eco-based materials selection*. Delft: VSSD. / Vogtländer, J.G., Baetens, B., Bijma, A., Brandjes, E., Lindeijer, E., Segers, M., Witte, F., Brezet, J.C. & Hendriks, Ch.F., 2010. *LCA-based assessment of sustainability: The Eco-costs/Value Ratio: EVR*. Delft: VSSD. / Vogtländer, J.G., Mestre, A., Van der Helm, R., Scheepens, A. & Wever, R., 2013. *Eco-efficient Value Creation for sustainable design and business strategies*. Delft: VSSD.

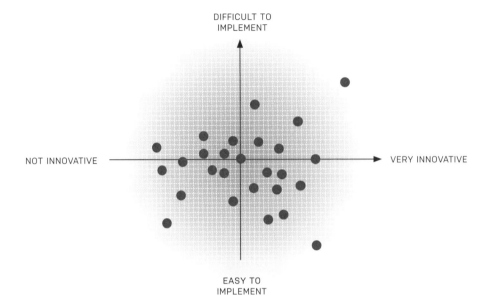

'Ora X' by total artist Bruno Munari (1907-1998) is a 'useless machine. An 'essentialists' clock where hands rotate thanks to a spring mechanism on a face without numbers. It belongs to the family of design objects where rules and chaos collide. Munari himself dedicated a poem to these two elements, which ended; 'Rules on their own are monotonous / chance alone makes us restless / The combination of rules and chance / is life is art is imagination / the balance'.

C-Box

C-Box is a method that uses a matrix that helps designers categorise and evaluate a great number of ideas. The ideas are mapped based on innovativeness and feasibility, other parameters on the axes can be chosen as well.

WHAT & WHY? C stands for creativity, and the paradox of creativity – also known as the Creadox – is that people focus on out-of-the-box thinking in divergent stages of the creative process, but once it comes to selecting ideas (converging), the innovative ideas are discarded because they seem too difficult to implement. To ensure novelty, the C-Box method was developed to create awareness about the level of novelty and feasibility of each idea. An overview can be created by mapping out the ideas along two axes.

MINDSET: Despite their fragility or novelty, all ideas should have an equal chance of surviving the selection phase. The C-Box method facilitates the consideration of each idea by giving it a chance to grow in the minds of all people participating. At this stage, the mindset should be positive, and you should remain a curious and focused mindset on inventorying and understanding each generated idea.

WHEN? A C-Box is commonly used in the early stage of idea generation when a Brainstorming session has generated a surplus of early ideas. Making a C-Box with a development team opens up discussion on the ideas and enhances the understanding of the solution space. It also helps you to reach an agreement with your team on the direction of the design process.

C-box can be a starting point for converging, such as selecting ideas once all are equally considered. It can also be a starting point for diverging, such as elaborating on ideas by moving an idea to a different quadrant. You can do this by answering questions such as 'How can I make idea X easier to implement?'

TIPS & CONCERNS

Some innovative ideas might be highly interesting but not very feasible. You could then choose to figure out ways to make such ideas more feasible without prematurely throwing them out.

Ideas that are placed closely together on the matrix are often not at all related or similar, so do not treat them as related ones.

Think of using other parameters, such as 'impact and effort of 'innovation potential and brand usability'

LIMITATIONS

C-box uses the lables 'innovativeness and feasibility' only.

181

HOW? The starting point of a C-Box is a multitude of early ideas (roughly 10 to 60). The outcome of a C-Box is an overview of these early ideas, arranged along the two axes of feasibility and novelty. Create a rough distinction between the ideas in four groups.

Step 1: Create two axes on a large sheet of paper, and construct this as a two-by-two C-Box matrix with the following as axes:
- X-axis (Novelty): Familiar ideas are at one end, while highly innovative ones are at the other end.
- Y-axis (Feasibility): One end represents 'difficult to imple-ment', and the other end represents 'easy to implement'.

Step 2: Make sure all ideas are written down or drawn on small pieces of paper, such as Post-it notes or A5 sheets.

Step 3: In your group, review and discuss the ideas, and place each idea in one of the four quadrants. Make sure

that ideas in one quadrant are situated closely to the criteria they meet best.

Step 4: Once you have placed all the ideas in the C-Box, you have created a first overview and can then reflect on it. Try asking questions such as; Are there any blind spots in the C-Box? Is there an area in the C-Box that needs further exploration?

Step 5: Proceed with one of the following steps (depending on the reflection in Step 4):
- Diverging: Elaborate on ideas by trying to move ideas from 'difficult to implement' towards 'easy to implement'.
- Diverging: Generate more ideas to fill certain gaps in the C-Box.
- Converging: Identify ideas in the 'sweet spot' of the C-Box, which is typically on the cross section of the axes; this point implies a fair amount of novelty but not too futuristic.

REFERENCES & FURTHER READING: Heijne, K.G. & van der Meer, J.D., 2019. *Road map for creative problem solving techniques. Organizing and facilitating group sessions.* Amsterdam: Boom. / Tassoul, M., 2006. *Creative Facilitation – a Delft Approach*, Delft: VSSD. / The C-Box is designed by Mark Raison (1997) and further developed and published in: Byttebier, I., Vulling, R., & Spaas, G., 2007. *Creativity Today. Tools for a creative attitude.* Amsterdam: BIS Publishers.

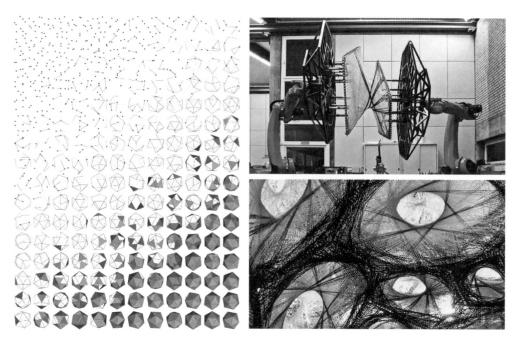

Computational design is a way to approach problems that require high-levels of complexity both from design and engineering perspectives. It enables its user to manage and coordinate many parameters at the same time, while keeping some specific constraints stable. This improves the design process since it can offer infinite alternatives. The design team can use large numbers of factors to evaluate the lifecycle performances. Feedback data can further improve the design. (images: the deterministic design workflow; carbon fibre robotic construction by Achim Menges / Institute for Computational Design)

Hyundai and Kia's new VR design evaluation system enables 20 individuals to simultaneously participate in design processes. The technology uses several development applications to carry out vehicle design quality assessments and development verification processes. A multitude of design concepts can be reviewed in ways that were previously physically impossible. It also opens tremendous potential for developing safety technologies, as participants can virtually test vehicles in a variety of simulated environments and situations. (Hyundai Motor Europe GmbH)

vALUe, IR, and PMI

The methods of vALUe, IR, and PMI are elementary means to evaluate and screen early design ideas in a systematic way. In this group of methods, vALUe stands for Advantages, Limitations, Unique elements, while IR stands for Itemised Response, and PMI means Plus, Minus, and Interesting.

WHAT & WHY? In the beginning of the ideation process, you want to find out what kinds of ideas have potential. Innovative ideas are fragile in these early stages of development, and they are easily killed by judgments such as 'too expensive', 'won't work', and 'does not fit our business'. Therefore, a structured way of evaluating early stage ideas was developed based on the convergent mindset 'affirmative judgment', which entails looking for what makes the idea good. Also, new insights in the solution space are provided by listing the pros and cons of an idea, such as new criteria or crucial parameters.

MINDSET: The principle mindset when converging is affirmative judgement. It needs a critical and analytical attitude, asking questions such as 'what makes...?' or 'why?'

WHEN? These evaluation methods are typically used during ideation when you need to screen a manageable number of ideas, such as after a brainstorm session. The methods of vALUe (also known as UALo), IR, and PMI allow ideas to be described in common terms. These methods work best just after you have selected 5 to 10 ideas from a great number of ideas. They can be used for more detailed concepts.

HOW? The vALUe, IR, and PMI methods are inventorying methods where they allow designers to review and validate ideas. By explicitly writing down the ideas in terms of pros, cons, and unique or interesting elements, designers can impose a common vocabulary on the ideas, thus making further selection easier.

Step 1: Start with a set of 5 to 10 early ideas or principal solutions.

Step 2: For each idea, list the positive features (advantages or plus) in the form of a list using questions such as: What is good about the idea? What are the strengths of this idea?

Step 3: For each idea, list the negative features (limitation or minus) using questions such as: *Which aspects would you need to improve? Which aspects may not work in its current form?*

Step 4: For each idea, list the unique (vALUe) or interesting (IR and PMI) qualities by asking

questions such as: What makes the idea interesting? What makes the idea unique? What does this idea have that other ideas don't have?

Step 5: For each idea, you now have three kinds of information:
- *Advantages* (Plusses): Use positive aspects for further development into concepts.
- *Limitations* (Minuses): Evaluate the negative aspects and try to overcome them or even turn them into opportunities.
- *Interesting*: Take the interesting aspects of the ideas to see whether you can develop them into other ideas.

Step 6: Decide upon your course of action: Are you going to develop the good ideas into concepts? If so, how many concepts? Perhaps you should combine some of the good ideas? Or will you continue with the early idea generation and seek more ideas? Will you combine interesting ideas with the good ideas, or maybe explore the interesting ideas further?

TIPS & CONCERNS:
vALUe is not a final selection method because it does not provide you with a set of requirements that is independent of your ideas.

Pluses and Minuses invites people to make decisions, but it is better to postpone that and become acquainted first with all possible ideas without deciding on which ones to discard.

PMI should be used before you set up the first version of your List of Requirements.

Once you have this LoR in place, it is a more powerful and methodically sound basis for the selection of design proposals.

LIMITATIONS:
Ideas might provide advantages in different areas. For example: idea 1 has the advantage of being lightweight. Idea 2 is not lightweight but is very cheap to manufacture. You cannot compare these ideas and select one if you do not know yet what is more important: weight or costs, or other factors.

REFERENCES & FURTHER READING: Heijne, K.G. & van der Meer, J.D., 2019. *Road map for creative problem solving techniques. Organizing and facilitating group sessions.* Amsterdam: Boom. / Isaksen, S.G. & Treffinger, D.J., 1985. *Creative problem solving: The basic course.* Buffalo, NY: Bearly Limited. / Gordon, W.J., 1961. Synectics: *The development of creative capacity.* New York: Harper & Row. / Tassoul, M., 2006. *Creative Facilitation: a Delft Approach.* Delft: VSSD.

	STAPLE	PAPERCLIP	WIRE-O
Speed	S	•	-
Costs (variable + fixed) 100 reports	S	D	-
Amount of sheets per report	+	A	+
Durability	+	T	+
Looks	S	U	+
Environment / material use	+	M	-
Σ +	3	•	3
Σ -	0	•	3
Σ S	3	•	0

BEST CONCEPT?

	STAPLE	PAPERCLIP	WIRE-O
Speed	•	S	-
Costs (variable + fixed) 100 reports	D	S	-
Amount of sheets per report	A	-	+
Durability	T	-	+
Looks	U	S	+
Environment / material use	M	-	-
Σ +	•	0	3
Σ -	•	3	3
Σ S	•	3	0

2 CONCEPTS WITH EQUAL SCORE

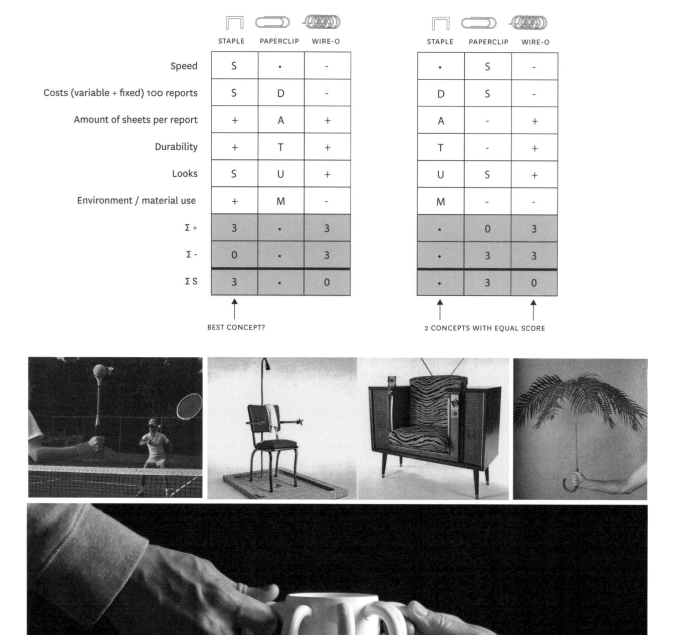

The Japanese term 'chindogu' describes a product that is un-useless: by solving one problem it creates another one. The treasures from artist Philip Garner's 'Better Living Catalog' fit in this category: Reversed Tennis, the Shower Chair, the Television Seat and the Portable Sunshade with a tropical flair to remind you of carefree island life. The Mug-a-Tron 8000 solves the age-old problem of how to hand someone a hot cup of tea or coffee without either person getting burned. However, its eight handles make it challenging to drink the hot tea or coffee.

Datum Method

The Datum Method enables designers to evaluate design alternatives using design criteria. One design is randomly chosen to be the 'datum', which by definition represents a neutral performance on each criterion. Designers need to evaluate each criterion against the datum to determine whether their design alternatives are less effective, the same, or better than the datum.

WHAT & WHY? The human mind is well equipped to intuitively compare alternatives. We designers have the innate tendency to constantly compare ideas against one another. Maybe at some point in the creative process, your first idea seems to be the best, or maybe it's your last one that is best. Maybe you got lost in the process and can't decide which one is best. In such a case, you can try the Datum Method, which is a formalised way to quickly evaluate a set of design proposals. Instead of comparing ideas randomly, a systematic approach is used so that the evaluation is complete and can be communicated well.

MINDSET: The value of the design proposals is determined on the basis of a quick judgment, and in such a case, the mindset is not analytical but holistic. After the procedure, you need an analytical approach again to determine how you can combine the positive properties of the different design proposals.

WHEN? The Datum Method is typically used after an idea generation phase in the design process whenever you need to compare a number of design proposals to arrive at a consensus or an intuitive decision. The method aims to provide you with confidence by guiding you through a systematic discussion of the criteria and by identifying the advantages and disadvantages of alternative designs.

HOW? Three judgment scores can be given: not as good (–); the same (S); or better (+). The sum of these three values will help you or your design team decide which to have the most confidence about.

The method starts with product concepts that have been developed to an equal and hence comparable level of detailing, along with a list of criteria suitable for use in this stage and in relation to the level of development. The expected outcome is a reasoned selection of design concepts that are suitable for further development.

Step 1: Arrange all the design alternatives and criteria in a matrix.

Step 2: Choose the datum, which can be a similar existing product.

Step 3: Compare the properties of the other designs with those of the datum:
– = Less good than the datum
+ = Better than the datum
S = Same as the datum

Step 4: Compare scores. If you see many pluses and few minuses, this means your alternative design is considered good. An equal spread of pluses, minuses, and sames may indicate vague and ambiguous criteria.

Step 5: Choose a new datum and iterate Steps 3 and 4. For example, take something that you consider to be a strong design from Step 4 and see whether it has many pluses.

Step 6: Repeat Steps 3, 4, and 5 until you reach consensus about the best design.

Step 7: To save time, weak designs can be omitted after the first session.

TIPS & CONCERNS

The alternatives need to be developed to an equal level and visualised as realistically as possible.

A criterion stating that the product should cost no more than € 15 or weigh no more than 800 grams cannot be judged in an early stage of the design process. Still, you may have some idea already about the differences in the cost prices of your design proposals.

When you have formulated a more general criteria, limit your number of criteria to no more than 10 items.

If Step 4 does not provide a strong profile, reformulate the criteria and make sure that a strong profile emerges.

LIMITATIONS

The method should not be seen as a sort of mathematically justified process but as a decision making aid.

Do not look at each score individually; you need to add up the totals. Each plus for a particular concept is offset by each minus given to the same concept.

A concept with two pluses, one 'S', and two minuses will have an end score of zero. Although this delivers an attractive outcome, you need to realise that this will nullify the results in the end and does not help the discussion of the concepts or criteria.

185

REFERENCES & FURTHER READING: Pugh, S., 1981. Concept selection: a method that works. In: Hubka, V. (ed.), *Review of Design Methodology*, pp. 497 – 506. Zürich: Heurista. / Roozenburg, N.F.M. & Eekels, J., 1995. *Product Design: Fundamentals and Methods*. Utrecht: Lemma.

	Weight	STAPLE Score	STAPLE Total	PAPERCLIP Score	PAPERCLIP Total	WIRE-O Score	WIRE-O Total
Speed	30	9	270	9	270	3	90
Costs (variable + fixed) 100 reports	25	7	175	8	200	2	50
Amount of sheets per report	20	6	120	2	40	10	200
Durability	10	6	60	3	30	10	100
Looks	10	4	40	3	30	9	90
Environment / material use	5	9	45	7	35	4	20
Total score	100		710		605		550

BEST CONCEPT (Staple)

	Weight	Score	Total	Score	Total	Score	Total
Environment / material use	30	9	270	7	210	4	120
Durability	25	6	150	3	75	10	250
Looks	25	4	100	3	60	9	225
Costs (variable + fixed) 100 reports	10	7	70	8	80	2	20
Amount of sheets per report	5	6	30	2	10	10	50
Speed	5	9	45	9	45	3	15
Total score	100		665		480		680

CLOSE SECOND (Staple)   BEST CONCEPT (Wire-o)

By attributing weight factors to design requirements, the choice of a certain design can be precisely motivated. Design proposals should be worked out in detail so that they can be scored. By analysing the scores, strong features of different proposals can be combined into a new one.

Many of the works of American artist Sol LeWitt explore the variations possible within the basic structure of a cube. He spoke of the cube as both the 'grammar' and the 'syntax' of the total work; literally the elemental building block from which limitless variants could be constructed. Rigorous arrays of designs, shapes, grids, and colors suggest a process of endless serial production in coherence with strict instructions and diagrams to be followed in executing the work.

Weighted Objectives

The Weighted Objectives method is an evaluation method for comparing design concepts based on the overall value of each design concept.

WHAT & WHY? Decision making is not a strong point for many designers, especially when things get complicated and alternatives seem to fairly resemble one another. The Weighted Objectives method helps you organise the discussion when a lot of detailed information is already on the table.

Like other methods for making a design concept choice, the idea behind Weighted Objectives is that decision making is not only about the outcome, but also about a way to organise the discussion. This method can provide you with an overview of parameters and opinions when the decision-making process becomes overly complicated. While discussing the matrix, new ideas and new combinations of properties can appear.

MINDSET: As the name indicates the method requires a systematic and analytical mentality, in which you rely on the assumptions and calculations.

WHEN? This method is best suited for situations when a decision needs to be made between a selected number of design alternatives, design concepts, or principal solutions. Usually, the Weighted Objectives method is used when you evaluate design concepts and when you decide which design concept should be developed in greater detail. The Weighted Objectives method enables you to sum up the scores of all criteria into a numerical value for each design alternative.

HOW? The Weighted Objective method assigns scores to the degree to which a design alternative satisfies a criterion. The criteria that are used to evaluate the design alternatives might differ in their importance. For example, the cost price might be of less importance than appealing aesthetics. The Weighted Objectives method allows you to take into account the difference in importance between criteria by assigning weights according to their importance for the evaluation. You can rank each of the weights on a scale from 1 to 5 or decide on a total sum of the weights of the criteria (usually 100). For example, the environmental impact is 20 and the production costst is 10.

Step 1: Select the criteria for evaluation; the selection will be made according to the items in the criteria.

Step 2: Choose three to five concepts for evaluation.

Step 3: Assign weights to the criteria. These could be up for discussion in the development team.

Step 4: Construct a matrix, with the criteria in rows and the concepts in columns.

Step 5 Attribute values to how each concept meets a criterion. Rank the scores of the concepts from 1 to 10.

Step 6: Calculate the overall score of each concept by summing up the scores on each criterion, and make sure you take into account the weight factor.

Step 7: The concept with the highest score is the preferred concept.

TIPS & CONCERNS

The team needs to review both the weights assigned to the criteria and the scores of the concepts according to all the criteria.

To determine the weight factors of the criteria. It is recommended that you compare the criteria in pairs to attribute a weight factor to each of them, for example, environmental versus production costs and production costs versus aesthetic pleasure.

LIMITATIONS

The numerical outcomes seem quite exact, but small differences in scores bear no significance to the decision to be taken.

Close results need to be discussed in the team.

A concept that scores low might still be chosen, because it has more potential for improvement in a later stage.

187

REFERENCES & FURTHER READING: Roozenburg, N.F.M. & Eekels, J., 1995. *Product Design: Fundamentals and Methods.* Utrecht: Lemma. / Roozenburg, N.F.M. & Eekels, J., 1998. *Product Ontwerpen: Structuur en Methoden.* 2nd ed. Utrecht: Lemma.

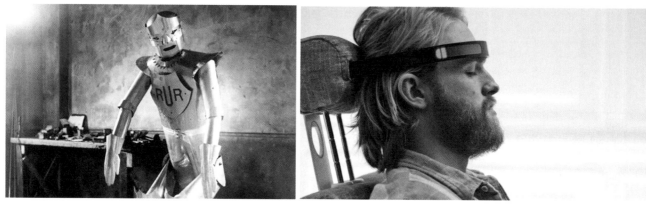

Science fiction has been called 'the literature of ideas', and often explores the potential consequences of scientific, social, and technological innovations. It started with Mary Shelley's 200-year-old Frankenstein creature who is more alive than ever in his new role as the bogeyman of artificial intelligence (AI). Supermale from 1902 is a novel by French author Alfred Jarry, revolving around a race between a train and a team of cyclists fuelled by perpetual-motion food, and the exploits of endurance and sexual athleticism. The word 'robot' entered world literature in 1921, via the Czech Karel Čapek's play RUR (Rossum's Universal Robots). Today series like Black Mirror (Netflix) further explore new techno-worlds through storytelling.

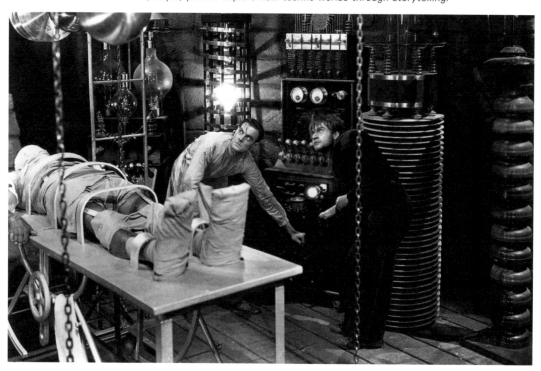

Storytelling

Storytelling is a method for designers to seek input from consumers and users on ideas early on in the design process. The narratives added to the designcocept enable consumers to immerse themselves either in a new world or in the use setting.

WHAT & WHY? Stories serve as early input for your innovative idea and can filter out conservative responses that are typically present when an idea is new. This input helps you to check whether your idea meets the consumers' needs (present or future) or whether it adds value to them. This consumer input is only valuable when the consumer understands the new idea well.

Stories trigger a special kind of imagination that is called narrative transportation. When we watch a movie or read, we sometimes forget the world around us, and while immersed in this story world, we may have a clear image of this world in our heads and can even share the feelings and thoughts of the main character that can feel like a real-life experience. You can explore research questions regarding general attitudes, believability, ease of use perceptions, benefits, or disadvantages. Try to explore the user's recognition and even their evaluation of current, new, or future needs and intended meanings. You can use this input to improve your idea, and a new story about the idea may emerge. Stories could be discussed with stakeholders so that they also can experience the use and benefits; this allows them to generate a clear picture of the idea and assess possible consequences for consumers' daily practices. Sometimes the story is accompanied by visualisations, which can either be in a text or video format.

MINDSET: The art of writing stories is to identify the main theme and the variation from the story's beginning to its end. One pitfall is to construct an overly compelling story with extraneous details.

WHEN? For really new product ideas, a story is a useful prototyping tool in the early phase of the design process.

HOW? Present multiple stories to the same participants (monadic or comparative testing). Visuals helps to distinguish the stories. participants tend to take the depicted content into account in their evaluation, and thus the mindset rules about avoiding emotions and rich details also apply here. Simple drawings are sufficient. Avoid facial expressions and use a consistent style.

Step 1: Determine how many ideas you want input on, what kind of input you would like to get, and from whom. Decide on the format (as in visualisations, text, or video).

Step 2: Write the story, and transform your need for input into a list of questions.

Step 3: Select and invite participants.

Step 4: Let them read or watch the story. Encourage attentive reading.

Step 5: Interview the participants or let them complete a survey. Encourage them to share their opinion and emphasise that there are no right or wrong answers.

Step 6: Analyse your data, improve your idea.

Step 7: Develop a new story.

Step 8: Discuss your findings and improvements with your stakeholders.

TIPS & CONCERNS

Develop writing skills and general development by reading books.

Use simple language and avoid the overuse of adjectives.

Avoid strong emotional fluctuations. Otherwise, you will get undesired 'emotion-in equals emotion-out' effects in the obtained consumer input.

First set the scene, followed by an imaginable plot with events and outcomes in the middle and concluding with a neutral ending.

Avoid an obvious happy ending for it will make your intentions unclear. You want an evaluation of the idea, not of the story.

LIMITATIONS

Valuable input is only possible when consumers understand the idea.

Misunderstandings that are resolved through discussion can be valuable input for improvement of your idea and story.

Having only textual explanations of product details in a story format will not allow all consumers to imagine them the same way. At that point, different prototyping methods will be more suitable.

189

REFERENCES & FURTHER READING: Van Laer, T., Edson Escalas, J., Ludwig, S., & Van Den Hende, E.A. (2018). What happens in Vegas stays on TripAdvisor? A theory and technique to understand narrativity in consumer reviews. *Journal of Consumer Research.* / Schweitzer, F., & Van den Hende, E.A. (2017). Drivers and consequences of narrative transportation: understanding the role of stories and domain⊠specific skills in improving radically new products. *Journal of Product Innovation Management,* 34(1), 101-118. / Van den Hende, E.A., & Schoormans, J.P.L. (2012). The story is as good as the real thing: Early customer input on product applications of radically new technologies. *Journal of Product Innovation Management,* 29(4), 655-666.

The Internet of Things (IoT) can effectively be defined as the grid of interconnected gadgets, sensors and devices that make up most of the modern internet which supplies us with big data. A Smart city is an urban area that uses all these sensors to collect data and then use insights gained to manage traffic and transportation systems, power plants, water supply networks, crime detection and other community services. Artificial intuition is an essential part of these systems, like in designing self-driving cars. Reinforcement learning and deep learning networks use big data to enable autonomous decisions about prediction, obstacle avoidance, path bending, and so on.

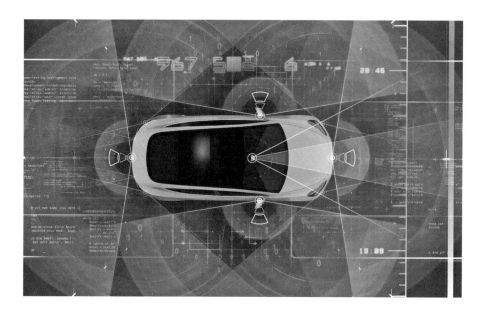

Usage Analytics

Usage Analytics is a set of methods for obtaining actionable knowledge for either designers, users, or other stakeholders. This information comes from quantitative data that products or services generate during the use stage of their lifecycle.

WHAT & WHY? Real-world usage of products and services does not always correspond to the expectations that you have envisioned. Having insight into actual usage can inspire the (re)design and (re)engineering process that results in products and services that better fit the users' needs. The approach of Usage Analytics comprises practices, methods, and tools to acquire, analyse, and interpret quantitative data from various sources. This can be done through surveys, observations, or maintenance reports. Thanks to the World Wide Web and the Internet of Things, effective large-scale detailed data collection is now possible from web logs and embedded sensors. Providing deeper insights into interaction behaviours and experiences of individuals, such as their handling of physical products and clicking on websites. Or aggregated behaviours of user populations, such as the average use of a product feature across all users.

MINDSET: Designers should anticipate that the actual use of products or services may reveal patterns that were unforeseen during the initial design process. You need to be open to use insights from Usage Analytics to improve the product or service and to recognise the opportunity to complement it using qualitative insights.

WHEN? Usage Analytics is an evaluative design approach that is applicable to intermediate prototypes throughout iterative, agile, or lean design processes, and even to fully-finished products or services after their deployment or sale. You can apply the methods whenever there is a need to gain generalised knowledge about the phenomena observable during the use of the product or service. Typical examples are:
- Recurring patterns in user actions and interactions: Previously unknown patterns can inspire redesigns or software updates by anticipating the patterns and thereby making use easier, more comfortable, or more efficient. Knowledge about patterns can also be interesting for users and can therefore be displayed on the product or in an external app.
- Trends in product performance: A product-performance decline can indicate a need for maintenance (which can be predictive) in order to reduce unnecessary downtime.

HOW? To utilise usage data, try using a rich set of mathematical analytics and data visualisation techniques that range from descriptive statistics to predictive or diagnostic ones, as well as machine learning and simulations. You can use sophisticated data analytics tools such as an open source tools called Orange and KNIME. Also, tailor-made analytics solutions can be developed using powerful analytics packages for programming languages such as Python.

Step 1: Identify possible needs for knowledge.

Step 2: Identify data items that can help resolve the knowledge needed.

Step 3: Identify and implement means to collect and record the data (e.g. sensors, reports, and data storage means.

Step 4: Identify, prototype, and evaluate the data-processing techniques. While processing the input data to obtain insights, the actual analytics process takes form. This step is iterative, and it may involve looping back to Step 2 or 3. Typically the first iteration involves data visualisation so that you can check for the presence and the nature of potentially interesting patterns. In the last step, you define how, from the raw data, so-called features are extracted that characterise meaningful use patterns.

Step 5: After consolidating the processing steps, implement them centrally (as in server or cloud-based) or decentralised (as in edge computing inside product units).

Step 6: Perform product analytics continuously or repeatedly to support information provision or decision making.

TIPS & CONCERNS:
Use descriptive statistics including average use duration or options most selected by users. Conventional spreadsheet software can usually do the job.

More advanced analytics can be done using off-the-shelf data analytics as well as visualisation tools and software libraries for various programming languages.

Additional pre-processing steps such as data cleaning and data reordering are often needed, since raw data seldom comes in a form that is ready for direct analysis.

When collecting data privacy regulations, such as the General Data Protection Regulation have to be observed.

LIMITATIONS:
There are no 'magic algorithms' that can be fed with all the data that happens to be available, nor are there any that can find interesting patterns without any human intervention.

191

REFERENCES & FURTHER READING: Klein, P., Van der Vegte, W.F., Hribernik, K., & Thoben, K.-D., 2019. *Towards an approach integrating various levels of data analytics to exploit product-usage information in product development.* Proceedings of the Design Society: International Conference on Engineering Design, Vol. 1, Issue 1, pp. 2627-2636 / Porter, M. E. & Heppelmann, J. E., 2015. How smart, connected products are transforming companies, *Harvard Business. Review*, 93(10), pp. 96-114, 2015.

Spirit airlines introduced new seating to make the most of space in economy class inspired by passenger feedback. They are built with a composite skeleton and padded with an ultra-light weight foam. Each one is 1,2 kilogram lighter than its predecessor, helping to improve fuel efficiency. The seats feature elevated literature pockets to offer an extra 50 mm of useable legroom and an additional inch of pre-recline compared to Spirit's current seating configuration.

'Seated Design' is a method of analysing our existing design infrastructure and encouraging implementation of functional, attractive and more comfortable design solutions for seated individuals. (Lucky Jones, Parsons School of Design, New York). 'Equal' makes independent, low-emission transportation possible for people who utilise a wheelchair. Most of us tend to take the comfort of unhindered walking, running and driving for granted. Since regular cars are not designed with a disabled person in mind these lack the features and comfort needed. (Absolute Design, Croatia)

Comfort Evaluation

Comfort Evaluation is a method for assessing the experienced comfort of either existing products or new design concepts.

WHAT & WHY? The term 'comfort' is often used in relation to the marketing of products such as beds, seats, cars, clothing, handles, and even airplane tickets; on the contrary, the term 'discomfort' is utilised in many scientific studies, as it is a predictor of musculoskeletal complaints. Methods to study (dis)comfort are useful in designing for comfort or for a reduction in discomfort. There are many definitions of comfort. Despite this ongoing debate, some issues are generally accepted:
- Comfort is a construct of a subjectively defined personal nature.
- It is affected by physical, physiological, and psychological factors.
- It is a reaction of a person interacting in the environment.

MINDSET: The starting point is that comfort is a desired quality. From this perspective, the method is normative, which assumes that discomfort is an undesired situation.

WHEN? Comfort Evaluation can be conducted at various points in the design process. It can be used early on for evaluating the comfort or discomfort in an existing situation, which indicates a direction of improvement. Once a new design has progressed far enough, Comfort Evaluation can be performed on prototypes and design concepts (mock-ups), or by comparing versions of products or environments.

HOW? A designer could consider the physical interaction such as force exertion, duration of a certain posture, or pressure on body parts to design healthy products that prevent musculoskeletal disorders. These aspects are often evaluated by discomfort questionnaires. Nonetheless, the absence of discomfort does not automatically result in comfort. As comfort is also related to emotional and cognitive factors and subjective experience, both dimensions are important to assess.

The underlying factors influencing comfort and discomfort differ per product. For chairs, a distinction can be made by factors influencing comfort and discomfort. For hand tools and aircraft interiors, this distinction is not always found.

Step 1: Determine the focus of your evaluation.

Step 2: Decide on the use of only a discomfort scale, a comfort scale, or both.

Step 3: Utilise the Localized Postural Discomfort (LPD) method. The advantage of the LPD method is that you obtain an indication of the area that needs attention, giving a rough redesign direction. For comfort aspects, consider the context, the direct and social environment, and climate.

Step 4: Beware that the LPD method is not useful for sessions that run for less than an hour, as it takes time for discomfort to be noticed, especially when differences should be recorded in well-designed products or environments with a rather good level of comfort.

For brief sessions, the LPD method can also be used in a simpler manner. After spending time with the product, subjects can be asked to put red crosses on the LPD body map where they feel discomfort, and green crosses where they feel comfort. For Comfort Evaluation, conducting a 'before use' evaluation is also important due to the influence of expectations.

TIPS & CONCERNS

Make sure to ask subjects to compare two products, given that human sensors do not record absolute values.

Evaluate comfort across an appropriate sample, and not with only a single participant, as major differences exist between the things that people experience as comfortable.

Comfort differs for various activities. Therefore, when testing the environment, your participants should perform the same activities.

Temporary discomfort can make you feel more comfortable after the short moments of discomfort; low comfort expectations can lead to higher comfort evaluation in case the situation is not too unpleasant.

Ensure that the duration of (dis)comfort evaluation is as close to reality as possible. For example: using a drilling machine during the day as a professional versus for a couple of minutes as a hobby.

Recognise that when discomfort factors are present, comfort factors become secondary in the perception.

LIMITATIONS

The method does not support the decision about the desired amount of comfort or discomfort in a certain situation.

193

REFERENCES & FURTHER READING: Dianat I., Nedaei M., Mostashar Nezami M.A. 2015. The effects of tool handle shape on hand performance, usability and discomfort using masons' trowels, *International Journal of Industrial Ergonomics* 45, pp.13-20. / Hiemstra-van Mastrigt, S. 2015. *Comfortable passenger seats: Recommendations for design and research.* Unpublished doctoral thesis, Delft University of Technology, The Netherlands. / Kuijt-Evers, L.F.M., Vink P., & Looze M.P. de, 2007. Comfort predictors for different kinds of hand tools: Differences and similarities. *International Journal of Industrial Ergonomics*, 37, pp. 73-84.

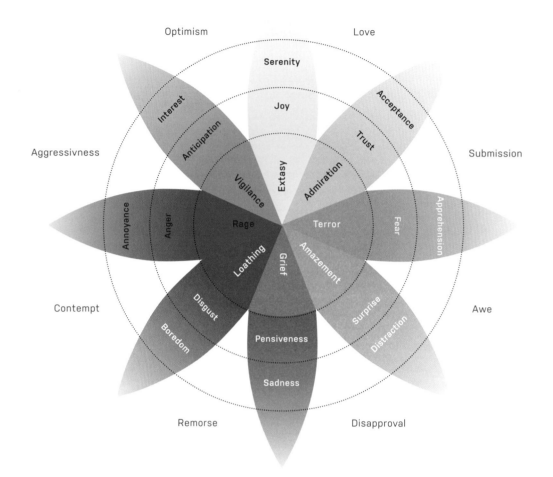

The Plutchik's wheel of emotions shows the relations between 8 primary bipolar emotions. The real challenge using emotions for design analysis is that people do not express what they think, how they feel and most importantly, they don't do what they say.

A lot of research is invested in Artificial Intelligence applications learning to decipher non-verbal cues such as vocal intonations, body language, and facial expressions. Yet instead of reliable readouts of our emotional states, they reflect our intentions and social goals. The face acts like a road sign to affect the traffic that's going past it. The relationship of expressions to emotion turns out to be very nuanced, complex and not prototypical. When shown photos of the standard Western face of fear, Trobriand Islanders saw an aggressive one. There are 19 types of smiles, but only 6 are for happiness.

PrEmo & Photo-Elicitation

Product Emotion Measurement Instrument (PrEmo) is a pictorial emotion self-report instrument. Photo-elicitation is a method of interview research that uses visual images to elicit comments. Even though we experience a range of emotions every day, it is often difficult to point out emotional expressions to show how we feel.

WHAT & WHY? Emotions are relevant to design because they influence the user experience and relation we have with a product or service. The heart of the PrEmo tool is a illustrated character that uses his face, body, and voice to express 14 different body and facial expressions that can be used for non-verbal measuring emotions.

The main purpose of photo-elicitation interviewing is to record how subjects respond to designs or products, attributing their social and personal meanings and values. The meanings and emotions elicited may differ from or supplement those obtained through verbal inquiry.

Our brain processes visuals differently from verbal communication. When the interviewer and subject collaborate to create an image sub-sets of data can be produced that are hard to capture by other traditional means of data gathering. Without these sub-sets, sometimes even the most important conclusions of research are empty when it comes to human emotion and expression.

MINDSET: Starting point for PrEmo is the believe that nuanced and mixed emotions in response to design can be measured, whereas Photo-Elicitation starts from the idea that emotions can be best understood through comprehensive stories about people's experiences.

WHEN? PrEmo can be used to increase understanding of how people feel about a particular stimulus, such as a product design, an image, a fragrance, an interior, or a service encounter. Likewise, it can also be used to ask people about how they would like to feel, how they are currently not feeling, or what they felt in previous events. Visual images can evoke emphatic understanding of how other people experience products and design. Photo-elicitation is common in participatory research with young children and marginalised communities. It is also an ideal method of qualitative research for those who are naturally visual learners. The results of a PrEmo or Photo-Elicitation study can produce a detailed profile, which can be used in various stages of a design process to assess the emotional impact of existing designs or new concepts.

TIPS & CONCERNS
Be curious and motivated to listen. Many people like to talk or share their experiences in other ways, but most people can feel when you are not curious and not listening well; when you are in a hurry, with your thoughts somewhere else; or if you are impatient. If you really want to know people's stories, they will feel it, and, if you are lucky, they will tell them to you.

LIMITATIONS
The PrEmo tool can only measure emotions, such as attraction, fascination, boredom, and dissatisfaction; it does not measure other design-relevant user information such as motivation, attitudes, and behaviour.

HOW? PrEmo has been developed for designers who are not experienced with measuring emotional responses to products or product concepts. It has the form of a card set that supports the generation of both qualitative and quantitative data.

Photo-elicitation uses photographs, video, illustrations, graffiti, or advertising, among others to support people in talking about their feelings. Either the interviewer or the subject may provide the images.

Some knowledge or experience is required for the analysis of PrEmo data. The analysis results can be used for different purposes, such as input for new product design to formulate an emotional benchmark, input for concept selection to select the concept that evokes the most positive emotions

----

PrEmo can also be used as a communication tool in design teams to achieve a shared understanding of the emotional impact of given products.

REFERENCES & FURTHER READING: Desmet, P.M.A., 2018. *Measuring Emotion: Development and Application of an Instrument to Measure Emotional Responses to Products.* In M. Blythe & A. Monk (Eds). Funology 2: From Usability to Enjoyment, 2nd Edition (pp. 391-404). New York: Springer. / Desmet, P.M.A., & Schifferstein, N.J.H., 2012. *Emotion research as input for product design.* In J. Beckley, D., Paredes, & K. Lopetcharat (Eds.), Product Innovation Toolbox: A Field Guide to Consumer Understanding and Research, pp. 149-175. Hoboken, NJ: John Wiley & Sons. / Laurans, G. & Desmet, P.M.A., 2017. Developing 14 animated characters for non-verbal self-report of categorical emotions. *Journal of Design Research*, 15(3/4), 214–233. Raijmakers, B. and Miller, S. (2016) *Viewfinders – Thoughts on Visual design research.* London: STBY Ltd. Raijmakers, B. & Miller, S. (2016) *Viewfinders – Thoughts on Visual design research.* London: STBY Ltd.

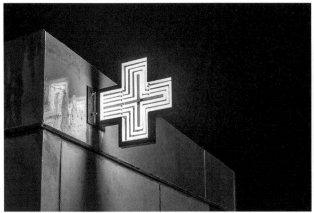

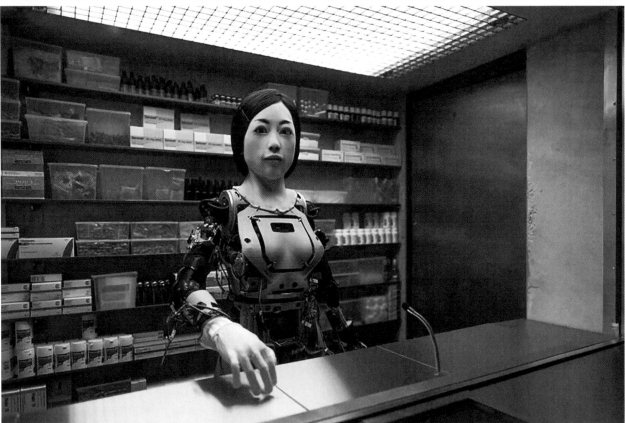

Dutch artist Dries Verhoeven created a human-like robot, named Amy, for his live installation 'Happiness'. She runs a drug store that can be visited to imagine a world in which drugs are part of daily life. Spectators will be informed in a businesslike manner about various options for self-medication to adjust the serotonin and dopamine levels in our brains. In healthcare, artificial aids are normal: when you wear, you get an artificial hip, your eyes get lasered. What if we start intervening in our brain, our emotional balance, our personality? (photography: Willem Popelier, Thorsten Alofs)

Role-Playing

Role-Playing is a form of simulation that helps designers to develop and determine the interaction between their design and its intended users.

WHAT & WHY? Users interact with products using their entire body, their senses, and their mind. Placing yourself physically in a user's shoes allows you to evaluate your own design according to their experiences, and this can also help you remove yourself from preconceived opinions that you might have about your own design. The method resembles acting in theatre – by acting out the tasks your intended user has to perform, you can better understand the complexity of the interaction.

MINDSET: Imagining yourself as the user and playing out several user scenarios can confront you with the flaws of your design. Try to find wrong assumptions and mistakes in your design proposal. These experiences can shed light on new insight and new ideas to solve problems you encounter as you use Role-Playing.

WHEN? You can use Role-Playing throughout the design process to develop ideas about how people would interact with the product you are developing. You can also engage in Role-Playing to understand the interaction qualities of an existing product, or you can use the method in a later stage when evaluating a concept. It can be particularly useful to put yourself in the role of your intended user when you do not belong to that user group. For example, by putting on semi-covered eyeglasses and taping up your joints, you can get a sense of how a visually impaired person with limited mobility experiences the world.

TIPS & CONCERNS:
When analysing data, pay attention to the sequences of tasks, motivations, and factors that could influence the interaction.

Participants will act more realistically if the physical environment is simulated as well.

Conduct a pilot test to explore the barriers and enablers of the Role Playing approach; you can try doing this with team members first.

LIMITATIONS:
You cannot replace completely the intended user with yourself.

Combine this method with other methods and techniques so that you can get to know the users and their interaction with existing systems, products, and services.

197

HOW? One of the major advantages of Role-Playing is that you use your entire body; this involves more like real interaction compared to using storyboards or scenarios. Role-Playing techniques enable you to explore the tangibility of the interaction as well as the appearance and attractiveness of graceful movement. Moreover, Role-Playing allows you to simulate an interaction walkthrough, which is usually captured using photography or video. Role-Playing starts with the first idea about the interaction between the product and its user.

The outcome of using Role-Playing techniques is that you will most likely have a good conceptual idea about the interaction, and you will also have visualisations or written descriptions of the interaction. Both visualisations and written descriptions can be used for communication and evaluation purposes.

Step 1: Determine the actors and the goal of the actors or the interaction.

Step 2: Determine what you want to portray through Role-Playing. Determine the sequence of steps.

Step 3: Make sure you have the costumes and props ready, and be prepared to record the Role-playing session while the activity is performed.

Step 4: Divide the roles amongst the team members.

Step 5: Perform the interaction and improvise. Be expressive in your movements. Think aloud when enacting motivations.

Step 6: Adjust the narrative or setting and repeat the Role-Playing task several times until different sequences have been enacted.

Step 7: View the recordings, transcribe data, and translate them into insights.

REFERENCES & FURTHER READING: Jacko, J.A. & Sears, A., 2002. *The Human-Computer Interaction Handbook: Fundamentals, Evolving Technologies and Emerging Applications.* New York, NY: Erlbaum and Associates.

Product Usability Evaluation

Product Usability Evaluation serves to validate product usability; it enables designers to understand the quality of their designs (ideas or concepts) in actual use conditions. The outcomes of the evaluation can help with modifications of the design.

WHAT & WHY? Designers make many assumptions on how people use the products they design and the extent to which users will understand how to use them. Evaluation is a key step for validating these assumptions and for getting inspiration on how to further improve the usability of a product.

MINDSET: Designers can be too optimistic about how well users are able to understand how to use their designed product or service. Product Usability Evaluation stimulates to challenge assumptions and provide an understanding of how people experience and use your designs. This will then help you in further improving the product.

WHEN? In each stage of the design process different areas can be evaluated. At the start test and analyse the use of existing similar products. In an early stage evaluate ideas and concepts using sketches, scenarios, or storyboards for simulation. Throughout the process evaluate the designs using 3D or partly interactive models that can simulate specific functionalities and forms. Towards the end evaluate the use of almost fully functioning prototypes. The outcomes help you generate requirements for efficiency, effectiveness, and satisfaction, or determine to what extent the product meets initial requirements. In the process, you may discover issues, possible improvements to resolve those issues, and opportunities to improve user experience.

HOW? Use a representation of your design and observe the usage in a realistic situation. Observe the 'use-cues' perceived and encountered (perception), the way of understanding (cognition), and the way intended users achieve their goal (perception and cognition). The result is a list of requirements for redesign.

Step 1: Make a storyboard of the expected, realistic users, and usage of your design.

Step 2: Decide which parts of product use you need to evaluate, how you process with the evaluation, and in which context.

Step 3: Describe your assumptions in detail: which product characteristics will users perceive, understand, and operate in a specified situation?

Step 4: Formulate open research questions, such as 'How do people use the product?' and 'What do they use as use-cues?'

Step 5: Set up your research. This includes representations of your product (storyboards and models), the research environment, instructions, and questions for the participants.

Step 6: Prepare your participants; remember to manage their expectations, including privacy issues, and conduct research. Record the activities, and observe both intended and unintended use.

Step 7: Analyse the results qualitatively (using issues and opportunities) and/or quantitatively, such as by counting occurrences.

Step 8: Communicate results and redesign the product accordingly. Ideas for improvements often emerge during the evaluation.

TIPS & CONCERNS:
Ask someone less involved in the design to conduct the evaluation to avoid influencing your users.

Specialists such as marketing and management may need to be convinced that valid results can be derived from small samples of participants.

The validity of your results will increase over time as you gain research experience.

You often do not need formal recruiting or testing facilities. Use your personal network to find unbiased participants.

For a simple qualitative evaluation, you need about 4 to 1 participants.

Any testing is better than none at all! Do 'guerrilla testing' if money and time are limited.

Handle privacy issues in advance.

Video has great value as a communication tool.

Ask a limited number of qualitative questions at the end of the evaluation session. Do not sidetrack your participants from their primary tasks.

LIMITATIONS: If evaluations are done using product models or prototypes, be aware that the results can only be valid for the tested functionalities.

Participants may have feelings of failure while being observed if they do not know how to use a product. They may be more tenacious in trying to use the product than they would be in reality.

199

REFERENCES & FURTHER READING: Boess, S.U., De Jong, A.M. & Kanis, H., 2004. *Usage research in the Delft Design Project Ontwerpen 4.* In P. Lloyd, N. Roozenburg, C. McMahon and L. Brodhurst (Eds.) Procs. EPDE, pp. 577-584. Delft: Fac IDE, TU Delft. / Boess, S.U. & Kanis, H., 2008. *Meaning in product use: a design perspective.* In H.N.J. Schifferstein and P.P.M. Hekkert (Eds.), Product experience, pp. 305-332. Amsterdam: Elsevier. / Kanis, H., 1998. Usage centred research for everyday product design. *Applied Ergonomics,* February, 29(1), pp. 75-82. / Kanis, H., Rooden, M.J. & Green, W.S., 2000. *Usecues in the Delft Design course.* Contemporary Ergonomics, 6 April, pp.75-82.

Bear-resistant containers come in all sizes and shapes, from ultra-light backpacker food containers weighing a few ounces to dumpsters able to hold 20 tons. Some of these products have been tested by trial and error through direct experience with bears, and actually meet the criteria for 'bear-resistance'.

Product Concept Evaluation

Product Concept Evaluation helps designers understand how intended users or other stakeholders value their concept design. This enables them to determine which aspects should be optimised, and they can then make a go/no-go decision or select concepts (also known as concept screening).

WHAT & WHY? In Product Concept Evaluations, various stakeholders evaluate the core ideas behind a product or service proposal, usually from various perspectives. This may be used for selecting which concept to proceed with or for evaluating whether to proceed in further developing a concept or not.

MINDSET: Designers generally have an a priori preference for one of the concepts. In such cases, an open mind for the preferences of the stakeholders is required, and it is especially important to make serious attempts to understand the reasons behind their preferences.

WHEN? Product Concept Evaluations take place throughout the design process. Concept optimisation takes place near the end of the design process when aspects of the concept need to be improved.

HOW? Product Concept Evaluations are carried out in a controlled environment where a panel of people judge product concepts based on a list of predetermined issues. The starting point is a number of concepts to be judged and a reason for conducting the evaluation. Concept screenings are often conducted by experts such as managers, engineers, and marketers instead of representatives from the user group. Concept optimisation aims to judge parts or elements of product ideas and concepts. The assumption is that preferred aspects or elements of the individual product concepts can be connected with each other, and this yields a concept that is regarded as optimal. Go/no-go decisions usually involve the choice between two or three product concepts. These are the types of concept representations you can use:

- *Textual concepts:* Scenarios describing how people can use the product, or an enumeration of the aspects of the product idea.
- *Pictographic concepts:* Visual representations of the product ideas, which can be sketches or highly detailed 3D CAD models, depending on the stage of development.
- *Animations:* Moving visual representations of the product idea or a user scenario.
- *Mock-ups (dummies):* 3D tangible representations of the product idea.

Step 1: Describe the aim of the Product Concept Evaluation.

Step 2: Determine what type of evaluation you want to conduct (such as personal interviews, focus groups, or discussion groups).

Step 3: Create the appropriate concept representations.

Step 4: Create a plan that includes the aims and type of evaluation, a description of the respondents, questions you want to ask them, aspects of the product concept that need to be evaluated, a description of the test environment, the means of recording the evaluation, and a plan for how you will analyse the results.

Step 5: Search for respondents and invite them to the evaluation.

Step 6: Set up the test environment, including recording equipment.

Step 7: Conduct the concept evaluation.

Step 8: Analyse the results and present the results concisely (such as using a report or a poster).

TIPS & CONCERNS
The invited respondents belong to one or more of the pre-formulated user groups. Select them based on sociocultural characteristics or demographic characteristics.

The respondents' level of knowledge of the product category is an important issue. Simply ask respondents about their experiences with similar products.

Check how tolerant the respondents are towards new products and new situations?

Structure the evaluation systematically with the questions you want to ask.

Don't forget to provide the respondents with some form of compensation!

LIMITATIONS
Generally in Product Concept Evaluations, unfinished products are used. They have to imagine how the finished product will function in reality and in various contexts. For that reason, it is important that further in the development process, designers regularly evaluate whether they are still on the right track.

201

REFERENCES & FURTHER READING: Antonides, G., Oppedijk – Van Veen, W.M., Schoormans, J.P.L. & Van Raaij, W.F., 1999. *Product en Consument.* Utrecht: Lemma. / Roozenburg, N.F.M. & Eekels, J., 1995. *Product Design: Fundamentals and Methods.* Utrecht: Lemma. / Schoormans, J. & De Bont, C., 1995. *Consumentenonderzoek in de productontwikkeling.* Utrecht: Lemma.

SAMPLE REGULAR RAZORS

Manufacturing cost price (incl. patents, materials, assembly, packaging)	€	6,10
Overhead costs / factory running costs 15%*	€	0,92
Selling costs 5%*	€	0,31
Factory margin (profit/risk) 25%*	€	1,53
Factory selling price	**€**	**8,86**
Distribution and wholesale margin 30%*	€	2,66
Buying price for retailer (Retail margin 50%**)	**€**	**11,52**
Selling price excl. VAT	€	17,28
VAT	€	3,63
Selling price for customer	€	20,91
Round off pricetag to:	**€**	**20,95**

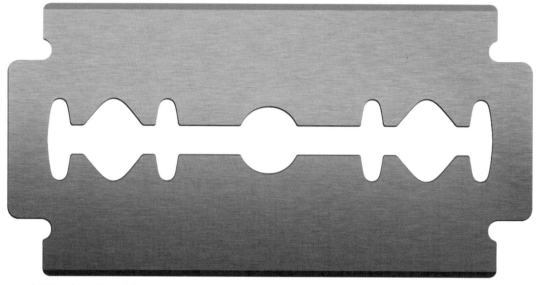

Cutting the price: Boldking razor blades offers a circular buisiness model where you receive 4 blades per month via mail. Used ones are send back to the company for recycling. A company cuts prices by more than 50% without cutting corners when it comes to quality. See the calculation below.

SAMPLE PRICE CUT RAZORS

Manufacturing cost price (no excessive design features, no patents)	€	4,40
Overhead costs / factory running costs 15%*	€	0,66
Selling costs 5%	€	0,22
Factory margin (profit/risk) 25%*	€	1,10
Factory selling price	€	6,38
Distribution and wholesale margin 0% (no wholesale in between)	€	0,00
Buying price	**€**	**6,38**
Boldking retail margin 30%* (website, online payment, profit/risk)	€	1,91
Selling price excl. VAT	€	8,29
VAT (in the Netherlands: 21%)	€	1,74
Selling price for customer	€	10,03
Round off pricetag to:	**€**	**10,00**

* average value, varies from case to case ** varies per branch, brand or shop from 20-300%

Cost Price Estimation

The Cost Price Estimation method helps designers define the cost price of their designs in a rough way at an early stage of the design process.

WHAT & WHY? It is important to know how cost prices and store prices are constructed and related to each other. Designers also need to know how early decisions in the development process can greatly influence the outcome. The cost price is the basis for determining the price of product-service systems and the rental or lease constructions.

MINDSET: Be aware that any decision in the conceptual stage of the product or service design can have a big effect on the store price or subscription price. The challenge is to balance functionality and quality versus costs in the same way as your target audience would.

WHEN? This method helps you estimate the cost price and provides you with a checklist of additional costs that should not be overlooked. You need detailed information, such as material choices, dimensions, packaging, and lot size. Avoid overlooking cost aspects that are hidden in the production and distribution chain. For instance, after buying the prototyping materials in the workshop for € 9, you might expect that the product can be sold in shops for € 10, yielding a profit of € 1 for you as the designer. This is actually not realistic at all! With some basic rules of thumb, you can estimate the selling price realistically within a certain range. You can also estimate what kinds of parts, materials, details, and extra features would make the design either more or less costly than your target figure.

HOW? You can estimate cost price qualitatively and quantitatively. The qualitative approach is based on existing products, where you compare your design proposal to existing products. The quantitative approach is based on adding up all the cost factors and margins that are needed to build and sell your product.

Qualitatively

- Compare your design proposal to what is already on the market. A bicycle designed with an electric motor is probably more expensive than a normal bicycle and less expensive than a scooter. A bigger engine would increase the cost, as would any added functionalities such as lightweight wheels.
- Usually, expensive materials such as titanium, carbon-reinforced epoxy, and veneer cause prices to increase. Over time, the cost of labour has become a much bigger component in the cost price. That's why labour-intensive parts such as welding instead of bending a tube can make products more expensive. Finishing steps are particularly costly, and these can include steps such as grinding away mould marks or polishing.

- Industrial production involves producing in series, ranging from several hundred to millions. Each lot size has a specific production method and manufacturing cost. A clever design can save on costs. The key is to find a balance between fixed costs (such as moulds) and variable costs (such as materials) as well as labour cost per product. Injection moulding involves expensive moulds, but in mass production they only add a few cents per product to the cost price.

Quantitatively

- Start by estimating how much your material will cost. You can do this with the Cambridge Engineering Selector program (http://www-g.eng.cam.ac.uk/125/now/ces.html)or a survey on the Internet. A rough estimate can be made with the rule of thumb that a consumer price is seven to eight times the material cost. We can state that the consumer price is three to four times the manufacturing cost which includes labour, packaging, and the manufacturer's profit.
- This checklist can help you estimate the cost price more precisely. Novice designers often overlook cost components such as packaging, transport, wholesale, and value added tax.

TIPS & CONCERNS

Do not overlook Cost Price Estimation as it is important to gain experience with this method during study projects.

With this method, you can also calculate the price for product-service systems or lease constructions. Man-hours are a logical part of the equation.

LIMITATIONS

The method can only provide a rough indication of the selling price. Estimates from producers can result in differences of 100%, to 300% in consumer price.

After going through this process several times, you will have a better idea about the surprises that lie ahead.

203

REFERENCES & FURTHER READING: Buiting-Csikós, C., Kals, H.J.J., Lutterveld, C.A., Moulijn, K.A. & Ponsen, J.M., 2012. *Industriële Productie.* Den Haag: Academic Service.

The Ocean Cleanup is a non-government engineering environmental organisation that develops technology to extract plastic pollution from the oceans. After a couple of years of various tests they deployed their first full-scale prototype. The organisation conducts scientific research into oceanic plastic pollution and was founded in 2013 by Boyan Slat, a Dutch-born and TU-Delft student, inventor-entrepreneur. (support the project: products.theoceancleanup.com)

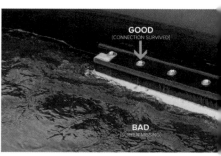

Interaction with the prototype:

A new ocean cleanup prototype is being deployed on the North Sea as one of the last steps to prepare the first full scale cleanup system in the Great Pacific Garbage Patch.

The purpose of the tests:

To gain experience in deploying offshore structures and to maximise the cleanup systems' capacity to handle the harshest conditions they could face in the Pacific Ocean. Instead of testing the full system, smaller 'slices' out of the bigger whole have been tested. If such a section can last at sea, this is a good indication that a full-length system will also be able to survive.

Important remaining question:

How to connect the floater pipe with the screen that is suspended below it? This connection forms a bridge between a rigid element and a flexible element, and as such will be subject to high loads and exotic, erratic motions.

Knowledge gained about technology:

A barrier design inspired by conventional oil containment booms won't be able to last at sea for a very long time. The inflatable air chambers showed a tendency to leak very quickly, and the connection between the boom and the mooring wasn't able to cope with the high loads.

Knowledge gained about the design process:

Unscheduled Learning Opportunities have put more pressure on the timeline, but we are happy that we discovered them last year on a small section of the system in the – much more accessible – North Sea, instead of with a screen 600 meters in length, 1200 nautical miles offshore.

Prototype Reflection Cards

Prototype Reflection Cards is a documentation format that helps designers in articulating and keeping track of the tacit knowledge acquired while prototyping.

WHAT & WHY? Designers learn from prototyping in a variety of ways. On the one hand, testing a prototype can explicitly validate a design assumption or answer a research question. On the other hand, through the prototyping process, designers can also develop diverse practical know-how, come up with new ideas, and obtain an intuitive understanding of the context they design for. Prototype Reflection Cards is a method that helps designers in capturing and documenting the diverse kinds of knowledge they obtain while prototyping. The method is particularly useful for articulating, structuring, and following up on intuitive hunches that often drive fast-paced prototyping processes. The method also helps designers in revealing blind spots and the implicit assumptions made while designing.

MINDSET: Prototype Reflection Cards method builds on the way of thinking as described in the Basic Design Cycle model. It requires designers to make their reasoning steps explicit.

WHEN? A card can be filled out any time after putting a prototype to some kind of use. Filling out a card can take as little as 10 to 15 minutes, yet it can trigger the need in you to take a step back from your hands-on prototyping or testing activities and to reflect on the 'big picture' of your project. Here, the format can structure the reflection around the concerns relating to the affected individuals, the involved technology, or the transformed organisation. The card also distinguishes insights, know-how, and ideas as three forms of tacit knowledge that are being accounted for throughout the design process. You can use a collection of prior prototype reflection cards to track the things you have learned throughout the project, identify knowledge gaps and implicit assumptions, and plan the next project steps accordingly.

HOW? Cards can be filled out on paper or digitally by individual designers or by teams. The structure of the form guides you to reflect on the recent activity that involves your prototype and to consider what this activity has taught. It is useful to keep prototype cards chronologically organised and to review prior cards upon every project reflection moment.

Step 1: Write a brief description of how your prototype was tried out, and illustrate it with a photo or drawing.

Step 2: Reflect on what this activity has taught about people, technology, or organisation that relate to your design concept. Focus especially on unexpected learnings that might have been in your blind spot earlier on.

Step 3: Reflect on obtained insights (you have learned something new about the design context), know-how (you have learned how to do something new) and ideas (you have learned what you want to do next).

Step 4: Choose and briefly summarise the three most important things you have learned.

Step 5: Reflect on your design process and make a note of it.

TIPS & CONCERNS
Keep your prototype reflection cards in a folder and browse through them regularly.

Make additional annotations on the back of the form or in a separate notebook or blog.

Do not describe your design concept using Prototype Reflection Cards.

Keep a separate account of the details and evolution of your designs.

If you are working on a team project, fill out the cards together with the whole team and discuss what each one of you has learned.

Choose to fill out and track Prototype Reflection Cards individually and use them to share your own reflections with the rest of the team.

LIMITATIONS:
Prototype Reflection Cards do not provide an exhaustive documentation of the knowledge acquired by designers.

REFERENCES & FURTHER READING: Jaskiewicz, T. & van der Helm, A., 2017. *Progress Cards as a Tool for Supporting Reflection, Management and Analysis of Design Studio Processes*. In proceedings of the conference: Engineering and Product Design Education, Norway. / Schön, D.A. & DeSanctis, V., 1986. *The reflective practitioner: How professionals think in action*.city: publisher?

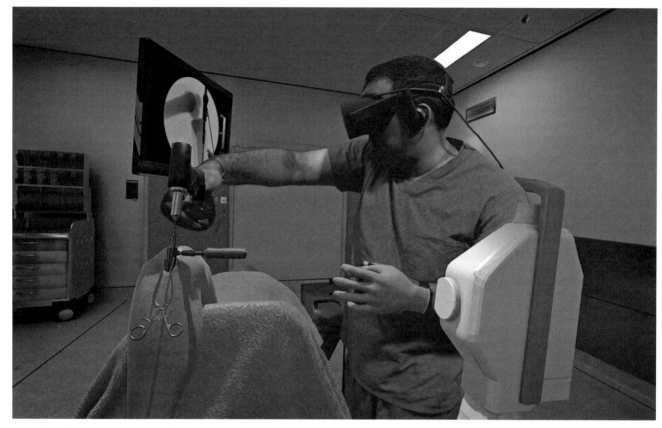

With advancing technology, there is now a way to conduct medical device human factors testing that doesn't require travel, allows for rapid iteration, and ultimately combines 'looks-like' and 'works-like' prototyping. Using VR during usability testing enables real-time design iteration in response to user feedback on a distance. These users can examine and hold the device in question as well as actually use it as a team in various scenarios to more accurately analyse the effectiveness of the user interface and the risk of misuse. (Image courtesy of Osso VR)

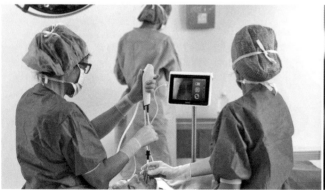

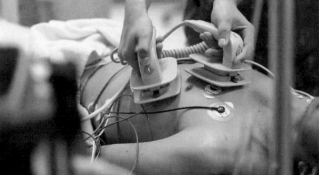

Product demonstration and device simulation videos can be a great way to both market your new medical device as well as to ensure a greater understanding of the application of the technologies at hand.

Cinematic Prototyping

Cinematic Prototyping is a method that enables the exploration and development of interactive products, systems, or service interactions without being restricted by the limitations of technical prototyping platforms. It uses filmmaking codes and techniques, interaction design, and sound design at its core.

WHAT & WHY? Cinematic Prototyping can be considered a form of design fiction, as it uses design as an instrument to generate awareness, highlight concerns, or our challenges values about new, emerging, and future technologies, products, and services. It does this using storytelling through designed objects. Rather than having a design process directed by the use of sensors, actuators, or Arduino boards, Cinematic Prototyping concentrates on freely exploring and designing the aesthetics, sensuous experiences, and meanings that are evoked when you interact with objects in a specific context of use.

MINDSET: The approach brings a 'lo-fidelity' narrative mindset to the design of interactive objects, as it involves the use of theatrical and expressive techniques such as enacting, animating, and puppeteering. You can use mundane materials such as foam, cardboard, and fishing lines to build and control objects that function as 'film props' in contextual stories rather than as stand-alone functional prototypes.

WHEN? Cinematic Prototyping is especially suitable in an early stage of the design process when designers research and develop applications of new and emerging technologies. This is typically done in teams consisting of the industrial, academic, and societal stakeholders. With its visual richness and intrinsic narrative structure, Cinematic Prototyping can help you create shared spaces for dialogue within each team, where members can work together to align goals and identify critical issues.

TIPS & CONCERNS:
Think about products and services as parts of stories.

Select your shot sizes, compositions, camera positions, and camera angles well, as this can greatly reduce the required fidelity of your mock-up.

Pay special attention to the design and synchronisation of the sounds that the object makes when it is in use, as these should be realistic and perfectly timed to be credible.

LIMITATIONS:
A potential pitfall is spending too much time on the technical quality of the video in order to impress a potential client. The main focus should be on the value of the video for the design situation at hand.

207

HOW? Cinematic Prototyping is performed in four consecutive phases:

Phase 1: Concepting - First, define the functionalities of an object, and construct a further specification of the object in a state-change diagram. This way you provide detail on the product's sensing and actuating capabilities. Make a first storyboard that depicts the intended user and context of use, as well as how the object influences and affects the user and the context in the story.

Phase 2: Embodiment - Create simple mock-ups of the object so that you can explore its expressiveness, size, overall shape, and material composition. Be sure to also explore the auditory qualities of materials and online sound libraries to determine possible sounds that the object might produce.

Phase 3: Enactment - Do some further exploration with the object's behaviour by animating it through human motion (such as puppeteering). This involves creating a motion-transfer mechanism to control the object and then enacting it to experience how the object would be understood and used by people in the specific context of use.

Phase 4: Production
Create the actual Cinematic Prototype, which is the production of a short film that should vividly and convincingly demonstrate the object in use. Go through the typical stages of pre-production, production, and post-production:
• Create a detailed storyboard
• Provide details for the mock-up by turning it into a 'film-prop'
• Select a real-world location that is accessible
• Check lighting conditions, and determine the shot sizes, camera angles, positions, and movements
• Rehearse and then perform the scenes
• Edit your shots and add in sounds and effects

REFERENCES & FURTHER READING: Pasman, G., Rozendaal, M. van Ramshorst, A., Quaedvlieg, F., Osako, M. & Aguirre Broca, D., 2018. *Cinematic Prototyping: Exploring Future Interactions without Prototyping Technology.* In Extended Abstracts of the 2018 CHI Conference on Human Factors in Computing Systems (CHI EA '18). ACM, New York, USA. / Pasman, G. & Roosendaal, M., 2017. *Designing Interactive Objects through Cinematic Prototyping.* In proceedings of the 16th International Conference on Engineering and Product Design Education, Oslo, Norway. / Pasman, G. & Roosendaal, M., 2016. *Exploring Interaction Styles using Video.* In proceedings of the 15th International Conference on Engineering and Product Design Education, Aalborg, Denmark.

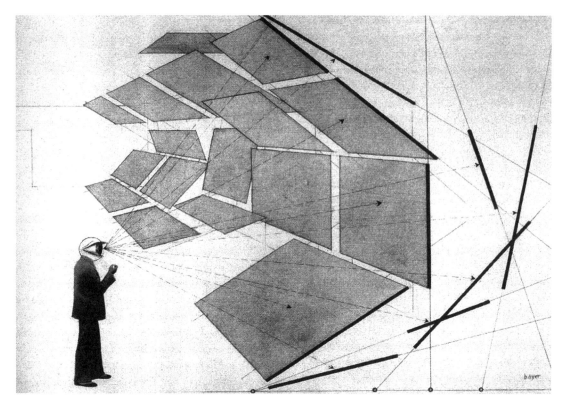

Concept delivery drawing by the Eames Office for the world's first Multimedia Instalation, entitled 'Think'. 12 films were projected simultainiously on a system of 12 tilted screens. The drawing presents the design of the screens which are positioned in carefully calculated view angles. The Eames office was responsible for the exhibitions, graphics, signage, and films for the IBM's presentation at the 1964 New York World's Fair. All of which focused on the influence of computers in contemporary society, and the similarity between the ways that man and machine process and interpret information. The images below show more drawings from Ray and Charles Eames in which they explore shapes, characters, silhouettes, details, materials and context.

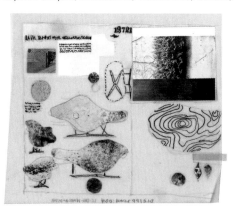

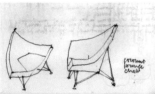

Design Drawing to Develop

In the Develop stage, you address and assert your creativity. You are encouraged to sketch out all your thoughts, no matter how premature. Drawing helps you with visual exploration, a process where you can think, reflect, and develop your ideas further. Simultaneously, drawings will help you present, assess, and compare ideas.

WHAT & WHY? As discussed in the Perspectives chapter, drawing serves as a visual language for exploration and communication. For both purposes, drawings in this stage can concern properties such as shape, aesthetics, size, interaction or use, relationship within a system, structure, working principles, ergonomics, and anything else that is relevant for the project or situation.

The Develop stage is characterised by multiple steps and activities. Sketching and drawing can be used for a diverging brainstorm or other exploration techniques (diverging). It can also be useful for aligning with stakeholders through presenting, steering and choosing (converging). The further the progress, the more detailed a drawing should convey the qualities of the design proposals at hand.

MINDSET: In this stage, creativity and imagination are required. The activity of sketching - which stimulates thinking in a visual manner - accommodates this well, and can help in communicating your ideas. The Develop stage is a transition from ideation to concept delivery, and thus entails both diverging and converging steps. The communicative power of drawings is a prerequisite from start to finish. Don't be too concerned with producing a 'beautiful' final drawing, focus on clarity and convincing power.

WHEN? Drawing during the Develop stage includes a range of steps; from free and rough sketches to rather concrete and detailed ones. Drawing represents a trajectory from ideation to concept delivery. Towards the end of this stage, sketching, graphic design, model-making, and CAD-modelling can be done in parallel. This is also the case for development sketches of different specific aspects related to a design such as aesthetics, assembly, and ergonomics.

HOW? Inspiration will not come about by itself! From the start of the creative process, use pen and paper or a tablet to develop your thoughts, iterations, and alternatives. Without externalizing your thoughts, your mind will fill up and you will find it difficult to reflect on and improve ideas.

Start in a simple way; you don't need to find the perfect polished idea with the first thing you put on paper. Warm up both your hands as well as your brain by sketching simple shapes, thoughts, and partial solutions. As you are sketching along, the ideas will inevitably get more elaborate and complete. Use the SCAMPER technique to multiply your ideas. Creativity can be sparked by collaboration, for example by brainstorming and association techniques executed in a group. Most importantly: execute these techniques in a visual manner. Put all that comes to mind on paper, if needed in combination with rough physical models. Feel free to explore. Share your sketches, even if you don't consider them to be any good. Use them to extract insights and inspiration from your colleagues and peers.

TIPS & CONCERNS
When drawing for exploration and ideation, sketch freely, iterate and adjust in any direction on a sheet of paper. Don't let the composition of a sketch hinder the creative flow. The results can even be comparable to a mindmap.

To help your creativity and exploration, it is worthwhile to go away from your workspace and into the street to observe, interview, and try things out.

Sketch anywhere you want and use all the tools available. Treat your work with respect and avoid folding, stains, smudgy paper.

LIMITATIONS
Sketches of human-product interaction can support a User-Centred Design approach. For solid testing and conclusions about ergonomics and use, it is necessary to build models in order to simulate and evaluate. With the results you can return to the drafting table and improve on your ideas.

209

REFERENCES & FURTHER READING: *Eissen, J. J., & Steur, R. (2009). Sketching: Bis. / Olofsson, E., & Sjölén, K. (2006). Design Sketching: KEEOS Design Books. / Robertson, S., & Bertling, T. (2013). How to Draw: Design Studio Press. http://www.delftdesigndrawing.com/basics.html*

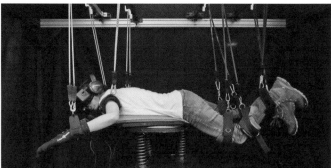

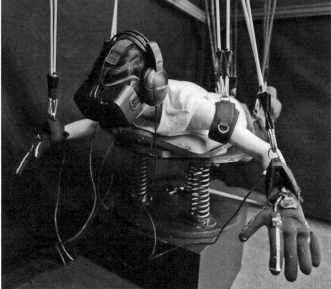

A quick cardboard model gives the designer feedback on how the design works and how users react and interact (left). A MIT virtual-reality project simulates scuba diving while also aiming to give users a sense of what it's like to experience deafness (right).

About 200 units were built of the Apple 1 (1976). They were originally sold without keyboard, monitor or even a housing for $666.66 each. After working with this prototype-style machine, a client asked for a protective cover. Apple founder Steve Jobs delivered it with a keyboard and a wooden case (left). Researchers at the Delft University of Technology use one or more layers of sandwich bags to simulate different degrees of blurred vision (right).

Experience Prototyping

Experience Prototyping involves situating a product or service prototype in a broader context of use. By doing so, designers can explore and communicate how everyday situations – in their complexity and unexpectedness – can influence people's engagement with the design.

WHAT & WHY? When creating an experience prototype, the focus is not on how this prototype works but on the experiential qualities that emerge from interacting with it. Experience Prototyping often involves make-believe props or 'faked' technology. The method analyses how a person who experiences a product or service is affected by the context in which this experience takes place. For example, the experience of taking a nap on the plane does not only depend on the airplane cabin design but also on what this passenger did before boarding the plane as well as the behaviour of other passengers and flight attendants. Experience prototyping involves bringing to life many possible aspects of the experience you design for. This may involve taking your prototype to an outside world setting.

MINDSET: Rather than testing a specific detail of your design, Experience Prototyping is best suited for grasping the intricacies of the situations you design for. Because of that, you need to prepare yourself to be surprised in how others engage with your prototypes in unexpected ways, and you should refrain from prescribing how others should or should not use the prototype.

WHEN? Experience prototyping is not bound to any specific stage of the design process. For example, in the fuzzy front end of designing, it can help you explore the existing and possible user experiences. Later in the design process, you can use it to assess whether the designed product contributes to the user experiences as you expected. At all stages of your design process, you can use Experience Prototyping to communicate your design intentions to others, such as to clients or collaborators.

HOW? Experience Prototyping can either involve bringing prototypes into real-life situations or simulating a real-life situation in an artificial setting. The goal of Experience Prototyping is to understand what people experience when interacting with your prototypes in these situations and why they experience it in this way. Experience Prototyping can be combined with most user research methods. Possible procedure:

Step 1: Specify the situations you are designing for:
- Visit the design context and explore possibilities for introducing your prototype there, or come up with a way to recreate encountered situations it in a more convenient setting.
- Describe the user experience you hope to achieve. You can do this using a scenario, an interaction vision, or a storyboard.
- List materials, props, proxy devices, and the people that are essential to enable this experience.

Step 2: Explore how to enable the intended experience:
- Situate your prototypes in the improvised setting and try them out; do this within the design team, potential users, or your client, and iterate towards delivering the experience you aim for.
- Try using low fidelity prototypes, as these can allow you to explore more variations.

Step 3: Study how people experience your prototype:
- Choose the design research methods most appropriate for your context, design challenge, and setup.
- Embrace all insights that challenge your assumptions about the situations in which your design is being experienced.

TIPS & CONCERNS:
Look towards simulation methods employed by theatre, movies, or media art, such as Role-Playing.

Practice on yourselves!

Do not worry if the prototype doesn't look like what you intend to design; the important thing is that it evokes the experience you are after.

Use existing products that deliver the required experiential qualities.

Simulating product experiences is a skill that will develop over time.

If some type of technology is required to create the desired experience, resort to Wizard of Oz prototypes.

Choreograph the introduction, use, and conclusion of your experience prototype.

LIMITATIONS:
It is impossible to simulate all possible aspects and variables that affect a person's experience. Identify the dimensions of your experience that are leading your design idea.

REFERENCES & FURTHER READING: Buchenau, M. & Suri, J.F., 2000. Experience prototyping. In *Proceedings of the 3rd conference on Designing interactive systems: processes, practices, methods, and techniques*(pp. 424-433). ACM. / Law, E.L.C., Roto, V., Hassenzahl, M., Vermeeren, A.P. & Kort, J., 2009. *Understanding, scoping and defining user experience: a survey approach.* In Proceedings of the SIGCHI conference on human factors in computing systems (pp. 719-728). ACM. / Buxton, B., 2010.*Sketching user experiences: getting the design right and the right design.* Morgan Kaufmann. / Boess, S., Saakes, D. & Hummels, C., 2007. *When is role playing really experiential?: case studies.* In Proceedings of the 1st international conference on Tangible and embedded interaction (pp. 279-282). ACM.

Invention is often associated with a pragmatic application. Yet up until the middle of the 19th century, invention was strongly linked to imagination. For the Belgian artist Panaramenko, invention is an adventure, a process of exploration. The airships he builds in his studio become uncontrollable. 'I built them all to fly, sail or drive,' he claims. Yet none of his vehicles do what they promise because at the end the works lose their original purpose. 'My objects are becoming too beautiful to really function.' According to Panamarenko's calculations the 'Scotch Gambit' aircraft shown above (1966-1999, MUKHA Antwerp) can reach a speed of 100 km/h using two air-cooled 370-hp Lycoming aircraft engines.

A Wizard of Oz prototype for a vision impaired navigation system that would support users using audio input in identifying obstacles while they're moving. Chemistry goggles are taped to blind the user. A compact camera module for supposed navigation purpose is attached to the headset with wires and a fake battery. Feedback from the navigation system is delivered through an earphone by the Wizard (the designer), but the blinded users are told that the navigation feedback comes from the AI navigator being tested.

Wizard of Oz Prototyping

Wizard of Oz Prototyping supports designing a user experience by involving a human operator who inconspicuously controls the prototype's behaviour. Wizard of Oz prototypes allow designers to try out a design idea in a quick, cheap, and technologically undemanding way.

WHAT & WHY? In the children's book *The Wonderful Wizard of Oz*, the evil wizard turns out to be a clever inventor who manipulates seemingly magical contraptions from behind a curtain. Inspired by this, the Wizard of Oz Prototyping involves a person who controls the prototype behaviour without being seen by the user.

This technique allows you to prototype and test your idea in a short time while using limited resources but without using advanced technology. It is a powerful way to validate your design assumptions before you embark on a full-fledged prototyping and development path. Wizard of Oz Prototyping can also help you in exploring various design directions, understanding your design context, and communicating your ideas to others.

MINDSET: These prototypes are built with a 'try quickly and see if it works' mindset. Therefore, when trying out Wizard of Oz prototypes, you need to be prepared for your prototype to not be successful on the first try, and you should be critical and inquisitive in your attempts to understand why it didn't work as you expected!

WHEN? Wizard of Oz Prototyping is typically used in the fuzzy front end of designing. Because these are quick and inexpensive to make, you can use them to test and validate multiple ideas for a specific user experience before converging on your final design direction. They can also be used at later stages of your design process. For example, when basic features of the prototype become autonomous in subsequent stages of the design process, the wizard can start to control more specific or advanced features.

HOW? Unlike the main designer in the similar 'paper prototyping' technique, in Wizard of Oz Prototyping, the human operator of the prototype is always hidden or inconspicuous, hidden in plain sight. In this way, while it may involve little or no technology, the prototypes can still have a polished look and feel that give people a fully believable product experience. For a successful Wizard of Oz Prototyping setup, there should be a suitable place and effective controls for the prototype 'wizard'; such a setup allows the operator to respond to the actions of users in a timely and adequate way without interrupting their experience. The 'wizard' may need to write scripts for possible situations and perform training beforehand. Do bear in mind that the difficulties experienced by the 'wizard' are the challenges that the eventual product design will have to address.

TIPS & CONCERNS:
You can look for Wizard of Oz inspiration in science fiction movies, such as R2D2 played by Kenny Bakker in Star Wars.

Wizard of Oz Prototyping can also integrate advanced technology. MAX/MSP is a popular software that can be used as an interface to control prototypes that include sensors and actuators.

Quickly built Wizard of Oz prototypes can help you overcome 'analysis paralysis', which often occurs when you feel that your otherwise elaborate research is still not complete enough to commit to a specific design idea.

LIMITATIONS:
Anything the Wizard cannot observe is impossible to simulate. To extend the wizard's seeing abilities, you may consider adding a camera and a monitor to your prototype setup.

There is a limit to the number of triggers and responses that a wizard can control. Fast-paced or nuanced actions of users are especially difficult for the wizard to respond to.

Design fixation and 'prototype love' often stand in the way of moving on from one Wizard of Oz prototype to the next.

213

REFERENCES & FURTHER READING: Buxton, B., 2010. *Sketching user experiences: getting the design right and the right design.* San Francisco: Morgan Kaufmann. / Buxton's Sketching user experiences (2010, p. 241)

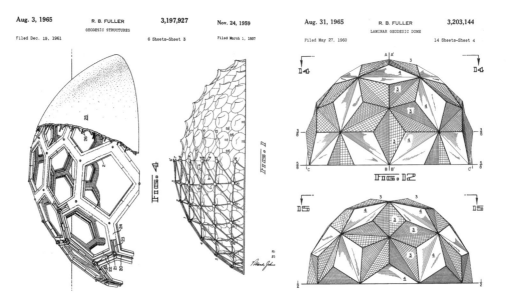

Two of Buckminster Fuller's 1965 patent drawings for the Geodesic Dome demonstrating that it was possible to create a liveable space using only one-fiftieth of the materials normally used in a conventional architectural design. The triangle is a natural mathematical figure that, in combination with other triangles, provides maximum efficiency with minimum structural effort.

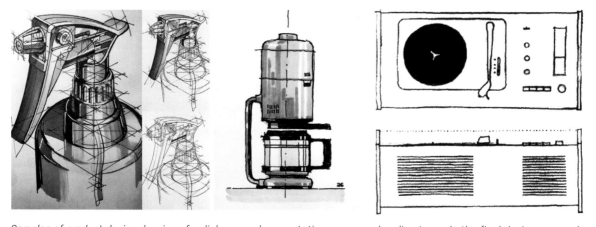

Samples of product design drawings for dialogue and presentation purposes, heading towards the final design proposal. German electronics company Braun is known for its outstanding minimalistic design. This attitude is reflected in the very efficient, suggestive yet accurate drawing of a recordplayer by designer Dieter Rams on the right. The opposite approach to this minimalism is photorealistic 3D computer rendering, using CAD modelling software. These CAD models can also be used as input for 3D printers and provide all reproduction data for final production.

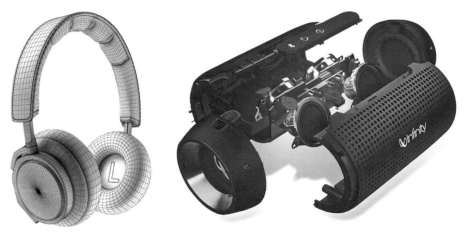

Design Drawing to Deliver

In the Deliver stage, visual representation supports the communication of a design concept. Drawings can help you to explain your design and to convince others. They can facilitate the selection process. Drawings made for this purpose mostly have an informative and appealing character; they should represent all underlying considerations in an understandable manner.

WHAT & WHY? In the Deliver stage sketches and other visual representations primarily have a communicative purpose rather than an explorative purpose. Each presentation or moment of delivery is part of a bigger development process: a presentation could result in a decision to redo or iterate on certain parts or stages of the process.

   The nature of a project determines whether delivery refers to a strategic roadmap or system to be delivered, or a service or product that is fully developed. They can be a representation of the chosen outcome, or to be judged among other alternatives. If a client needs to decide on one of the proposed options or on the continuation of the project, drawings should be detailed, clear and convincing regarding the design properties and preferably presented in context.

MINDSET: Sketches in the Deliver stage help define and present the specific qualities of a design. Advantages of the medium of drawing are its flexibility, the option to mix scales, views and cross sections. You can create and present a certain atmosphere, and the designer's signature style adds personality. Always remember who your audience is and why you are presenting. What is the purpose of your presentational drawings and how can they enforce that purpose?

WHEN? Detailed visual representations of design proposals are used in the Deliver stage, where are used to evaluate how the design alternatives perform with regards to the main design criteria and support the selection process.

HOW? Each project has a different scope, which is why a presentation should entail and highlight different aspects or features. Depending on various factors such as the initial criteria of a project, a final delivery presentation could focus on the human-product interaction that was established or on the unique working principle. It could also highlight certain features, such as the sustainable energy consumption, its support system, its aesthetics, the assembly plan, or its suitability for the pre-defined context. Pay attention to the viewpoint and perspective to be applied to the scene that you are about to visualise. Choosing a suitable point of view and perspective helps you bring your message across in a clear way. For example, to evaluate how users will experience a bus stop is more clearly represented by choosing a vantage point at eye-level. For modelling or prototyping purposes it could be more informative to choose a bird's eye view.

TIPS & CONCERNS

The presentation medium can have different forms, such as a digital presentation, a poster, or a booklet. These could be accompanied by a physical model and technical information. Drawings in this stage are often created digitally (perhaps with a scanned underlay) with a sketching tablet and pen, using software such as Photoshop or Sketchbook. Compositions can be adjusted and improved according to what needs to be conveyed.

 A sketch can have the power to steer the process. It can emphasise certain subjects that you want to emphasise, as it can draw attention away from the areas that you consider less relevant. The visual representation can influence the perception of design proposals.

There are many ways to compose and emphasise specific sketches, they usually need to be integrated in a presentation medium, in order to highlight and select them for the next development step. Graphic design aspects should be considered, like differences in line weight, adding background effects, text, or applying differences in hue, saturation, and brightness.

LIMITATIONS

Drawings of human-product interaction can be helpful in this phase of the design process. For solid testing and conclusions about ergonomics and use, you need to build 3D-models and simulate usage. This can prompt you to revisit the drafting table.

In this near finalisation stage, you will need other documentation and representation media, such as physical models, video, CAD, etcetera, depending on the character of the project.

215

REFERENCES & FURTHER READING: Eissen, J. J., & Steur, R., 2009. *Sketching.* Bis Publishers. / Olofsson, E., & Sjölen, K., 2006. *Design Sketching.* KEEOS Design Books. / Robertson, S., & Bertling, T., 2013. *How to Draw.* Design Studio Press. / http://www.delftdesigndrawing.com/basics.html

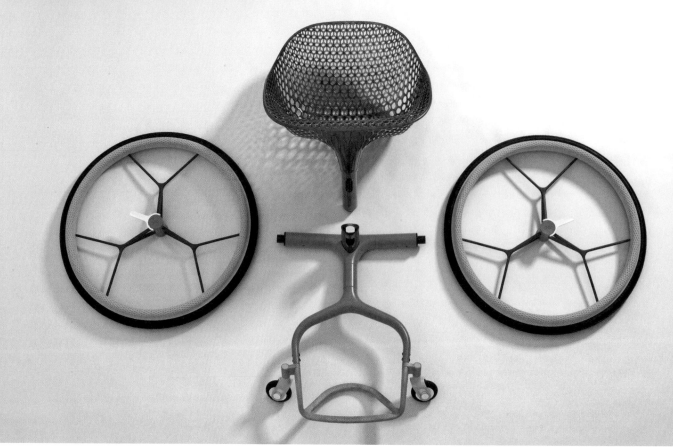

Prototyping is often broken into two categories: 'Looks-like' prototyping looks similar to the anticipated finished product but does not necessarily have its functionality. 'Works-like' prototyping doesn't necessarily look like the finished product but achieves the desired result. Benjamin Hubert of design agency Layer collaborated with Materialise to create the true-to-life prototype for the GO Wheelchair, the world's first 3D-printed consumer wheelchair.

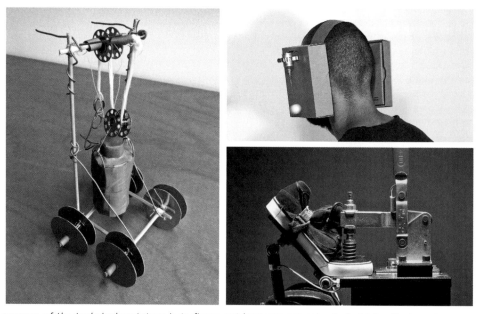

The purpose of the technical prototype is to figure out how you are going to build the final version – so you are experimenting and testing your assumptions. A technical prototype does not need to be beautiful, or simulate a full user experience. It is about making something work. Final protypes are as close tot the real product as possible and will be physically tested to study how it performs,

3D Physical Models

A Three-Dimensional Physical Model is a manifestation of a product idea – it is a hand-built physical model that represents a final product. In the design process, designers use Three-Dimensional Physical Models to simulate product ideas and concepts.

WHAT & WHY? Next to a pen or pencil, the workshop is the most important tool for the a designer. This space allows you to explore shapes that you cannot draw, and it lets you test properties of materials, shapes, constructions, connections, and systems that you are designing. For instance, 3D-printers make it possible to iterate complex shapes many times in a short period of time.

MINDSET: During modelmaking, the hands partly take over the thinking process. The feeling of materials, shapes, textures, strength, stiffness, softness, or the workings of a complex machine simply cannot be calculated or evaluated on paper. On the other hand, prototypes provide objective test results.

WHEN? Models are often used in the practice of design, and they play a vital role in the product development process. In industries, models are used for testing product aspects, changing constructions and details, and helping a company reach consensus on the final form of a product. In mass production, working prototypes are used for testing functionality and ergonomics. Changes that need to be made later are often expensive and time consuming. The final prototypes thus facilitate the preparation and planning of production. The first phase in the production process is called the null series – these first products are used to test the production process, even though they are to a certain extent still prototypes.

HOW? 3D physical models can be useful for three reasons:
1. Generating and developing ideas and concepts: Sketch models are used frequently when generating ideas and concepts. Simple materials are used, such as paper, cardboard, foam, wood, tape, glue, wire, and solder. With sketch models, you can quickly visualise early ideas and develop them into better ideas and concepts. An iterative process often occurs between sketching, making sketch models, drawing, and making a second generation of sketch models.

2. Communicating ideas and concepts in design teams: A *dummy mock-up,* or Visual Model (VISO), is a 1:1 scale model of the product idea. A dummy only has the external characteristics of the product idea, not the technical working principles. It is often built at the end of the idea generation phase to visualise and present final concepts.
A detailed model is used in the concept generation phase to show particular details of the concept. A detailed model is much like a dummy – both are 1:1 scale models with predominantly external characteristics of high quality. A detailed model can also have some limited functionality.
The final model is a prototype that has a high-quality look. It is built of wood, metal, or plastic, and it features real buttons as well as high-quality paint or finishing. The final model should preferably also include some of the technical working principles.

3. Testing and verifying ideas, concepts, and solution principles: *Proof-of-concept prototypes,* Functional Models (FUMOs), are used to verify whether certain technical principles actually work. They are simplifications – often details are left out, and only rudimentary forms and working principles are built. The level of detail and materials are determined based on what is required at that stage of the idea generation phase.

Step 1: Determine the purpose of your model before you start building.

Step 2: The required level of detail has to be chosen prior to collecting materials, devising a plan, and building the model.

Step 3: Make simple sketch models at the beginning of idea generation using the materials that you find around you. Working prototypes or presentation models require a detailed plan for how to build them!

TIPS & CONCERNS
Look for examples of sketch models for inspiration.

Paper-and-tape sketch models are often very helpful during idea generation when the two dimensions of drawing are not enough.

In design schools, you can often find examples of presentation models on display or in the workshop.

Harness the expertise of the people who work in model workshops.

Practice makes perfect – practice and practice some more!

LIMITATIONS
Spending resources on model building during the development phase is time consuming and costly but will help you find mistakes that would cost a lot more time and money to fix later on in your project.

217

REFERENCES & FURTHER READING: Hallgrimsson, B., 2012. *Prototyping and Modelmaking for Product Design.* London: Laurence King. / Thompson, R. 2011. *Prototyping and Low-Volume Production.* London: Thames & Hudson.

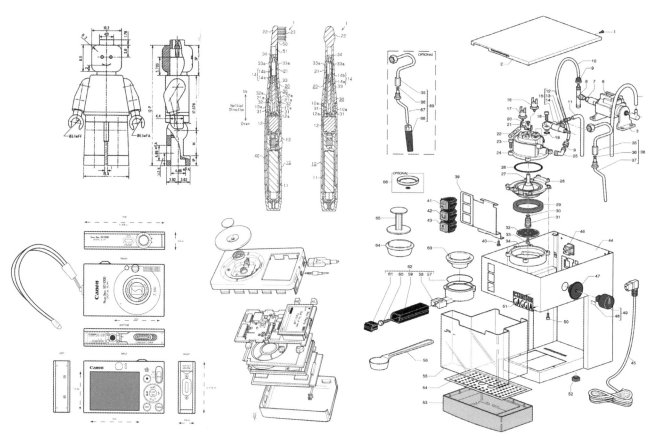

A technical drawing Lego man; a cross section electric toothbrush; an exploded view Cubica Jet Black Espresso machine;
a size drawing Canon digital camera; an exploded view iPod and CAD, and a drawing of the Airbus Double-deck jet airliner A380

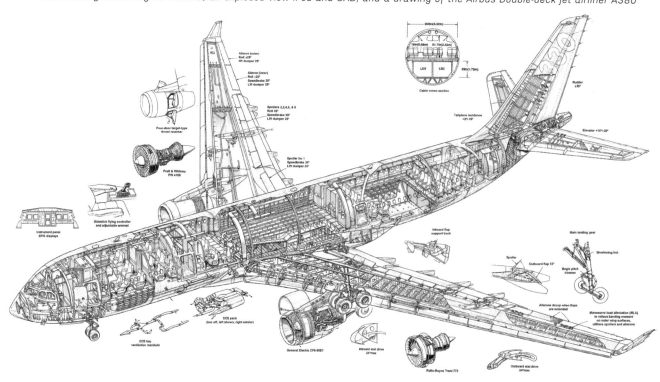

Technical Documentation

Technical Documentation is the unambiguous recording of designs using standards-compliant digital 3D models and technical drawings. The 3D model data can also be used to simulate and control manufacturing processes and the assembly of products or parts. Rendering techniques or animations can be applied for presentation purposes.

WHAT & WHY? Technical drawings and 3D models are a standardised way of communication between designers and workshops or manufacturing. In theory, the workshop should be able to make exactly what you have in mind. Even in the age of 3D printers and computer-driven manufacturing, this is often a vital documentation step in the development process of products or as a communication tool when asking quotations from outside parties.

MINDSET: Imagine being on the receiving end of the drawings: what information do you need to manufacture the part or product? In your drawing or document, there should be no lack of information, nor should there be a flood of information.

WHEN? Technical Documentation is applied when research is needed to determine what production techniques and materials can be used to manufacture a component or product. It also provides support in an earlier stage to quickly generate concept variants or to determine what production processes are possible. To model basic components, such as batteries or an internal frame that will be applied (bottom-up design). Paper prints of these models can serve as an underlay when doing a form study by clearly outlining the geometrical space limitations of your design. Tangible models can be created through rapid manufacturing techniques to support moulded shells or housings. Finally, Technical Documentation can be applied when using digital 3D models of outer parts, such as product housings (top-down design).

HOW? Design software such as SolidWorks is used for generating parametric digital 3D models. These must be based on the feature-modelling concept: separate parts are built by combining or extracting basic forms, such as cylinders, spheres, or more organically shaped bodies. The 3D shapes can be solids (volume-based geometries) or surfaces (zero thickness) when organic shapes are required. A 3D model of a product can be built from separate parts. Parts, assemblies, and features in parts are dependent on each other and are linked through their relations. To guarantee and certify quality and tolerances, technical drawings must be made according to valid standards. To this end, you must have the skills to read, write, and speak this manufacturing language.

Step 1: Make a first digital 3D model during the conceptualisation phase. In earlier stages, the 3D model can be used to study the behaviour of possible mechanisms through animations.

Step 2: Within the materialisation phase, choose materials that allow you to predict a component's behaviour during manufacturing processes (such as mould filling or cooling). Perform failure analyses such as strength calculations, and examine the form, colours, and texture.

Step 3: At the end of the design process, generate an evolved digital 3D model and a final set of technical drawings to safeguard the manufacturing processes and valid product properties and functions.

Step 4: After completion, use the digital 3D model to control production machines or to produce production-related tools.

Step 5: Finally, generate renderings, 'exploded views' of the (de)assembled product, and animations; this can be used to support product presentations and manuals or to develop and produce packaging.

TIPS & CONCERNS
Develop a modelling strategy and time schedule in advance.

Develop a strategy for product data management, such as management of files and part/product revisions.

Build your 3D models of parts and assemblies as symmetrically as possible.

Think about manufacturing at an early stage.

Start with completely new 3D-CAD models when entering the materialisation or final detailing stage.

Use drawing standards to produce proper technical drawings that are legally sound.

A combination of 3D modelling and sketching can be very useful.

While the level of detailing increases both modelling and drawing will take more time accordingly.

Always make backups!

LIMITATIONS
Digital forms can exist virtually, but not always in reality. Perform a reality check after your digital modelling step.

On screen objects can float without being attached to anything.

219

REFERENCES & FURTHER READING: Bertone, G.R. & Wiebe, E.N., 2002. *Technical Graphics Communication*. Blacklick, OH: McGraw-Hill College. / Breedveld, A., 2011. *Producttekenen en –documenteren: van 3D naar 2D*. The Hague: Academic Service. / Bremer, A.P., 2004. *Technisch documenteren*. Delft: Delft University of Technology.

'The main
question each
student should ask
him- or herself after
graduation is if they
want to make money
or sense.'
BUCKMINSTER FULLER

FINALE

Index

223

COLOPHON

Publisher

BIS Publishers
Borneostraat 80-A
1094 CP Amsterdam
The Netherlands

T +31 (0)20 515 0230
F +31 (0)20 515 0239
bis@bispublishers.com
www.bispublishers.com

ISBN 978 90 6369 540 8

Editors
Annemiek van Boeijen
Assistant Professor in Design, Culture & Society at the faculty of Industrial Design Engineering at TU Delft, where she obtained her Master's degree and PhD. Her research focuses on the role of culture in design processes.

Jaap Daalhuizen
Associate Professor in Design Methodology at the Technical University of Denmark. He obtained his Master's degree in Integrated Product Design as well as his PhD at Delft University of Technology.

Jelle Zijlstra
Industrial designer and head of the Motion department at the Design Academy Eindhoven. He teaches design at IPO Rotterdam and design didactics at the Delft University of Technology.

Graphic design, Image reserach and compiler/editor of left pages
Yvo Zijlstra / Antenna-Men

Reference
van Boeijen, A.G.C., Daalhuizen, & J.J., Zijlstra, J.J.M. (Eds.), (2020, Rev. ed.). *Delft Design Guide: Perspectives-Models-Approaches-Methods.* Amsterdam: BISPublishers.

For questions and suggestions please contact us via ddg-io@tudelft.nl.